NEW FARMHOUSE FARE

NEW
FARMHOUSE FARE

Recipes collected by
Farmers Weekly

HAMLYN

*Star-marked recipes are the
winning entries to the Farmers Weekly
seasonal recipe contests.*

Cover and inside illustrations by Anthony Sidwell

Published in 1985 by the Hamlyn Publishing Group Limited
a division of the Octopus Publishing Group
Michelin House, 81 Fulham Road, London SW3 6RB

ISBN 0 600 32478 8

Set in Linotron 202 Old Style
by Wyvern Typesetting Ltd, Bristol

Printed in Hungary

CONTENTS

Foreword	6
Soups	7
Starters	15
Fish and Seafood	27
Meat Dishes	38
Poultry and Game	96
Savoury Pies and Pasties	119
Supper Dishes	135
Picnic Fare	145
Salads	151
Vegetable Dishes	161
Hot Puddings	170
Cold Puddings	199
Tea Breads, Cakes and Biscuits	247
Preserves	257
Quick and Easy Dishes	263
Index	274

FOREWORD

For more than half a century, *Farmhouse Fare* has held pride of place among country cookbooks. Brainchild of the late Mary Day, first editor of Farmers Weekly's Home Section, it was published in 1934 and has since sold more than half a million copies. The secret of *Farmhouse Fare*'s success is that the recipes were supplied by Farmers Weekly readers. For who better than those who live and work in the countryside to devise delicious ways of serving home-grown produce?

In 1982 *Farmhouse Fare* went into its seventh edition but we were convinced that our readers had more culinary treats still to share with us. So in the past couple of years Farmers Weekly has run a series of seasonal recipe contests, as well as a competition sponsored by Food from Britain. It is from these competition entries that the bulk of *New Farmhouse Fare* has been compiled. References to "high tech" implements and a smattering of foreign names for dishes set these recipes firmly in the 'eighties. But we are sure you will find this collection contains the same blend of originality and common sense as its forerunner.

British farming is the best in the world and *New Farmhouse Fare* proves our farmers' wives can outcook all comers too.

Mary Wagner, Farmlife Editor, Farmers Weekly.

SOUPS

MEAT AND VEGETABLE SOUP

450 g/1 lb stewing steak or minced steak	2 large onions
seasoned flour	1 large leek
fat to fry	1 small swede
225 g/8 oz carrots	1 beef stock cube
225 g/8 oz parsnips	1 tablespoon flour
	1 tablespoon gravy browning

HAVE ready a large saucepan and put in the steak, cut into small pieces, if necessary, and rolled in seasoned flour. Brown it in a little fat, then cover with water. Add all the vegetables, sliced or diced, and the stock cube. Also, in spring gather young nettles (with gloves on), put in the leaves and add 1 tablespoon of cider vinegar. Cook the soup, covered, until the meat is tender, about 1½–2 hours, adding more water if needed.

When cooked, lift meat out. Mix together the flour and gravy browning in a little water. Add to soup, stir well and add more water if needed, not too thick or too thin. Return the meat to the soup and serve. Makes the mouth water.

Mrs J. M. McKeown, Shipley, nr Wolverhampton

LETTUCE SOUP

1 large onion	1 stock cube
butter or oil to fry	salt and pepper
2 large potatoes	about 150 ml/¼ pint creamy milk
3 lettuces	parsley

CHOP the onion and soften in the butter. Add the potatoes, cut into small pieces, and the lettuces, separated into leaves. Cover with water, add the stock cube and seasoning. Cover and simmer gently, until potatoes are soft. Cool and put through the liquidiser. Add the milk and reheat gently. Serve garnished with parsley.

Mrs Sheila Jerrard, Oldhamstocks, East Lothian

TOMATO AND ORANGE SOUP

1 large onion	2 396-g/14-oz cans tomatoes, or
1 large green pepper	1 kg/2 lb fresh tomatoes
1 clove of garlic	1 140-g/5-oz can tomato purée
knob of butter	salt
2 large oranges	1 carton pure orange juice

FINELY chop onion and pepper, crush garlic. Fry gently in butter, do not brown. Add grated zest of orange rinds, the juice of the oranges and the flesh. Then add the tomatoes and the purée, breaking up the tomatoes into small pieces. Stir, cover and simmer for about 20 minutes. Add salt to taste and use the orange juice to adjust to the consistency required. This is quite a thick and lumpy soup but could be given a much smoother texture by putting through the liquidiser. SERVES 6–8.

Mrs Joyce Cook, Kelso, Roxburghshire

MOTHER-IN-LAW'S MUSHROOM SOUP

PEEL and chop plenty of mushrooms. Place in a pan and cover with cold water. Bring to the boil and simmer until tender. Add milk, desired quantity. Make a paste with plain flour, salt and pepper and a little cold milk. Stir into the soup until it thickens, add a knob of butter to serve.

Mrs Maureen Dinsdale, Leyburn, Yorkshire

MUSHROOM AND WATERCRESS SOUP

50 g/2 oz butter
40 g/1½ oz plain flour
600 ml/1 pint chicken stock
450 ml/¾ pint milk
225 g/8 oz mushrooms, wiped and finely chopped

2 tablespoons chopped watercress
salt and freshly ground pepper
croûtons to garnish

MELT the butter in a saucepan, add the flour and cook gently for 3–4 minutes. Blend in the chicken stock and heat, stirring continuously, until soup thickens and boils. Add the milk, mushrooms and watercress. Cook for 5 minutes, season to taste. Serve hot, garnished with croûtons.

Miss D. Sherwin, Knutsford, Cheshire

WAYFARERS' SOUP

½ bucket young spring nettles
4 sticks celery
1 carrot
1 medium onion

1 medium potato
150 ml/¼ pint milk
salt and pepper

USE gloves when picking the nettles, and strip leaves from stems. Wash nettle leaves, simmer in salted water for 15 minutes, then remove from water to liquidise.

In 600 ml/1 pint salted water, simmer the roughly chopped celery, carrot, onion and potato until soft (about 30 minutes) then liquidise the contents. Add the nettle purée and milk, season to taste, return to the saucepan and reheat.

Serve with croûtons of toast. Delicious!

Mrs J. Francis, Seal, nr Sevenoaks, Kent

CREAMED LEEK AND POTATO SOUP

2 potatoes, peeled
450 g/1 lb leeks
100 g/4 oz butter
salt and black pepper
25 g/1 oz flour

600 ml/1 pint milk
450 ml/¾ pint stock
150 ml/¼ pint single cream or
    1 small tin evaporated milk
chopped mint leaves or parsley

BOIL the potatoes and the white parts of the leeks until tender. Drain and slice. Melt half the butter and fry the potatoes and leeks with salt and pepper to taste. Make a white sauce with the remaining butter, the flour and milk. Cook for a few minutes then add to the vegetables. Stir in the stock and cook for 15 minutes. Pass through a sieve or purée in an electric blender, then reheat until boiling. Add the cream, chopped mint or parsley to taste and serve at once.

Mrs Rosemary Mackie, Alford, Aberdeenshire

CREAM OF VEGETABLE SOUP

This is a recipe that seems to have evolved in our family over the last few years, using any vegetables left in the garden. It is so simple to make that I often prepare it for lunch, together with some bread and cheese, for my two young children. It is also quite elegant, and could be served quite easily at a dinner party.

1 large or 2 small potatoes and
    1 leek (the only essential
    vegetable ingredients)
selection of available chopped
vegetables, e.g. carrots, turnips,
    swedes, sprouts etc.

salt and pepper
about 300 ml/½ pint creamy milk

WASH and prepare the vegetables in the usual way, then roughly chop them into smallish pieces. Put into a large saucepan and just cover with water. Add salt and boil until tender, taking care to maintain the water level. Purée the contents of the saucepan, then add the milk (and cream if desired) until the required consistency is reached. Adjust seasoning, reheat and serve with fresh bread.

Mrs Mary Osborne, Bontnewydd, nr Aberystwyth

SWEDE AND PARSNIP SOUP WITH CINNAMON

2 onions
1 small swede (about 450–675 g/1–1½ lb weight)
450–675 g/1–1½ lb parsnips (equal weight to swede)
25 g/1 oz butter
salt and pepper
1 chicken stock cube
good pinch cinnamon
up to 150 ml/¼ pint milk
croûtons or chopped parsley

CUT the onions into quarters. Cut the swede into 2.5-cm/1-inch cubes and the parsnips into thick slices. Fry in the butter for a few minutes to soften. Add salt and pepper, 600 ml/1 pint water and the stock cube. Cover and cook gently for 50–60 minutes, until the vegetables are tender.

Liquidise the vegetables with sufficient of the liquid in which they were boiled to produce a thin purée. Return to the pan. Add a good pinch of cinnamon and dilute with enough milk to make a thick soup consistency. Reheat gently. Serve with croûtons or freshly chopped parsley.

Mrs A. D. Wrapson, London NW7

DAD'S BROTH

450 g/1 lb carrots
450 g/1 lb potatoes
1 medium swede
1 large onion
1 chicken stock cube
mixed herbs
salt and pepper
leftover cooked chicken or turkey
250 ml/8 fl oz white wine (optional)

PREPARE and coarsely grate the vegetables. Place in a large pan, add stock cube, herbs and seasoning. Cover with water, bring to the boil, reduce heat and simmer gently, covered, for at least an hour. Meanwhile finely chop meat, add to pan towards the end of cooking along with the wine.

The timing for this recipe is only approximate, as the longer it can be left to cook, the better it tastes.

Mrs Carol Dickinson, Coton-in-the-Elms, Staffordshire

WINTER VEGETABLE SOUP

1 medium onion	25 g/1 oz flour
2 medium carrots	1.15 litres/2 pints beef stock
1 medium potato	salt and pepper
2 sticks celery	2 sachets mixed herbs or bouquets
25 g/1 oz lard	garnis

FINELY chop the vegetables. Melt the lard in a heavy pan or pressure cooker and sweat the chopped vegetables gently for 5–10 minutes with the pan lid on. Add the flour and stir until dissolved then add the stock slowly, stirring all the time. Add the salt and pepper and mixed herbs. Simmer for approximately 30 minutes, or 5 minutes at 15 lb pressure for a pressure cooker, until the vegetables are cooked. Remove herb sachets.

At this point you have two choices:

1.   Add a cup of mixed frozen vegetables e.g. peas, runner beans, small cauliflower florets, and simmer for a further 5 minutes. Alter thickness and seasoning as necessary and serve as chunky soup with crusty bread.

2.   Cool slightly and liquidise or sieve. Reheat and alter seasoning and thickness as necessary. Pour into bowls and serve with a swirl of cream and a sprinkle of chopped parsley for more special occasions.

Mrs M. D. Jones, Holywell, Clwyd, North Wales

FARMHOUSE BROTH

1 kg/2 lb brisket	2 onions
225 g/8 oz split peas, soaked	3 or 4 slices swede
overnight	3 or 4 sprigs cauliflower
3 or 4 carrots	12 small suet dumplings

PLACE the brisket and soaked split peas in a large saucepan. Cover with water, bring to the boil and simmer for 2 hours. Chop all the vegetables into small pieces and add to the pan. If more water is needed, add liberally. Continue to keep well simmering for an hour or more, then add the dumplings and keep simmering until ready.

Keep the meat to serve as a main course after the soup, accompanied by some buttery mashed potatoes. This is really delicious, substantial and warming, and is a great favourite with my family.

Mrs Stella Lobb, Falmouth, Cornwall

FARMHOUSE BEAN AND BACON SOUP

350 g/12 oz dried haricot beans
350 g/12 oz streaky bacon
2 medium onions
2 sticks celery
1.4 litres/2½ pints water
3 chicken stock cubes

1 medium carrot
1 bay leaf
¼ teaspoon pepper
pinch ground cloves
1 396-g/14-oz can tomatoes

SOAK the haricot beans overnight in enough cold water to cover.
Chop the bacon finely and fry in its own fat until browned.
Spoon most of fat from the pan but leave about 4 tablespoons.
Chop onions and celery and add to pan, fry for 10 minutes until
tender. Put the beans (with the water they have been soaking in),
onion, celery and bacon into a large saucepan. Add the water,
crumbled stock cubes, sliced carrot, bay leaf, pepper and cloves,
cover and simmer for 1½–2 hours. Stir in canned tomatoes and
break into small pieces. Simmer gently for 30 minutes, stirring
occasionally until beans are cooked (very tender). Remove bay leaf
and serve immediately.

Mrs L. C. Mitchell, Hambledon, Hampshire

☆ FINNAN CHOWDER ☆

2 Finnan haddocks
2 onions, sliced
2 carrots, chopped
2 sticks celery, chopped
1 bay leaf
1.75 litres/3 pints water
600 ml/1 pint milk
450–675 g/1–1½ lb potatoes, cooked
and mashed with butter

1 carrot, grated
100 g/4 oz ham or crisply fried
bacon
salt and pepper
parsley to garnish

POACH haddock with vegetables and bay leaf in water for 5
minutes. Remove haddock, take best of fish from the bones and
reserve. Return bones to pan and simmer with the vegetables for
30–40 minutes.

Strain stock and return it to a clean pan. Heat milk and add to
the stock with the mashed potatoes, grated carrot, chopped ham or
bacon and flaked fish. Season to taste, reheat and simmer for 5–10
minutes. Garnish with parsley before serving with warmed oatcakes or wholemeal rolls. SERVES 8–10.

Mrs S. Harrison, Aberdeen

☆　VARIETY FRUIT SOUP　☆

Choose any one from each of the following groups:

(A) 100 g/4 oz strawberries,
　raspberries or blackberries
(B) 1 apple or pear
(C) 1 large orange or grapefruit

(D) 2 ripe bananas, 100 g/4 oz
　redcurrants or blackcurrants
(E) 100 g/4 oz cherries or grapes or
　1 peach

You will also need:

juice and pared rind of 1 lemon
50 g/2 oz sugar
300 ml/½ pint ginger ale
2–3 tablespoons liqueur, Kirsch or
　Grand Marnier (optional)

6 ice cubes
fresh mint leaves or thinly sliced
　cucumber

PLACE an opened 1-litre/1¾-pint food flask in the refrigerator.

Mash or liquidise fruits from (A) and (D). Peel and chop fruit from (B). Peel and segment, cutting smaller if necessary, fruit from (C). Stone fruit from (E); if peach is chosen, peel and slice.

Make a syrup by simmering together the lemon rind and sugar in 300 ml/½ pint water for 10 minutes. Strain and leave to cool.

Combine all fruits, add lemon juice, cooled syrup and ginger ale. Add liqueur if used. Pour into cooled flask and cover tightly until needed.

Serve in frosted glass dishes, add ice cubes and decorate with mint or cucumber. To frost dishes, dip edge in lightly beaten egg white and then in castor sugar. Refrigerate until set and needed. SERVES 6.

Mrs J. Peters, Ormskirk, Lancashire

STARTERS

CARROT AND WATERCRESS MOUSSE WITH TARRAGON CREAM

350 g/12 oz new carrots
4–5 tablespoons fresh orange juice
1 bunch watercress
2 eggs

150 ml/¼ pint double cream
a little butter
1 teaspoon chopped tarragon
1 teaspoon white wine vinegar

PEEL and slice the carrots and cook in boiling salted water until tender. Drain. Place carrots in a pan with the orange juice and simmer, uncovered, until reduced by half. Discard the tough stalks from the watercress. Add the leaves and tender stalks to the carrots and cook for a further 2 minutes. Drain. Liquidise the carrots and watercress to a purée with eggs and all but 2 tablespoons cream.

Butter four ramekin dishes and divide the mixture between them. Cover each dish with foil and place in a bain-marie (roasting tin of hot water). Cook in a moderate oven (160 c, 325 F, gas 3) for 40 minutes.

Mix the remaining cream with the tarragon and vinegar. When the mousses are cooked turn out onto a warm plate and serve with a little of the tarragon cream. SERVES 4.

Mrs M. E. Denny, Enfield, Middlesex

CAULIFLOWER STARTER

1 medium cauliflower
1 small onion, chopped
100 g/4 oz mushrooms, sliced
50 g/2 oz margarine
25 g/1 oz breadcrumbs

25 g/1 oz plain flour
250 ml/8 fl oz milk
75 g/3 oz mature English Cheddar
salt and ground black pepper
freshly chopped mint

COOK cauliflower whole in boiling salted water, about 20 minutes.

Fry onion and mushrooms in half the margarine. Place in an ovenproof dish with chopped cooked cauliflower sprigs and breadcrumbs. Melt the remaining margarine, stir in the flour and then the milk to make a sauce. Add the grated cheese, seasoning and mint to taste. Pour over the cauliflower mixture. Grill to brown the top. SERVES 4.

Caroline Hobbs, Chesterfield, Derbyshire

☆ CRUSTY BAKED ☆ TOMATOES

4 slices brown bread
50 g/2 oz butter
1 tablespoon freshly chopped
  herbs (parsley, thyme, basil)
FILLING
25 g/1 oz butter
2 spring onions, chopped
1 small cooking apple, peeled and
  grated

4 tomatoes, peeled, seeded and
  chopped
25 g/1 oz fresh breadcrumbs
100 g/4 oz smoked mackerel fillet,
  flaked
1 teaspoon chopped thyme
squeeze of lemon juice
salt and pepper

USING a pastry cutter, cut four rounds from the slices of bread (use the trimmings to make the breadcrumbs). Cream together the butter and fresh herbs and spread over each round of bread. Place in a patty tin and bake in a moderate oven (180 c, 350 f, gas 4) until golden and crisp.

Meanwhile prepare the filling. Melt the butter in a pan, add the spring onion and apple and cook until soft. Add the remaining ingredients, reserving a little of the chopped tomato. Mix well and heat thoroughly, seasoning to taste. Divide filling between the crusty bread cups and garnish with the reserved chopped tomato. Serve immediately. SERVES 4.

Mrs D. Gray, Chilton, Buckinghamshire

MUSHROOMS IN GARLIC

450 g/1 lb small fresh button
  mushrooms
250 ml/8 fl oz natural yogurt
250 ml/8 fl oz mayonnaise
1 teaspoon tomato sauce

3–4 cloves of freshly crushed
  garlic
salt and pepper
bunch of watercress
chopped parsley

WASH the mushrooms and slice thinly. Set aside. Mix together yogurt, mayonnaise, tomato sauce and crushed garlic. Add salt and pepper to taste. Wash and prepare a bed of watercress for each portion. Mix the sauce and mushrooms gently together and spoon out portions on top of the watercress. Garnish with chopped parsley.

For best results and added freshness the sauce and mushrooms should be kept separate in the fridge until about half an hour before needed. SERVES 6.

Joanna Fredenburgh, Norwich

☆ GREEN PEA WITH MINT ☆ SAVOURY ICE CREAM

225 g/8 oz shelled green peas
sprig of mint
100 g/4 oz cream cheese
150 ml/¼ pint double cream

1 teaspoon grated lemon rind
1 tablespoon finely chopped mint
½ teaspoon salt

COOK peas in lightly salted water with a sprig of mint. Refresh with cold water. Put through sieve then blend to a purée in food processor or liquidiser. Mix in all other ingredients until well blended. Place in container suitable for the freezer and with sufficient room to stir in a couple of times before completely frozen.

Serve as a first course with Cotswold Cheese Crescents, and a sprig of mint for decoration.

Cotswold Cheese Crescents

Puff pastry cut into small triangles, lightly brushed with egg and milk, sprinkled with grated Cotswold Cheese (Double Gloucester with chives), rolled and shaped into small crescents. Bake at 200 c, 400 F, gas 6 until golden.

Mrs R. F. Wilkinson, Spexhall, Suffolk

SALMON-STUFFED COURGETTES

4 large or 8 small courgettes
100 g/4 oz cooked flaked salmon
50 g/2 oz cream cheese
salt and pepper

lettuce
tomato
chopped parsley

BLANCH courgettes for 10 minutes in boiling salted water. Lift out. When cold, halve lengthways and cut into 5-cm/2-inch slices. Spoon out centres, chop finely and mix with salmon, cheese, salt and pepper. Pile stuffing back into courgette slices. Serve on a bed of crisp lettuce and thinly sliced tomato, sprinkle with parsley and accompany with a dish of mayonnaise. SERVES 4.

Mrs M. A. Brooks, Newent, Gloucestershire

TUNA SURPRISE

1 198-g/7-oz can tuna
2 tablespoons plain yogurt
2 tablespoons salad cream
2 sticks celery, finely chopped
1 small onion, finely chopped

25 g/1 oz stoned dates, finely
   chopped
1 dessert apple, finely chopped
lettuce and tomato

FLAKE the tuna fish finely and add the yogurt and salad cream. Mix thoroughly before adding the other ingredients. Serve chilled, on a bed of lettuce and tomato, with crusty brown bread and butter. SERVES 4.

Mrs Patricia Gillespie, Kings Knowe, Edinburgh

☆ LEMON AND TUNA ☆ BASKETS

3 large lemons
1 198-g/7-oz can tuna fish, flaked
3 tablespoons dry white wine
2 tablespoons chopped chives

salt and pepper
2 tablespoons natural yogurt
chopped parsley to garnish

CUT lemons in half, scoop out flesh. Strain juice, then blend tuna fish, lemon juice and wine. Add chives, seasoning and blend in yogurt. Pile mixture back into lemon shells and garnish with parsley. Only 60 calories per portion. SERVES 6.

Mrs E. A. Rayburn, Great Shoddesden, Hampshire

SMOKED TROUT PÂTÉ

4 small smoked trout
150 ml/¼ pint single cream
2 tablespoons horseradish sauce
sea salt and freshly ground black
  pepper

1 Iceberg lettuce
½ cucumber
4 tomatoes
1 lemon

FLAKE the trout flesh into a blender, add half the cream and whizz. Put the horseradish into the blender and add more cream to give a smooth pâté consistency. Add sea salt and black pepper to taste. Cut the lettuce into small wedges, peel and thinly slice the cucumber and slice the tomatoes. Arrange salad on four plates, place a dollop of pâté on each, accompanied by a lemon wedge. Serve with fresh baked brown bread or thick oatcakes.

This is a delicious lunch or first course for dinner on a hot day and goes down well with chilled white wine. Should smoked trout be unavailable, a combination of smoked haddock and mackerel may be substituted. SERVES 4.

Susan Lawrence, Newmarket, Suffolk

CHEDDAR MACKEREL PÂTÉ

450 g/1 lb smoked mackerel
75 g/3 oz finely grated Cheddar
  cheese

225 g/8 oz melted soft margarine
1 teaspoon lemon juice
seasoning

REMOVE skin and any bones from mackerel and break flesh into small pieces. Put into liquidiser or food processor (or even a large bowl with the use of hand mixer). Add all other ingredients and whizz until well mixed.

Turn into suitable container for putting in refrigerator for use in a couple of hours, or into deep freeze for future use.

Mrs D. Campbell, Cromarty, Ross-shire

EGG PÂTÉ

8 hard-boiled eggs
400 g/14 oz cottage or cream
  cheese
1 teaspoon powdered mace or
  nutmeg

salt and freshly ground black
  pepper
2 teaspoons finely grated onion
a little extra powdered mace to
  garnish

PURÉE the hard-boiled eggs in a blender or grate on a very fine grater. Add the cheese and blend to a creamy mixture. Beat in the mace, salt, pepper and onion. Spoon the mixture into eight individual ramekins, smooth the top and sprinkle with a little mace. Chill for 30 minutes before serving. SERVES 8.

Mrs F. M. Alderwick, Haverfordwest, Pembrokeshire

EGG AND TOMATO BOATS

4 large tomatoes
4 large hard-boiled eggs
100 g/4 oz chopped ham
2 teaspoons chopped chives
2 teaspoons chopped parsley

1–2 tablespoons salad cream or
  mayonnaise
lettuce
¼ cucumber, sliced
2 tablespoons grated red cheese

CUT tomatoes and eggs in half. Scoop out tomato centres and egg yolks. Mix to a pulp and add chopped ham, chives, parsley and salad cream. Pile filling back into tomatoes and egg whites.

Arrange on a bed of lettuce leaves and sliced cucumber, and top with grated cheese. SERVES 4.

Mrs Betty Alcock, Brixworth, Northampton

SALUMBER

1 sachet aspic jelly crystals
225 g/8 oz fresh salmon
1 wineglass white wine
15 g/½ oz powdered gelatine
2–3 tablespoons water
¼ cucumber, peeled

3 tablespoons mayonnaise
4 tablespoons double cream
1 teaspoon lemon juice
salt and pepper
watercress sprigs to garnish

MAKE up aspic jelly and use to coat a ring mould generously. Put aside to set firmly.

Cook salmon in the wine in a greased ovenproof dish covered with foil for approximately 30 minutes at 190 C, 375 F, gas 5.

Sprinkle gelatine on to the water in a cup, leave for a few minutes to soften, then place the cup in a pan of hot water to dissolve the gelatine.

Dice cucumber very small, flake fish and stir into the mayonnaise with the cream, lemon juice, salt and pepper, cooking liquid and dissolved gelatine, Pour into the mould and put in refrigerator to set.

Turn out and serve garnished with watercress. To make turning out easier dip the mould first into hot water; this helps to loosen the aspic. This starter serves four.

Mrs Susan Jervis, Oswestry, Shropshire

SALMON MOULD

150 ml/¼ pint natural yogurt
2 tablespoons thick mayonnaise
2 tablespoons salad cream
2 teaspoons tomato sauce
1 tablespoon lemon juice
1 teaspoon Worcestershire sauce
salt and pepper
2 teaspoons powdered gelatine

2 tablespoons water
1 212-g/7½-oz can pink salmon
1 small onion, finely chopped
1 hard-boiled egg, chopped
2 gherkins, chopped
6 slices cucumber, chopped
cucumber and tomato slices to garnish

COMBINE yogurt, mayonnaise, salad cream, tomato sauce, lemon juice and Worcestershire sauce, and season with salt and pepper. Dissolve gelatine in the water in a basin over hot water. Stir into yogurt mixture. Mix together flaked salmon, onion, egg, gherkin and cucumber and fold into yogurt mixture when it is on point of setting. Spoon into a fish mould and decorate when set with thin cucumber and tomato slices. This makes a lovely starter to a dinner party, and can be prepared well in advance. SERVES 4.

Mrs Mary Clanachan, Cranfield, Bedfordshire

SALMON AND AVOCADO MOUSSE

Salmon mousse

100 g/4 oz fresh cooked salmon
150 ml/¼ pint cold béchamel sauce
4 tablespoons mayonnaise

1½ teaspoons powdered gelatine
1½ tablespoons cold water
3 tablespoons double cream

POUND the fish until smooth, blending in the sauce and mayonnaise. Dissolve the gelatine in the water over a very low heat and add to the above mixture. Stir in the cream.

Avocado mousse

1½ teaspoons powdered gelatine
1½ tablespoons cold water
1 avocado pear
2 teaspoons finely grated onion
2 teaspoons Worcestershire sauce

½ teaspoon salt
150 ml/¼ pint hot chicken stock
3 tablespoons mayonnaise
3 tablespoons double cream

DISSOLVE the gelatine in the water over a very low heat. Halve the avocado and scoop out all the flesh into the liquidiser goblet, or mash in a bowl with a fork. Add the onion, Worcestershire sauce and salt. Pour the hot chicken stock onto the gelatine, add to the avocado mixture and blend until smooth. Pour into a bowl and stir over ice until cold, then fold in the mayonnaise and cream.

To assemble

Oil an 18-cm/7-inch ring mould. Pour in half the salmon mousse and place in the freezer or freezing compartment of the refrigerator to set. Meanwhile leave the rest of the mousse mixtures at room temperature. In about 10 minutes the salmon will have set firm enough to pour on half the avocado mixture. Repeat setting process as before then add the remainder of the salmon followed by the final layer of avocado. Leave all in the refrigerator to set.

When required, turn out mousse and garnish with cucumber twists around the top and halved hard-boiled egg slices around the base. Serves four as a starter.

We also enjoy this salmon and avocado mousse as a light luncheon dish, with a tossed salad of lettuce, green and red peppers, cucumber and green and black grapes. Normally I make twice this mixture as the mousse freezes very well and I feel then it is worth the effort.

Mrs Janet Brown, Carrutherstown, Dumfries

PRAWN AND CIDER MOUSSE

15 g/½ oz butter
15 g/½ oz flour
300 ml/½ pint cider
75 g/3 oz Cheddar cheese, grated
2 eggs, separated
2 tablespoons tomato ketchup
2 tablespoons chopped fresh
  parsley

salt and freshly ground pepper
225 g/8 oz peeled prawns, roughly
  chopped
15 g/½ oz powdered gelatine
150 ml/¼ pint double cream
cucumber and tomato slices to
  garnish

MELT butter in saucepan, stir in flour and cook gently for 1 minute, stirring. Remove pan from heat and gradually stir in all but 3 tablespoons of cider. Bring to boil slowly and continue to cook, stirring until the sauce thickens. Add the cheese, egg yolks, tomato ketchup, parsley and seasoning, and stir the mixture until the cheese has melted. Fold in the prawns.

Sprinkle the gelatine over the reserved cider in a small bowl and leave to soften for a few minutes. Place the bowl over a pan of hot water and stir until dissolved.

Whip the cream until softly stiff. Stir into the cheese mixture and then add the dissolved gelatine, mixing well. Whisk the egg whites until stiff and gently fold into the mixture. Pour into a large dish or individual dishes.

Put in refrigerator to set. Garnish with slices of cucumber and tomato. SERVES 4.

Miss D. Sherwin, Knutsford, Cheshire

CUCUMBER MOUSSE

1 lime jelly
3 tablespoons cider or wine
  vinegar
2 teaspoons sugar
150 ml/¼ pint natural yogurt or
  salad cream

salt and pepper
dash of Worcestershire sauce
  (optional)
½ large or 1 medium cucumber

MAKE up jelly with 300 ml/½ pint boiling water. Stir in all the remaining ingredients except cucumber and turn into mould. When nearly set stir in finely chopped cucumber, leaving on a little of skin to give colour. Turn out to serve on lettuce, and decorate with tomato cups, radish, beetroot and sliced hard-boiled eggs.

Mrs N. Freeman, Newport, Isle of Wight

TUNA MOUSSE

1 envelope powdered gelatine
3 tablespoons hot water
175 ml/6 fl oz double cream
2 tablespoons lemon juice
2 drops red food colouring

2 198-g/7-oz cans tuna fish
2 heaped tablespoons salad cream
salt and pepper
lettuce, cucumber and tomato to garnish

DISSOLVE gelatine in hot water. Whip cream until nearly stiff then add lemon juice and colouring, whip again until stiff. Mix in the drained mashed tuna fish and salad cream, and add seasoning to taste. Stir in the cooled dissolved gelatine. Pour into a small Swiss roll tin lined with greased greaseproof paper, smooth top and cover with cling film. Chill until set.

Cut into eight to serve as a starter or six for a light lunch. Garnish with salad and accompany with brown bread and butter.

Mrs E. M. Kirkpatrick, Hawick, Roxburghshire

SRING SALAD RING

1 lime jelly
1 tablespoon lemon juice
1 cucumber
225 g/8 oz cream cheese, softened
3 tablespoons mayonnaise
1 376-g/13¼-oz can crushed pineapple

2 tablespoons minced onion
½ teaspoon grated lemon peel
TO DECORATE
lettuce
watercress
green grapes
lemon and lime wedges

DISSOLVE jelly in 450 ml/¾ pint hot water. Add lemon juice. Measure 300 ml/½ pint jelly, pour into a wetted ring mould. Chill until almost firm.

Peel cucumber, halve and scrape out seeds, grate and drain. Blend softened cream cheese and mayonnaise. Stir in grated cucumber, undrained crushed pineapple, minced onion and lemon peel. Mix well. Stir in remaining jelly. Chill until partially set. Pour over jelly in the mould. Chill until firm.

Dip mould into hot water and turn out carefully on to a fancy glass dish or plate. Decorate with lettuce all round, filling cavity ring with lettuce and watercress. Finally finish with bunches of grapes and lemon and lime wedges around the edge of dish.

Mrs G. A. Daines, Bunwell, Norwich

☆ CUCUMBER CHEESECAKE ☆

½ cucumber
225 g/8 oz Philadelphia cream
cheese
2 eggs, separated
grated rind of ½ lemon

150 ml/¼ pint soured cream
salt and black pepper
15 g/½ oz powdered gelatine
thin slices of cucumber to garnish

PEEL and chop cucumber, put in cloth to remove excess moisture. Cream the cheese in a bowl. Beat in egg yolks, lemon rind, soured cream, salt and pepper. Stir in cucumber.

Put gelatine into a little cold water and leave to dissolve in a bowl over hot water, stir. When dissolved, beat the gelatine into the cheese mixture. Leave on one side until the mixture is on point of setting. Whisk egg whites until stiff and fold in thoroughly.

Spoon into a mould and chill overnight. Remove from mould, garnish with thin slices of cucumber. This freezes well – garnish after defrosting.

Mrs R. Robinson, Yaddlethorpe, South Humberside

CHICKEN MOUSSE

DISSOLVE 2 tablespoons powdered gelatine in a little chicken stock, taken from 600 ml/1 pint. Combine rest of stock with 6 egg yolks and seasoning, in a double boiler over hot water. Beat to blend thoroughly and stir until thick. Pour in the dissolved gelatine in a thin stream, stirring constantly. Cool and when half-set, stir in 50 g/2 oz minced cooked chicken, 150 ml/¼ pint whipped cream mixed with 150 ml/¼ pint mayonnaise, plus asparagus tips or peas, or whatever small pieces of cooked vegetable you have available. Spoon into a mould, cover and leave to set in the refrigerator. Turn out and serve with triangles of hot toast for a starter or light luncheon dish.

Mrs L. Balfour Paul, Kiltarlity, Inverness-shire

SPINACH CHEESE SOUFFLÉ

225 g/8 oz fresh or frozen spinach	¼ teaspoon mustard powder
75 g/3 oz butter	300 ml/½ pint milk
salt and freshly ground pepper	2 egg yolks, beaten
50 g/2 oz flour	100 g/4 oz Cheddar cheese, grated
½ teaspoon salt	2 egg whites, stiffly whisked
¼ teaspoon cayenne pepper	

IF using fresh spinach discard coarse stalks from stems. Wash and drain well and place in saucepan with 25 g/1 oz butter, salt and freshly ground pepper; cover and cook for 7 minutes, shaking pan occasionally until spinach has collapsed. Drain thoroughly, pressing out excess moisture; chop roughly. If frozen spinach is used, cook as per packet instructions.

Sift the flour with the salt, cayenne and mustard and place in a saucepan with the milk and remaining butter. Whisk with a balloon whisk over moderate heat, bring to boil and cook for 2–3 minutes. Cool slightly and mix in the egg yolks, grated cheese and spinach. Using a metal spoon fold in the egg whites. Spoon into a buttered 1.15-litre/2-pint soufflé dish or 4–6 small ramekins. Place on a baking sheet and bake in the centre of a moderately hot oven (190 C, 375 F, gas 5) for 30–40 minutes, or 25–30 minutes for the individual ramekins. Serve immediately with watercress sprigs and wholemeal toast. Serves 4–6 as a starter or snack.

Mrs Elizabeth Hern, Billingborough, Lincolnshire

COURGETTE PIE

PASTRY	FILLING
225 g/8 oz plain flour	450 g/1 lb courgettes, grated
2–3 tablespoons olive oil	1 large onion, finely chopped
water	1 egg, beaten
	100 g/4 oz cheese, grated

PUT the flour in a large bowl and make a well in the centre. Add the oil by pouring into the well, stir with fingertips until well mixed, add water until a soft dough (not sticky). Do not knead. Cut in half. Roll out half and line a well-buttered round 20-cm/8-inch pie dish. Fill with grated courgettes, onion, beaten egg and cheese on top. Cover with the remaining pastry and prick top of pie well with a fork. Cook in a moderately hot oven (200 C, 400 F, gas 6) until golden brown, about 30–40 minutes. Serves 6 as a starter.

Mrs Jane Stanley, Harvington, Worcestershire

FISH AND SEAFOOD

BAKED STUFFED HERRINGS

4 herrings
1 small onion
25 g/1 oz fresh breadcrumbs
1 large soft herring roe
½ teaspoon dried mixed herbs

1 teaspoon finely chopped parsley
salt and pepper
100 g/4 oz mushrooms, chopped
a little melted butter

REMOVE heads, clean and wash fish. Split open and remove back bones. To make the stuffing chop onion finely, add breadcrumbs, roe, herbs, parsley, seasoning, mushrooms and a little melted butter. Mix well. Sprinkle the inside of each herring with salt and pepper and spread on a little of the stuffing. Roll up and tie with cotton. Place in a greased pie dish and cover with buttered greaseproof paper. Bake in a moderately hot oven (190 c, 375 f, gas 5) for 25 minutes, then remove paper and allow to brown for a further 10 minutes. SERVES 4.

Mrs D. Winterburn, Heddon on the Wall, Newcastle-on-Tyne

SAVOURY MACKEREL

2 good-sized mackerel	½ onion, finely chopped
2 tablespoons fresh breadcrumbs	salt and pepper
1 teaspoon chopped parsley	breadcrumbs to sprinkle
1 teaspoon chopped mixed herbs	butter to dot

THOROUGHLY cleanse the fish, split and remove back bones, fins, heads and tails. Mix without moistening the remaining ingredients, seasoning to taste, and lay this stuffing on one fish. Place the other on top, skin side upwards, and sprinkle over a few breadcrumbs. Place on a greased baking tray, dot with butter and bake in a moderate oven (180 C, 350 F, gas 4) for about 30 minutes. Serve with a fennel sauce. SERVES 2.

Dorothy Skinner, Bala, Gwynned, North Wales

TROUT SOUCHET

BOIL four or five parsley roots in a pint and a half of water for five minutes; add a teaspoonful of finely grated horseradish and a teaspoon of salt. Put in the trout (5 or 6 small ones). Boil up, skim, simmer for twelve minutes. Serve in the water (with the parsley) in a deep dish, a dish of nicely cut thin brown bread and butter served with it. From: *The Young Housewife's Daily Assistant 1864.*

Mrs Shirley Harris, Eastington, Gloucestershire

TROUT FRICASSÉE

Trout

1 kg/2 lb rainbow trout, cleaned and with eyes removed	1 blade of mace
	1 tablespoon vinegar
1 bay leaf	1 teaspoon salt

IF you are using a fish kettle, lay the trout on the grid gently curled into an S-shape. If you have no fish kettle and are using a round pan, curl the fish round on a piece of folded clean cloth and place in the pan with the cloth overlapping the sides of the pan, so that you can lift the trout out by it when it is cooked; the ends of the cloth must not trail too much, and must be well away from the flame, but long enough to grasp. Cover the fish completely with water and add the bay leaf, mace, vinegar and salt. Bring to the boil very slowly indeed; it should take about 40 minutes. Put on the lid and boil rapidly for 3 minutes. Take off the heat and leave the fish in the water for 15 minutes. Lift out the fish on the grid and rest it above the fish kettle while you remove the skin. Remove the flesh from the bones and place in a buttered ovenproof dish.

Parsley sauce

25 g/1 oz butter
25 g/1 oz flour
300 ml/½ pint liquid (150 ml/¼ pint
  milk, 150 ml/¼ pint fish stock)

salt and pepper
2 tablespoons freshly chopped
  parsley
a dash of vinegar

MELT the butter, stir in the flour to form a roux and cook for 1–2 minutes, without browning. Add the liquid a little at a time, stirring well to keep the mixture smooth, and bring to the boil, stirring all the time. Cook for 2–3 minutes, beating the sauce to make it smooth and glossy. Add seasoning and parsley. Pour this over the trout.

Puff pastry leaves

1 212-g/7½-oz packet frozen puff
  pastry, thawed

beaten egg to glaze

ROLL out the pastry thinly. Cut into leaf shapes, place on a dampened baking tray and glaze with the beaten egg. Bake in a hot oven (230 C, 450 F, gas 8) for about 15 minutes.

Garnish

2 hard-boiled eggs
¼ cucumber

1 lemon

SLICE the hard-boiled eggs, place on the trout fricassée and return to a moderate oven (180 C, 350 F, gas 4) to heat through. Heat the pastry leaves at the same time if they were made earlier. Just before serving, garnish with slices of cucumber and lemon and accompany with freshly cooked new potatoes, asparagus cooked and prepared in the usual way, and the pastry leaves. SERVES 4.

Mrs E. M. Joules, Loynton, Stafford

☆ SUMMER TROUT ☆

575 g/1¼ lb rainbow trout, cooked
350 g/12 oz courgettes
1 tablespoon chopped fresh dill
2 teaspoons freshly grated
   horseradish
1 198-g/7-oz packet frozen puff
   pastry, thawed

beaten egg to brush
lemon wedges to garnish
SAUCE
40 g/1½ oz butter
40 g/1½ oz flour
300 ml/½ pint milk
salt and pepper

SKIN, bone and flake the trout. Slice the courgettes, place in boiling salted water and cook for 5 minutes. Drain and refresh (run under cold water to set colour and prevent further cooking).

Make the sauce. Melt the butter in a saucepan, add the flour and stir for 2 minutes. Draw the pan off the heat, pour in the milk and mix well. Return the sauce to the heat and stir continually until boiling. Simmer for 2–3 minutes and season with salt and pepper. Allow to cool.

When cool add the trout, courgettes, dill and horseradish. Season to taste.

Roll the pastry into a 30-cm/12-inch square. Place the trout mixture in the centre. Brush the edges of the pastry with beaten egg and fold over into a parcel. Crimp the edges together. Place on a dampened baking tray, glaze with beaten egg and bake in a moderately hot oven (200 C, 400 F, gas 6) for 20–30 minutes, until the pastry is golden and cooked. Serve garnished with lemon wedges. SERVES 4.

Jane Hale, Bough Beech, Kent

SOLE SUPRÊME

8 small fillets of lemon sole
juice of ½ lemon
salt and pepper
100 g/4 oz mushrooms
butter to fry

40 g/1½ oz butter
40 g/1½ oz flour
300 ml/½ pint milk
1 425-g/15-oz can mushroom soup
paprika

WASH and wipe dry the fish, squeeze lemon juice over fillets and add a little salt and pepper. Roll up each fillet and place in shallow square or oblong ovenproof dish. Peel and cut up mushrooms and fry in a little butter for a few minutes, then arrange these between fish in dish.

Melt the 40 g/1½ oz butter in a saucepan, add flour and gently cook for 1 minute. Stir in milk and mushroom soup, also salt and pepper to taste. Cook until sauce thickens. Pour sauce over the fish and mushrooms in dish. Place in a moderate oven (180 c, 350 f, gas 4) for 30–40 minutes, or until it turns golden brown on top. Before serving sprinkle over a little paprika. Serve hot with vegetables. SERVES 4.

Mrs S. E. Morgan, Narberth, Dyfed

SURPRISE BAKED FISH SOUFFLÉ

450 g/1 lb white fish, skinned and boned	1 teaspoon orange juice
300 ml/½ pint milk	100 g/4 oz button mushrooms
1 large slice onion	25 g/1 oz butter and extra butter to fry
1 bay leaf	15 g/½ oz flour
4 peppercorns	2 eggs, separated
salt and pepper	25 g/1 oz grated cheese
pinch of thyme	1 tablespoon breadcrumbs

GREASE a 900-ml/1½-pint ovenproof dish. Cook the fish in the milk with the onion, bay leaf, peppercorns and seasoning for about 12–15 minutes. Remove the fish and finely flake it into a bowl. Add the thyme and orange juice, mix well and leave to cool. Strain and reserve the milk.

Lightly fry the mushrooms in a little butter and put them aside. Melt the 25 g/1 oz butter in a pan and blend in the flour. Cook for about 2 minutes and then gradually stir in the reserved milk. Cook the sauce for a further 2 minutes until smooth and creamy, adjusting the seasoning as necessary. Blend the fish into the sauce and then add the egg yolks, one at a time. In a separate bowl whisk the egg whites and when they are stiff, fold them into the fish mixture.

Put half the fish mixture into the ovenproof dish and arrange the mushrooms in a layer on top. Spoon over the rest of the fish mixture and sprinkle with cheese and breadcrumbs. Bake in a moderately hot oven (200 c, 400 f, gas 6) for about 45 minutes. SERVES 2–4.

Mrs H. Karran, Castletown, Isle of Man

BUTTER BEAN AND FISH PIE

450 g/1 lb plaice, skinned
100 g/4 oz mushrooms, quartered
450 ml/¾ pint milk
sea salt and black pepper
50 g/2 oz butter
50 g/2 oz flour

3 tablespoons freshly chopped
  parsley
1 425-g/15-oz can butter beans,
  drained
3 hard-boiled eggs, halved
675 g/1½ lb creamy mashed potato

POACH fish and mushrooms in 300 ml/½ pint of the milk, well seasoned with freshly ground sea salt and black pepper, until cooked. Strain fish and mushrooms and reserve milk.

Make a white sauce by melting butter and then adding flour. Cook for 1 minute. Remove from heat and gradually add milk reserved from fish plus remaining 150 ml/¼ pint. Boil and thicken, stirring. Adjust seasoning if necessary. Add flaked fish, parsley, mushrooms and butter beans to sauce mixture. Gently stir in the hard-boiled eggs.

Place mixture in a large ovenproof dish and cover with creamy mashed potato dotted with a little butter. Cook in a moderately hot oven (190 C, 375 F, gas 5) until potato is nicely browned, about 30 minutes.

Serve on its own with crunchy garlic bread for a light lunch or supper, or for a more substantial meal accompany with green vegetables. SERVES 4.

Carolyn Heeps, Crossenny, Gwent

SMOKED FISH BAKE

100 g/4 oz long-grain rice
450 g/1 lb yellow fish (smoked cod
  or Finnan haddock)
350 ml/12 fl oz milk
2 tablespoons chopped parsley
20 g/¾ oz butter

20 g/¾ oz flour
100 g/4 oz grated Cheddar cheese
1 teaspoon made mustard
salt and pepper
4 eggs
sprigs of parsley to garnish

COOK the rice, rinse and drain well. Cook the fish gently in half the milk in a covered pan. When cooked remove fish and reserve liquid. Remove any skin and bones from the fish and flake. Mix the fish and rice together in a casserole dish. Stir in the chopped parsley. Melt the butter, stir in the flour and then the milk and reserved liquid to make a sauce. Add three-quarters of the cheese, the mustard and seasoning to taste. Mix the cheese sauce into the fish and rice, and sprinkle remaining cheese on top.

Bake until warmed through and top bubbles and turns golden brown, approximately 20 minutes at 180 c, 350 f, gas 4.

While casserole is cooking lightly poach the eggs. Remove casserole from oven, pop eggs on top, season and garnish. Serve with fresh crusty bread and butter for lunch, or with peas and grilled tomatoes for supper. It should serve four but has been eaten by two; the ingredients can be expanded or reduced to suit individual needs.

Mrs Pauline Mackinder, Chetton, Shropshire

FISH SUPRÊME

675 g/1½ lb fresh or frozen cod or haddock
225 g/8 oz smoked haddock
100 g/4 oz mushrooms, sliced
1 large or 2 small leeks, sliced
salt and pepper

450–600 ml/¾–1 pint thick white sauce (made with butter, flour, milk, fish stock and 1 egg yolk)
2 teaspoons grated Parmesan cheese
parsley to garnish

REMOVE skin and bones from the fish and reserve these to make fish stock for another occasion. Break up the fish into roughly 5-cm/2-inch squared pieces and place in ovenproof dish. Add sliced mushrooms and leeks. Season. Pour over sauce and lightly sprinkle this with Parmesan cheese. Bake in a moderately hot oven (200 c, 400 f, gas 6) until golden brown and bubbling. Allow 30 minutes for fresh fish and 45 minutes if frozen fish is used. Serve garnished with parsley. SERVES 6.

Mrs J. Winter, Leighton Buzzard, Bedfordshire

SCAMPI À LA LIVORNESE

25 g/1 oz butter	celery salt
½ clove garlic	1 teaspoon sugar
1 rounded tablespoon flour	1 227-g/8-oz can tomatoes
4 tablespoons chicken stock	1 99-g/3½-oz can tuna fish
1 teaspoon tomato purée	100 g/4 oz prawns
¼ teaspoon dried oregano	chopped parsley

MELT butter, sauté crushed garlic and stir in flour to form a roux. Add stock, purée, oregano, celery salt to taste and sugar. Add tomatoes and stir together until cooked. Add tuna fish (including liquid) and just before serving fold in prawns to heat – or they may be heated in a little butter and used to top as garnish. Sprinkle with chopped parsley.

Serve with cooked rice and green salad as a luncheon or supper dish, or with garlic bread as a starter. Double quantities for a more substantial main course dish for four.

Mrs V. Rowlands, Mickle Trafford, Chester

SALMON PUDDING

1 212-g/7½-oz can salmon	2 tablespoons wine vinegar
100 g/4 oz fresh breadcrumbs	2 eggs, separated
2 tablespoons melted butter	salt and pepper

MIX the flaked salmon, breadcrumbs, butter, vinegar and egg yolks together. Fold in the stiffly beaten egg whites and seasoning. Turn into a buttered pudding basin, cover with greaseproof paper tied down with string and steam for 30 minutes. Serve cold with salad and potatoes. SERVES 2–4.

Mrs J. P. Brand, North Berwick, East Lothian

SPECIAL SALMON PUFF

1 454-g/1-lb can salmon or 450 g/ 1 lb fresh salmon poached in a little milk with a dash of vinegar	100 ml/4 fl oz whipped cream
	1 142-g/5-oz carton mandarin yogurt
100 g/4 oz softened butter	salt and pepper
2 eggs, separated	2 tablespoons flour

FLAKE salmon and mash with a fork. Beat to a paste with softened butter. Add egg yolks and mix well.

Combine cream, mandarin yogurt, salt, pepper and flour and beat to a creamy consistency. Add salmon and butter mixture to cream and combine thoroughly. Fold in stiffly beaten egg whites and pour into a buttered casserole dish. Set in a roasting pan of hot water and bake in a moderate oven (180 c, 350 f, gas 4) for about 1 hour.

This is delicious served with creamed potatoes and garden peas, or as a light tea with lettuce or rice and sweetcorn salad as an accompaniment. SERVES 4.

Mrs I. E. Matthews, Bangor, County Down

BAKED SALMON AND TOMATO SAUCE

1 kg/2 lb fresh salmon (middle)	TOMATO SAUCE
salt and pepper	1 heaped teaspoon arrowroot
grated nutmeg	250 ml/8 fl oz canned tomato juice
2 small shallots	1 small onion or shallot
1 teaspoon chopped parsley	salt and pepper
little butter	grated nutmeg
1 small glass cider or claret	lemon juice
(optional)	sugar

CUT fish into two or three even pieces, place in a well-buttered ovenproof dish and season with salt, pepper and a little grated nutmeg. Chop shallots and sprinkle over with the parsley. Dot a little butter on top of the fish and moisten with wine or cider (if used). Cover and cook in a moderately hot oven (190 c, 375 f, gas 5) for about 1 hour, basting fish often. Dish up and pour tomato sauce over slices of salmon, using any juices left in dish to flavour the sauce. SERVES 6–8.

TOMATO SAUCE. Blend arrowroot with a little of tomato juice. Slice the onion and simmer in remainder of tomato juice for 10 minutes. Stir in the blended arrowroot and boil for 1 minute. Season the sauce. Add nutmeg and a few drops of lemon juice and sugar to taste. Strain the sauce before serving.

Anon

SALMON CUSHION WITH HOLLANDAISE SAUCE

THE CUSHION
1 tablespoon oil
1 teaspoon lemon juice
1.3 kg/2¾ lb tail end of salmon
   trout
175 g/6 oz button mushrooms
50 g/2 oz butter
50 g/2 oz plain flour
150 ml/¼ pint dry white wine

300 ml/½ pint milk
3 eggs
salt and ground black pepper
50 g/2 oz peeled prawns
HOLLANDAISE SAUCE
100 g/4 oz butter
2 eggs
1 tablespoon lemon juice
¼ teaspoon salt

FIRST make the cushion. Whisk the oil with lemon juice, use to brush the insides of four 300-ml/½-pint shallow, ovenproof round containers. Line bases with greaseproof paper. Remove the tail and fins from salmon and remove skin using a sharp knife. Cut salmon lengthways, parallel to the bone, into thin slices. Line base and sides of containers with salmon, then chill.

Wipe mushrooms, melt butter in a pan, add mushrooms and cook over a low heat for 3 minutes. Stir in flour, cook for 1 minute. Gradually add wine and milk and bring to the boil, stirring all the time. Cool slightly. Blend in the beaten eggs and seasoning until almost smooth.

Set oven to moderate (180C, 350F, gas 4). Divide prawns between containers, pour over mushroom mixture. Place in roasting tin and half-fill with hot water. Bake for 45 minutes until filling is firm.

Meanwhile make sauce. Heat butter until bubbling but not browning. Blend eggs, lemon juice and salt in a liquidiser until mixed. While still running, pour melted butter through hole in liquidiser lid until all is added and sauce is smooth and fairly thick. Turn out cushions onto warmed serving plates, remove greaseproof paper and spoon sauce over. Serve with new potatoes and French beans. SERVES 4.

Miss D. Sherwin, Knutsford, Cheshire

☆ SALMON AND PRAWN ☆
SLICE

1 212-g/7½-oz packet frozen puff
  pastry, thawed
1 egg, beaten
1 tablespoon grated Parmesan
  cheese
1 tablespoon finely chopped
  cucumber
1 tablespoon chopped watercress

1 tablespoon freshly chopped
  herbs (parsley, chervil, chives,
  tarragon)
300 ml/½ pint mayonnaise
175 g/6 oz fresh salmon, cooked
225 g/8 oz peeled prawns
chopped parsley to garnish

ROLL out pastry and divide into two oblong strips. Place on baking
sheet, lightly score one strip in diamonds. Brush with beaten egg
and sprinkle with the cheese. Bake in a hot oven (230 c, 450 f, gas
8) for about 10 minutes. Split each strip horizontally in half and
leave to cool.

Combine the cucumber, watercress and herbs with the mayonnaise. Add the flaked salmon and prawns.

Just before serving, place one strip of pastry on a serving dish.
Spread with one-third of the filling. Repeat twice more, finishing
with the decorative pastry strip. Garnish with parsley and serve
with green salad.

Mrs D. Gray, Chilton, Buckinghamshire

MEAT DISHES

SUMMER STEAK PARCEL

4 or 5 small young onions
450 g/1 lb new baby carrots
1 kg/2 lb braising steak, in one
   piece
dripping

225 g/8 oz small tomatoes
seasoning and mixed herbs
300 ml/½ pint beef stock (or water
   and a stock cube)

PREPARE onions and carrots and leave whole. Trim gristle and
surplus fat from meat and fry in dripping to seal on both sides.
Place on a large piece of foil in a roasting tin, add carrots, onions
and halved tomatoes, season with salt, pepper and herbs and pour
over the stock. Join and turn over the edges of the foil to make a
parcel. Bake in a moderate oven (180 c, 350 f, gas 4) for 2–2½ hours
or until the meat is tender. Delicious served with new potatoes and
fresh garden peas. SERVES 4–6.

Mrs Margaret Cooper, Edwinstowe, Nottinghamshire

B.B.C. CASSEROLE
(Beef, Basil and Cider)

2 tablespoons corn oil
2 large onions
1 or 2 cloves garlic (optional)
1 kg/2 lb cheapest stewing beef
salt and freshly ground black
 pepper
2 tablespoons plain flour
1 beef stock cube dissolved in
 300 ml/½ pint water

300 ml/½ pint dry cider
1–2 teaspoons sweet basil
ALTERNATIVE ADDITIONS
chopped root vegetables of your
 choice e.g. parsnip, turnip,
 swede, carrot
medium whole potatoes, enough
 for each person

HEAT corn oil in a large saucepan. Chop onions, crush garlic and add to hot oil. Remove from pan when onions are transparent, do not allow to go brown. Trim fat and gristle from meat and chop what is left into bite-sized chunks. Grind black pepper over meat and add to pan of oil. Brown meat nicely all over, remove with a slotted spoon and place with onions. Remove the saucepan from the heat and add the flour. Stir well with a spring whisk until the flour has absorbed all the lovely, tasty juices. Return to the heat, add the stock and cider slowly, stirring with the spring whisk. Season to taste and add the sweet basil. When it has all thickened, replace onions and meat and stir again to distribute all the succulent ingredients evenly. Adjust flavour if necessary. Pour the contents of the saucepan into a large buttered casserole dish, cover and cook in a moderate oven (160 C, 325 F, gas 3) for 2–3 hours, until the meat is tender.

If you are going to use the alternative additions this is all you do: dice root vegetables and place in a saucepan with enough water to cover. Bring to boiling point and allow to cook for 1 minute. Add these par-cooked vegetables and whole scrubbed (not peeled) potatoes to the casserole about ¾–1 hour after the casserole has been in the oven.

This recipe is guaranteed to stoke up the system, or alternatively send you to sleep in contentment. A glass or two of homemade cider will complement this meal. SERVES 6.

Mrs A. S. Bartlett, North Wootton, Somerset

FAMILY CASSEROLE

2 beef stock cubes
25 g/1 oz beef dripping
1 kg/2 lb stewing beef, cubed
1 large onion, sliced
2 large carrots, sliced
½ small turnip or swede, diced

3–4 tomatoes, skinned
few slices of green and red pepper
½ teaspoon salt
pepper
bouquet garni

MAKE up 1.15 litres/2 pints stock with the stock cubes. Melt dripping in a flameproof casserole and brown meat, onion, carrot and turnip. Pour off excess fat. Add stock, tomatoes, peppers, seasoning and bouquet garni. Bring to the boil then cover and cook in a cool oven (150c, 300f, gas 2) for 3 hours.

Serve with creamed or jacket potatoes and dumplings. Just before serving remove bouquet garni and thicken gravy as desired. SERVES 6.

Mrs J. Robinson, Wilberfoss, Yorkshire

BEER STEW

This is the Sneyd family's favourite winter meal; it is easy to keep hot and it reheats extremely well. Nothing needs precise weighing, as long as you have roughly equal amounts of meat and onion. I find 2–3 onions and 175 g/6 oz meat per person is a rough guide, but I use whatever I have. It really is foolproof.

stewing steak
onions
fat for frying

salt and pepper
beer
bread

FIRST trim the meat of gristle and excess fat. Cut the meat into slices 1.5 cm/¾ inch thick, then into pieces about 2.5 × 5 cm/ 1 × 2 inches. Slice the onions.

Fry the onions until transparent, drain and set aside. Brown the meat on both sides, a few pieces at a time so that they do not get "wet" but retain a good colour. Make sure you have the same amount of fried onion and browned meat. Drain off the extra fat, and arrange alternate layers of meat and onions in a casserole, adding salt and pepper to each layer, and finishing with onions. Pour beer over the contents of the casserole, so that the top layer is well covered. Cut the bread into slices about 1.5 cm/¾ inch thick, having removed the crusts, and make a lid of bread, shaping the side pieces so that the onions are all hidden. Press the bread down so that it soaks up the beer, it must be thoroughly damp but not floating!

Cook slowly in a moderate oven (160 c, 325 f, gas 3) for 3 hours or longer, keeping an eye after the first 2 hours so that if it dries out too much you can add a little more beer. The top should be rich and crisp, combining the fat from the meat with the flavour of the beer.

Mrs Henry Sneyd, Menheniot, Cornwall

Farmhouse Beef Casserole

50 g/2 oz butter
100 g/4 oz bacon, chopped
1 medium onion, chopped
3 carrots, chopped
675 g/1½ lb stewing steak
1 tablespoon flour
1 stock cube
1 tablespoon tomato purée
1 tablespoon demerara sugar
300 ml/½ pint boiling water
300 ml/½ pint Guinness (or other stout)
salt and pepper

Melt the butter in a pan and fry bacon, onion and carrots for 6–7 minutes. Drain and place in a large casserole dish. Chop stewing steak into chunks and fry in the butter until sealed, drain off and put in casserole. Blend the flour with remaining butter in pan and cook until brown. Remove from heat and gradually stir in the crumbled stock cube, tomato purée, sugar, boiling water and Guinness. Bring to the boil, stirring continuously. Season to taste and pour over casserole. Cover and cook in a cool oven (150 c, 300 f, gas 2) for 2½ hours. Season to taste and serve with piping hot creamed potatoes. Serves 4.

Mrs Barbara Newton, Coton Clanford, Stafford

IRÍSH HOT POT

oil to fry
675 g/1½ lb stewing steak, cubed
2 tablespoons pearl barley
900 ml/1½ pints stock, made with 2
   stock cubes
salt and black pepper
225 g/8 oz onions, finely chopped

225 g/8 oz leeks, finely chopped
2 sticks celery, chopped
1 medium parsnip, finely diced
1 medium carrot, finely diced
1 kg/2 lb potatoes, sliced
1 bay leaf
3 tablespoons chopped parsley

HEAT a little oil in a frying pan and brown meat. Transfer to a large flameproof casserole, add barley, stock and seasoning to taste. Bring to a simmer, cover and cook gently for 30 minutes. Add all other ingredients except parsley. Mix well, bring to boil, cover and simmer very slowly on top of stove, without stirring, for 1¼ hours. Remove bay leaf and add parsley before serving.

Mrs E. Jamison, Eglinton, Londonderry

☆ FRUITY SCOTCH BEEF ☆

25 g/1 oz lard
1.5-kg/3-lb piece of silverside or
   brisket
2 onions, sliced
1 tablespoon brown sugar
salt and pepper
6 tablespoons whisky
1 teaspoon ground cloves

4 tablespoons water
175 g/6 oz dried stoned prunes,
   soaked overnight
175 g/6 oz dried apricots, soaked
   overnight
15 g/½ oz plain flour
chopped parsley to garnish

MELT lard in a large flameproof casserole and brown beef all over. Add the onions, sugar, seasoning, whisky, cloves and water, and bring to the boil. Lower the heat, cover and simmer for 2½ hours, turning occasionally. (If you are feeling extravagant, add a little more whisky!) Add the prunes and apricots to the casserole half an hour before the end of cooking time.

Remove the meat and fruit with a slotted spoon, place on a heated serving dish and keep hot. Blend the flour with a little water until smooth, then gradually stir into the cooking juices. Cook, stirring constantly, until the gravy has thickened. Serve with the meat and fruit and garnish with chopped parsley.

Mrs Doreen Forsyth, Warkworth, Northumberland

FAMILY WARM-UP CASSEROLE

1 large oxtail
450 g/1 lb skirt beef
salt and pepper
50 g/2 oz flour
50–75 g/2–3 oz dripping
2 large onions, sliced
1 medium turnip or swede, diced
2 medium carrots, sliced
1 stick celery, chopped
100 g/4 oz bacon, diced

225 g/8 oz haricot beans, soaked
   and cooked
450 g/1 lb skinned tomatoes or
   1 425-g/15-oz can tomatoes
600 ml/1 pint boiling stock
2 peppercorns
2 cloves
pinch of mace
bouquet garni
1 glass wine

CUT up oxtail and skirt. Season the flour and coat each piece of meat. Melt dripping in a large frying pan until sizzling then brown the pieces well and transfer to a large casserole dish. Fry the onion, turnip, carrot, celery and bacon in the hot fat and add these to the casserole. Add the cooked haricot beans, tomatoes, stock, peppercorns, cloves, mace and bouquet garni. Stir gently and season, going easy on the salt because too much will make the beans go hard. Cover and cook in a cool oven (150 C, 300 F, gas 2) for about 3 hours, or until tender. Allow to cool overnight.

Next day, scrape unwanted surface fat off the top of casserole. Reheat for at least 1 hour in a moderately hot oven (190 C, 375 F, gas 5). Stir in a glass of wine and serve with boiled potatoes, cabbage and a knob of butter. SERVES 6.

Mrs Susan Simpson, Crediton, Devon

BEEF CASSEROLE SURPRISE

1 small onion
½ green pepper
½ red pepper
450 g/1 lb lean stewing steak
25 g/1 oz fat

2 teaspoons cornflour
300 ml/½ pint beef stock or water
1 227-g/8-oz can tomatoes
salt and pepper

DICE onion and slice peppers. Cut meat into cubes and brown in melted fat in a flameproof casserole. Remove meat. Gently fry onion and peppers until soft. Blend cornflour with stock or water. Place all ingredients in the pan and bring to the boil, stirring all the time. Season to taste. Cover and simmer on top of the cooker or in a moderate oven (180 C, 350 F, gas 4) for 1–1½ hours, until meat is tender. SERVES 4.

Mrs Linda McTurk, Lochfoot, Dumfries

BRISKET HOT POT

8 button onions
100 g/4 oz celery
225 g/8 oz carrots
225 g/8 oz new potatoes
25 g/1 oz dripping
1.5-kg/3-lb joint brisket, boned and rolled

salt and pepper
300 ml/½ pint beef stock (or stock cube and water)
2 teaspoons made English mustard
1 egg yolk
150 ml/¼ pint natural yogurt

PREPARE onions and leave whole. Wash celery and cut into 5-cm/ 2-inch lengths. Peel and cut up carrots and potatoes.

Melt dripping in a large flameproof casserole or saucepan. Sprinkle the meat with salt and pepper and fry until brown all over. Put on one side. Fry the vegetables for 3 minutes then remove. Add the stock to the pan and blend in the mustard. Return meat, bring to boil, cover and simmer for 1–1½ hours, or until tender. Add vegetables for the last 15 minutes.

Transfer the joint to a serving dish and keep hot. Blend egg yolk with yogurt, stir into vegetables but do not boil. Arrange vegetables around meat and pour over the sauce.

Mrs N. Burton, Brailsford, Derby

STEAK AND KIDNEY WITH SAVOURY CRUST

1 kg/2 lb lean stewing steak in one piece
2 lamb's kidneys
seasoned flour to coat
300 ml/½ pint stock
SUET CRUST
225 g/8 oz self-raising flour

100 g/4 oz shredded beef suet
¼ teaspoon salt
½ teaspoon bicarbonate of soda
1 tablespoon chopped parsley
1 teaspoon chopped thyme
a little sour milk

CUT steak and kidneys into thin slices and dip each in well-seasoned flour. Place a slice of kidney on each slice of steak and roll up.

Prepare a suet crust with the flour, beef suet, salt, bicarbonate of soda, parsley and thyme. Mix all well together and make into a fairly moist dough with sour milk.

Roll out three-quarters of the dough to line a well-greased 1.15-litre/2-pint pudding basin. Fill with the steak rolls and gently pour on the stock. Roll out the remaining dough to make a lid and press the edges together firmly to seal. Fold a pleat in a square of greaseproof paper, place over the pudding and then cover the top with a clean cloth, securing it with string below the rim. Place in a saucepan of boiling water and steam briskly for 2½–3 hours, replenishing the water as necessary. SERVES 4–6.

Mrs R. E. Bishop, Colwall Green, Worcestershire

BEEF COSMOPOLITAN

675 g/1½ lb best chuck steak, cut into 3.5-cm/1½-inch cubes
50 g/2 oz melted or clarified butter (unsalted butter is best)
100 g/4 oz onions, chopped
2 tablespoons curry powder made into a paste or 1 tablespoon curry paste
450 g/1 lb tomatoes, peeled and chopped
MARINADE
½ teaspoon salt
1 teaspoon freshly milled black pepper
1 teaspoon ground cinnamon
1 teaspoon ground cumin
1 teaspoon dry mustard
1 teaspoon garlic powder (or 3 cloves crushed garlic)
1 teaspoon cayenne pepper
1 teaspoon ground allspice
100 g/4 oz onions, finely chopped
300 ml/½ pint brown ale or stout

FIRST prepare the marinade. Mix the dry spices with chopped onions. Toss in the meat cubes, add the stout or ale, give it a stir and let it stand covered in a cool place for at least 12 hours.

When ready to cook, heat the clarified butter in a very thick pan or flameproof casserole and fry the onions until transparent. Add the curry paste. Fry the mixture until spices take on a granulated appearance and look golden brown, and the butter is separated from the spices. Add the tomatoes and keep stirring over a very low heat for a further 10 minutes. Remove from heat and stir in the meat and marinade. Place in a large warmed casserole dish, if not already using one, put on a well-fitting lid and cook in a moderately hot oven (200 c, 400 F, gas 6) for 1 hour. Test the meat and if not quite tender cook for a further half hour, adding a little water if the liquid has evaporated.

Serve with cooked pearl barley, fresh green peas, runner beans and cucumber cubes in natural yogurt. This casserole can also be cooked and frozen for use at a later date. SERVES 4.

Mrs Pushpa Darashah, Over, Cambridge

SUMMER CURRY

On previous day

IN 25 g/1 oz butter fry for 3–4 minutes, 1 large onion (or 12 shallots) and 1 clove garlic, both finely sliced. Then add the following spices mixed to a stiff paste with weak vinegar:

1 tablespoon ground coriander	¼ teaspoon ground chillies
1 teaspoon ground turmeric	generous pinch of fenugreek
1 teaspoon ground cumin seed	black pepper

OR *2 teaspoons good curry powder*

Cook spices with onion and garlic for 3–5 minutes. Add to this 450 g/1 lb stewing beef cut into 2.5-cm/1-inch cubes. Stir around and leave on low heat until gravy appears. Add 300 ml/½ pint hot water and half a peeled, chopped cooking apple. Cover pan and simmer until the meat is cooked, about 1½–2 hours, adding a little more water if necessary. Cool and leave for flavour to emerge until the next day.

The following day

Prepare individual dishes containing: sliced tomatoes, sliced cucumber, radishes, sliced green peppers, spring onions, raw grated carrots, cooked beetroot, lettuce, homemade chutney and sliced banana (NB NO OIL OR DRESSING).

Prepare white or brown rice, 2 cups washed rice to 4 cups water.

Reheat meat. Add liquid squeezed from ½ cup grated fresh or desiccated coconut covered with boiling water and allowed to stand for 1 hour. Add also 1 tablespoon homemade chutney, 1 dessertspoon homemade marmalade and the juice of ½ lemon.

Serve the curry on a bed of cooked rice, sprinkle sultanas and peanuts on top and accompany with all the side dishes. SERVES 4.

Mrs G. P. Edwards, Creamore, Shropshire

STEAMING HOT POT OF CHILLI CON CARNE

450 g/1 lb minced beef
2 onions
½ teaspoon salt
½ teaspoon pepper
2 sticks of celery
2 432-g/15¼-oz cans red kidney beans, drained

600 ml/1 pint water
1 beef stock cube
1 198-g/7-oz tube tomato purée
1 tablespoon chilli powder
100 g/4 oz grated Cheddar cheese

THE first thing I do is to find a big flameproof casserole and a large frying pan. I place the frying pan on the cooker and start to brown my well crumbled minced beef. I then chop up the onions into little pieces and add them with the salt and pepper to my cooking minced beef. I give it a good stir, add a little water and set it to simmer while I prepare the rest of the ingredients.

While I am in a chopping mood I chop up the celery and set it to one side. Into the casserole dish I place the red kidney beans and cover them with water (about a pint will do but use your own judgement; some people like to have their chilli a bit thicker so use a little less water). To the kidney beans add the crumbled beef stock cube and I squeeze in the whole tube of tomato purée. Now add the chilli powder and stir all of these ingredients together.

It is now time to add the minced beef, onion and celery to the casserole dish. Place the dish on the cooker and bring the chilli to a boil, stirring while you do so. Taste and add another tablespoon of chilli powder if you like it really hot. Now cover the casserole, put into a moderately hot oven (200 c, 400 f, gas 6) and let its juices make themselves into one delicious hot pot of chilli.

I usually make up some nice hot scones just about now so that they will be ready when the chilli is done. After about half an hour of cooking your chilli is ready but you can let it cook longer if you want to; just put it in a cooler oven and check occasionally to make sure it is not too dry, if it is add more water.

When it is ready to serve, dish out into bowls and sprinkle generously with the grated cheese. Serve with hot buttered scones or buttered bread. I hope you enjoy it as much as my family does. SERVES 4.

Mrs Ellen Marland, Hetheringtham Fen, Lincolnshire

AUTUMN SLOW BAKE

1 medium onion	mixed herbs
25 g/1 oz fat	1 447-g/15¾-oz can baked beans
450 g/1 lb minced beef	450 g/1 lb potatoes, sliced thin
2 beef stock cubes	225 g/8 oz carrots, sliced thin
1 tablespoon plain flour	100 g/4 oz peas
black pepper and salt	

SAUTÉ chopped onion in fat using a large frying pan. Add minced meat, turning it over with a wooden spoon for 5 minutes. Take from heat, stir in stock cubes, flour, salt and pepper, sprinkle on herbs then add can of beans. Mix together.

Line a large greased ovenproof dish with sliced potatoes and pour mixture on top. Layer carrots and peas and put another layer of potatoes on top to cover. Cover the dish with foil and bake in a moderate oven (160 c, 325 f, gas 3) for 1½–2 hours. The cover can be removed for the last 15 minutes to brown. Freezes well. SERVES 6.

Eileen M. Crooks, Ockbrook, Derbyshire

NETHERCOTT NOSHUP

675 g/1½ lb lean minced beef	salt and pepper
2 finely chopped medium onions	2 447-g/15¾-oz cans baked beans

MIX together beef and chopped onion and cook gently in enough water to cover, stirring occasionally. When the meat is cooked (about 45 minutes), season to taste and strain off most of the liquid to make gravy. Spread the moist meat and onion mixture into a shallow baking dish, making it level and even. Spread the baked beans evenly over the top. Heat through in a moderately hot oven (190 c, 375 f, gas 5) until piping hot, the meat mixture beginning to bubble up through beans here and there. Serve from the dish, best eaten with turnip tops and sliced carrots, adding gravy as liked. SERVES 6.

This dish was a great winter favourite with my five children, and made a nourishing simple meal, with nothing wasted as all of it was always eaten. It can be made with any meat leftovers minced, but is best with fresh meat.

Mrs Daphne Phillips, Combe Florey, Somerset

CURRIED SPAGHETTI MINCE

450 g/1 lb minced beef
2 teaspoons curry powder
1 large onion
2 large carrots

1 396-g/14-oz can tomatoes
150–300 ml/¼–½ pint water
salt and pepper
225 g/8 oz spaghetti

BROWN mince in pan. Add curry powder, chopped onion and cut up carrots. Cook for 5 minutes. Add tomatoes, water and seasoning. Simmer gently, stirring occasionally, for approximately 1 hour.

Cook spaghetti and either chop up and add to mince in pan or serve separately with the mince sauce on top. SERVES 4.

Mrs Doris Shearer, Stronsay, Orkney Islands

MEAT SAUCE CONCOCTION

3 rashers bacon, chopped
2 onions, chopped
3 tablespoons oil
2 carrots, grated
2 cooking apples, peeled and
    grated
100 g/4 oz minced beef
175 g/6 oz bean shoots
3 tablespoons tomato sauce
1 64-g/2¼-oz can tomato purée
dash soy sauce

dash Worcestershire sauce
shake of marjoram
salt and pepper
450 ml/¾ pint water
1 396-g/4-oz can chopped
    tomatoes
BASE
cooked spinach
TOPPING
50 g/2 oz grated cheese
parsley

FRY bacon and onions in oil until onions are soft. Add carrots, apples, mince and bean shoots and cook for a further 3 minutes, turning frequently. Add all the rest of ingredients for the meat sauce. Bring to boil, stirring frequently, then reduce heat and cook for 30 minutes over a very low heat, stirring occasionally until the meat is tender.

Place meat sauce on top of cooked spinach. Top with grated cheese and decorate with parsley. SERVES 4.

This is the sort of thing I throw together quite often and when my family ask what's for dinner I just say one of my concoctions. I vary the base between pasta, rice, potatoes and vegetables.

Mrs A. J. Harrison, Easenhall, Warwickshire

COUNTRY TIMBALE WITH
TOMATO SAUCE

Mushroom sauce

225 g/8 oz mushrooms, sliced
1 clove garlic, halved
25 g/1 oz butter
1 small glass brandy

150 ml/¼ pint stock
1 teaspoon cornflour
salt and black pepper

SAUTÉ mushrooms and garlic in melted butter for 3 minutes. Discard garlic, sprinkle mushrooms with brandy and stand for 1 minute. Slowly add stock and cook until mixture thickens, if necessary adding cornflour mixed with a little cold stock. Season to taste.

Meatballs

175 g/6 oz minced beef
50 g/2 oz minced ham
25 g/1 oz fresh breadcrumbs,
    soaked in milk and squeezed
    dry
1 egg yolk

2 tablespoons grated Parmesan
    cheese
salt and grated nutmeg
flour to dust
butter to fry

MIX all ingredients together, add salt and nutmeg to taste. Shape into walnut-sized balls, dust with flour and fry in butter until golden brown.

Risotto

1 onion, chopped
50 g/2 oz butter
350 g/12 oz long-grain rice
about 900 ml/1½ pints stock

2 eggs
4 tablespoons grated Parmesan
    cheese

SAUTÉ onion in butter. Add rice, cook until transparent, add three-quarters of stock. Cook, stirring occasionally, adding extra stock slowly if needed, until rice is just tender. Remove from heat, add eggs and Parmesan cheese. Spread on to an oiled baking sheet to cool.

To assemble

butter
few dried breadcrumbs

175 g/6 oz Ricotta cheese (or any
    good cooking cheese)

BUTTER a high-sided dish and dust lightly with breadcrumbs. Line the base and sides with risotto, reserving enough for the top. Fill mould with alternate layers of meatballs, mushroom sauce and sliced Ricotta cheese. Finally cover with remaining risotto, sprinkle with breadcrumbs and dot with a little butter. Bake for 30 minutes in a moderately hot oven (200 c, 400 f, gas 6). Turn mould on to a warm dish and pour over the tomato sauce. SERVES 4.

Simple tomato sauce

450 g/1 lb fresh tomatoes, scalded, skinned and chopped, or 1 452-g/15-oz can tomatoes

salt, pepper and sugar
2 tablespoons double cream

LIQUIDISE tomatoes and simmer gently until they begin to thicken. Season to taste. Add cream slowly just before serving.

Mrs D. Harvey, Great Haywood, Staffordshire

PEANUT CHOP

450 g/1 lb minced steak or lamb
cooking oil
300 ml/½ pint water
1 large onion, sliced
1 large carrot, sliced
100 g/4 oz salted peanuts
salt and pepper
1 clove garlic, sliced
1 teaspoon coriander powder

1 teaspoon cumin powder
1 teaspoon turmeric powder
1 bay leaf
1 226-g/8-oz can pineapple chunks
1 large cooking apple, peeled and sliced
2 tablespoons tomato chutney
1 teaspoon garam masala
2 teaspoons chopped parsley

COOK and brown mince in a little oil in a large pan. Add water, onion, carrot, peanuts, salt and pepper. Stir well and add garlic, coriander, cumin, turmeric and bay leaf. Stir and bring to boiling point. Cover and cook gently for 25–30 minutes. Add pineapple and juice, sliced apple and chutney, and cook gently until apple is soft but not broken down to a sauce-like consistency. Thicken if desired with cornflour and gravy browning, approximately 1 teaspoon of each in a little water. Remove from the heat and add garam masala and parsley as final flavouring. Discard bay leaf and serve with boiled rice and vegetable marrow. SERVES 4.

Mrs Martha Smith, Mawdesley, Lancashire

BARBECUE MEAT LOAF

900 g/2 lb finely minced beef
1 packet French onion soup mix
6 tablespoons milk
1 egg

3 tablespoons brown sugar
1 tablespoon prepared mustard
3 tablespoons tomato ketchup

MIX meat, onion soup mix, milk and egg together. Press mixture firmly into an ungreased 1-kg/2-lb loaf tin. Loosen edges with spatula and unmould loaf into ungreased baking tin, 33 × 23 × 5 cm/13 × 9 × 2 inches. Mix remaining ingredients and spoon over the loaf. Bake uncovered in a moderate oven (180 c, 350 F, gas 4) for 1 hour. Serve hot or cold with jacket potatoes and green salad.

Mrs E. Harris, Strathaven, Lanarkshire

SHEPHERD'S HARVEST

350 g/12 oz cooked minced lamb
1 large onion, sliced
2 or 3 slices of vegetable marrow, chopped
butter or oil to fry
3 or 4 tomatoes, chopped
100 g/4 oz mushrooms, chopped
2 large carrots, grated
450 ml/¾ pint gravy or water and stock cube

salt and pepper
FOR TOPPING YOU NEED:
450 g/1 lb cooked mashed potato mixed well with a small beaten egg, 1 tablespoon chopped fresh mint, about 25 g/1 oz chopped monkey nuts and 50 g/2 oz grated cheese

PUT meat into a large ovenproof dish. Fry onion and vegetable marrow lightly in the butter, then the tomatoes and mushrooms. Place on top of the meat. Add carrots to the stock or gravy and boil for about 2 minutes. Season the dish with salt and pepper and pour over the carrots and stock. Cover the contents with the potato mixture and rough up with a fork. Dot with butter or margarine and bake in a moderate oven (180 c, 350 F, gas 4), until brown on top, about 30–40 minutes. Add more gravy if needed when serving.

Enough for 4–6.

Mrs Dora Jackson, Austwick, Lancaster

LEFTOVER LAMB

100 g/4 oz macaroni or other pasta
salt and black pepper
1 large onion
1 clove garlic
dripping or butter to fry
225 g/8 oz cooked lamb
4 tomatoes, fresh or canned

pinch of thyme or rosemary
vegetables of choice (see method)
3 eggs
150 ml/¼ pint milk
50 g/2 oz grated cheese
chopped parsley

COOK the pasta in boiling salted water until just soft. Drain. Chop the onion, crush the garlic and fry gently in the fat. Cut the meat into small pieces and stir into the onion with the chopped tomatoes. Season with salt, pepper and the thyme or rosemary. At this stage add any leftover vegetables, chopped, or a few tablespoons of frozen peas or sweetcorn, in fact any small or chopped vegetables to add colour.

Arrange alternate layers of pasta and meat mixture in a deep ovenproof dish. Beat the eggs, season and add the milk. Pour this gently over the top, sprinkle with grated cheese and bake for 45 minutes in a moderately hot oven (190 c, 375 f, gas 5), until well risen and golden. Sprinkle with chopped parsley and serve straightaway.

This is very nutritious, a complete meal-in-a-pot, freezes well at the stage before the eggs are added, and when cooked in individual small dishes has made a warming starter for a lighter main course. It feeds a family of four.

Mrs Sarah Hellon, Middle Watch, Cambridge

LAMB AND LEEK CASSEROLE

8 lamb cutlets
fat for frying
2 leeks, sliced
1 onion, sliced
1 turnip, diced
225 g/8 oz carrots, sliced

100 g/4 oz peas
600 ml/1 pint stock, or water and
    stock cube
salt and pepper
2 sprigs of mint

PREPARE and trim the cutlets, fry in the fat for 5 minutes to brown, drain and place in a casserole. Add all the vegetables with stock, seasoning and mint. Cover and cook in a moderate oven (180 c, 350 f, gas 4) for 1½ hours. SERVES 4.

Mrs M. C. Pears, Mindrum, Northumberland

WENCESLAS WASSAIL

This is a recipe handed down from my great grandmother. I am intrigued to know whether the name was derived from the red and green sacrificial lamb or the spiced beer which invariably accompanied this dish.

50 g/2 oz dripping	900 ml/1½ pints stock
1 kg/2 lb neck of lamb, cut into pieces	1 bouquet garni
salt and pepper	tomato purée
25 g/1 oz flour	GARNISH
4 carrots, sliced	3 carrots, sliced and glazed
2 onions, sliced	100 g/4 oz garden peas, cooked
	12 button onions, glazed

HEAT the dripping in a large pan. Season meat with salt and pepper and fry to a golden colour. Drain well and place in a deep flameproof casserole. Dust with the flour and mix in with a wooden spoon. Fry the carrots and onions and add to the meat. Pour stock over all and add the bouquet garni and a squeeze of tomato purée. Cover and simmer gently on top of the cooker for 20 minutes, then transfer to a moderate oven (180 C, 350 F, gas 4) for 1½ hours.

Place the meat on a heated serving dish and remove any loose bones. Keep warm. Bring sauce to boil, adjust seasoning and thicken with a little cornflour if necessary. Pour over the meat, sprinkle with the prepared carrots and peas and arrange the button onions around the border of the dish. SERVES 4.

Edith Goulbourne, Hollingworth, Cheshire

CASSEROLED CHOPS AND MUSHROOMS

4 best end neck of lamb chops	1 tablespoon lemon juice
100 g/4 oz button mushrooms	pinch of nutmeg
40 g/1½ oz butter	salt and pepper
2 tablespoons redcurrant jelly	2 teaspoons flour
1 tablespoon Worcestershire sauce	150 ml/¼ pint meat stock

TRIM any excess fat from lamb chops. Peel or wipe mushrooms.

Heat the butter in a frying pan and brown chops quickly. Transfer to an ovenproof casserole and put the mushrooms on top. In a saucepan slowly melt the redcurrant jelly with the Worcestershire sauce and lemon juice. Add nutmeg and seasoning. Add the flour to the fat left in the frying pan and blend in the stock and melted jelly mixture. Bring to the boil and cook for 2 minutes. Adjust seasoning and pour over the lamb.

Cover and cook in a moderate oven (160 c, 325 f, gas 3) for 1¼ hours. When cooked, cool and chill in the refrigerator overnight. Skim off any fat and reheat in a moderate oven for 30–40 minutes. SERVES 4.

Mrs Mary Cundy, Lamerton, Devon

SPRING LAMB PARCEL

4 gigots of spring lamb (chump lamb chops)
2 onions
½ red or green pepper, finely chopped
salt and freshly ground black pepper
sprig of mint or rosemary (optional)

4 tablespoons apple juice or rosé grape juice
2 tablespoons redcurrant jelly
2 teaspoons cornflour mixed with 2 teaspoons cold water
1 170-g/6-oz tin cream
50–75 g/2–3 oz mushrooms, cooked and chopped

SEAR the lamb chops quickly in a hot oiled pan. Place a large piece of clear cooking film (similar to the material used for roasting bags) in a small roasting tin and transfer the chops on to it.

Cut off the top and bottom of the onions and remove any loose skins, leave rest of skin on (this gives maximum flavour and helps to keep the onions a better shape). Halve the onions and place one half cut side down on each chop. Sprinkle with the chopped pepper, season and add the sprig of mint or rosemary. Mix the apple juice and redcurrant jelly together, heating to blend if necessary, and pour over the meat. Fasten the ends of the cooking film with wire ties after forming a loose parcel.

Cook in a moderate oven (180 c, 350 f, gas 4) for 1½ hours. Carefully open the parcel. Remove outer skin from onions, still leaving a half on each chop. Transfer to a hot serving dish along with the drained peppers. Decant off any excess fat and make the juices up to approximately 200 ml/7 fl oz with water. Heat through and thicken with the cornflour paste, seasoning well. Add the cream and mushrooms. Reheat, taking care not to allow the sauce to boil. Serve separately to accompany the lamb. This gives a sweet succulent meat without the smell of cooking pervading the whole house. SERVES 4.

Mrs M. G. Kirkwood, Mouswald, Dumfries

SHEPHERD'S CASSEROLE

25 g/1 oz butter	1 tablespoon flour seasoned with
1 tablespoon cooking oil	salt and pepper
4 large or 8 small lamb chops	150 ml/¼ pint medium sweet cider
2 medium onions, chopped	300 ml/½ pint stock
1 clove garlic, crushed	1 tablespoon tomato purée
4 medium carrots, sliced	good pinch thyme

MELT butter, add oil and gently fry the chops until browned. Add the onions, garlic and carrots and continue frying for a few minutes. Sprinkle over the seasoned flour and cook for a further 2–3 minutes. Then pour in the cider and stock, add the tomato purée and thyme and gently stir in. Transfer to a suitable casserole, cover and cook in a moderate oven (180 C, 350 F, gas 4) for about 1–1½ hours, until the vegetables and meat are tender and the liquid reduced by a third. Adjust seasoning. SERVES 4.

Miss J. Attwood, Stonehouse, Gloucestershire

FRISKY LAMB CHOPS

4 lamb chops	SAUCE
6 tablespoons whisky	40 g/1½ oz butter
25 g/1 oz butter	40 g/1½ oz flour
freshly chopped or dried mint	450 ml/¾ pint milk
2 onions, finely chopped	2 cloves garlic, crushed
75 g/3 oz cheese, grated	salt and freshly milled pepper
breadcrumbs to sprinkle	

PLACE chops in a shallow dish and pour over the whisky. Allow to stand overnight. Drain and reserve liquid. Brown chops in a pan in the butter. Place in an ovenproof dish and sprinkle with the mint and onions.

Melt the butter for the sauce in a pan over low heat and stir in the flour. Cook gently for 2 minutes then stir in the milk a little at a time. Bring the sauce to the boil and add garlic and seasoning. Cover and simmer for 5 minutes. Remove from the heat and stir in the whisky liquid.

Pour the sauce over the chops and top with the grated cheese and a sprinkling of breadcrumbs. Cook in a moderately hot oven (190 C, 375 F, gas 5) for 30–40 minutes. SERVES 4.

Mrs Laura Cromarty, St Margaret's Hope, Orkney

LAMB CHOPS IN CREAM SAUCE

6 lamb chops
1 clove of garlic (optional)
oil or butter to fry
2 medium onions
2 tablespoons plain flour

250 ml/8 fl oz stock
100 ml/4 fl oz single cream
salt and pepper
herbs such as thyme, parsley or
    bay leaf

RUB chops with split clove of garlic and fry both sides to seal. Transfer to the oven to keep hot. Slice onions and pull into rings. Fry until slightly browned. Stir flour into fat then pour in stock and cream. Add seasoning and herbs. Cook, stirring all the time, till sauce thickens. Return chops to pan, cover and cook for about 30 minutes over a low heat. SERVES 6.

Verna Roberts, Ellesmere, Shropshire

LAMB CHOPS AND PEPPER-STYLE OMELETTE

1 green pepper
2 red peppers
1 tablespoon olive oil
1 onion, sliced
4 eggs
pinch each of thyme and sage

1 teaspoon chopped spring onions
1 tablespoon breadcrumbs
4 lamb chops
100 g/4 oz button mushrooms
watercress and tomato for garnish

PREPARE the peppers and slice thinly. In a large frying pan heat the oil over a moderate heat. Add onion and peppers and cook without colouring. Transfer to a plate and set aside.

Beat the eggs, herbs and spring onions together. Add the pepper mixture and breadcrumbs. Pour into the frying pan and allow to cook slowly for 20–25 minutes. Meanwhile, heat the grill, place the lamb chops under and cook slowly until ready. Grill the mushrooms and keep hot. Finally place the egg mixture under the grill until golden brown. Top with the lamb chops and mushrooms and garnish with watercress and tomato. Serve cut into portions. SERVES 4.

Miss Doreen Davies, Llansawel, Dyfed

LAMB AND MAÎTRE D'HÔTEL BUTTER

4 large loin lamb chops
50 g/2 oz button mushrooms,
   quartered
50 g/2 oz butter
50 g/2 oz ham, chopped
grated rind of 1 lemon
salt and freshly ground pepper
25 g/1 oz fresh breadcrumbs

1 beaten egg
1 tablespoon oil
MAÎTRE D'HÔTEL BUTTER
100 g/4 oz butter
2 tablespoons chopped parsley
1 teaspoon lemon juice
salt and pepper

USING a sharp knife, slit the lean eye of each chop horizontally through the fat edge.

Fry the mushrooms in half the butter until soft, add ham, lemon rind, seasoning and breadcrumbs. Bind with a little beaten egg. Allow to cool then stuff the mixture into the incisions in the chops. Secure each chop with string. Heat the oil and remaining butter in a large frying pan and fry the chops well on both sides over a high heat. Reduce heat and continue cooking for 20 minutes, turning once.

Meanwhile make the maître d'hôtel butter. Beat the butter until soft, add the parsley, lemon juice and seasoning and beat in well. Form into a long roll, using greaseproof paper, and chill until required.

Place the chops on a heated serving dish, discarding the string, and top each with several 1-cm/½-inch slices of maître d'hôtel butter. SERVES 4.

It is often a good idea to make up the maître d'hôtel butter well in advance, as the longer it has to chill, the easier it is to slice and the more professional it looks.

Anne Evans, Rhiwlas, Shropshire

LAMB CHOPS AND APRICOTS

1 425-g/15-oz can apricots
3 medium onions, thinly sliced
oil to fry
4 chump lamb chops
dried or fresh rosemary

2 teaspoons cornflour
3 tablespoons single cream
1 glass of white wine (optional)
salt and pepper

DRAIN the apricots, reserving the juice. Fry onions gently until soft but not brown. Fry the chops briefly to brown, then place in an ovenproof dish. Add a sprinkling of rosemary, the onions and the juice from the apricots. Cover with foil and cook in a moderate oven (180 C, 350 F, gas 4) for 30–45 minutes, depending on size. Mix the cornflour with the cream, wine and seasoning, add to the chops along with the apricots and cook for a further 15 minutes. Serve with jacket or creamed potatoes, carrots and peas. SERVES 4.

Mrs Joan Frisby, Oakham, Leicestershire

FRUITY LAMB CHOPS

4 loin lamb chops
butter for frying
1 small onion, chopped
50 g/2 oz flour
2 oranges
450 ml/¾ pint orange juice

225 g/8 oz courgettes, sliced
salt and black pepper
1 teaspoon fresh rosemary
2 fresh peaches
2 fresh apricots
2 tablespoons Cointreau liqueur

BROWN lamb chops on both sides in hot fat in a flameproof casserole. Remove from pan and cook chopped onion until transparent. Stir in flour and cook for 1 minute, stirring continually. Cut orange peel into fine strips and blanch in boiling water. Gradually stir the orange peel and 450 ml/¾ pint orange juice into the onion. Bring to the boil, add sliced courgettes, seasoning and rosemary. Return the lamb chops to the pan, cover and simmer for about 50 minutes, turning chops once.

Slice the peeled oranges, peaches and apricots and add with Cointreau to the casserole. Spoon sauce over chops and cook for a further 15 minutes. Stir sauce well, adding more orange juice if it becomes too thick.

Adjust seasoning and serve with new potatoes, leeks and buttered cabbage. SERVES 4.

Elaine Wilson Jones, Llanidloes, Powys

FRUITED LAMB STEAKS WITH RISOTTO

2 tablespoons corn oil
1 large clove garlic, minced
1 shallot, finely chopped
1 teaspoon grated carrot
1 tablespoon cider vinegar
3 tablespoons unsweetened orange juice
3 tablespoons canned unsweetened pineapple juice
1 teaspoon ground ginger
4 dashes soy sauce
4 lamb steaks
1 Navel orange, peeled and cut into chunks
3 canned unsweetened pineapple rings, cut into chunks
2 teaspoons arrowroot, dissolved in 2 teaspoons water

PLACE all ingredients, with the exception of meat, fruit chunks and arrowroot, in blender. Purée for 1 minute to make marinade. Wipe lamb steaks dry with kitchen paper. Place in a shallow baking dish in one layer. Pour over puréed marinade, cover and leave for 2–3 hours.

Cook, covered, in a moderate oven (180 C, 350 F, gas 4) for 45 minutes. Add orange and pineapple chunks, cover and cook until tender, about a further 20 minutes.

Transfer meat to a serving platter and keep warm. Pour the cooking juices into a saucepan and sprinkle in arrowroot mixture a little at a time. Stir well, using only enough to thicken gravy lightly. Pour over meat and serve with risotto (below). SERVES 4.

RISOTTO

250 ml/8 fl oz chicken or veal stock
250 ml/8 fl oz water
175 g/6 oz white rice
2 tablespoons corn oil
225 g/8 oz mushrooms, sliced
2 cloves garlic, chopped
2 shallots, finely chopped
2 teaspoons cider vinegar
225 g/8 oz fresh or frozen peas, cooked
$\frac{1}{4}$ teaspoon dried oregano
$\frac{1}{4}$ teaspoon dried marjoram
salt to taste
3 pinches cayenne pepper
1 tablespoon freshly chopped parsley

BRING stock and water to boil. Add rice and cook partially covered for 15 minutes (all liquid should be absorbed).

Heat $\frac{3}{4}$ tablespoon oil in a large non-stick frying pan until hot. Add half the mushrooms and sauté until lightly browned, turning often, about 3 minutes. Transfer with a slotted spoon to a bowl. Add a further $\frac{3}{4}$ tablespoon oil to pan and cook rest of mushrooms. Transfer to bowl. Heat remaining oil in same pan until hot. Add garlic and shallots and sauté until lightly browned. Stir in cider vinegar and cook for 1 minute. Add cooked rice, peas, mushrooms, herbs, salt and cayenne, and toss gently until heated through. Transfer to a heated serving dish and sprinkle with parsley.

P. E. North, Milton, Hampshire

RED-GLAZED LAMB

1.25-kg/2½-lb fillet end leg of lamb	225 g/8 oz redcurrants
4 tablespoons finely chopped mint	4 tablespoons dry white wine
salt and pepper	1 tablespoon brown sugar

MAKE four deep cuts in the lamb and open them out carefully. Fill each with 1 tablespoon chopped mint, season well and place the meat in a roasting tin with 3 tablespoons water. Cook in a moderately hot oven (200 C, 400 F, gas 6) for 1½ hours.

Meanwhile cook the redcurrants with the wine and sugar until soft. Sieve and set aside.

When meat is cooked lift on to a serving dish and skim off the fat from the juices in the tin. Mix juices with redcurrant purée and heat, stirring well. Spoon over the meat.

Arrange small whole cooked potatoes and baby carrots around the meat and garnish with sprigs of mint. Accompany with lettuce and sliced tomato in a vinaigrette sauce, and diced cucumber in a yogurt and mint dressing. Can be served hot or cold.

Mrs G. M. Cox, Stevenage, Hertfordshire

HONEYED WELSH LAMB

1 leg Welsh lamb	1 tablespoon ground rosemary
salt and pepper	2 tablespoons honey
1 teaspoon ground ginger	300 ml/½ pint dry cider

RUB joint with salt, pepper and ginger. Line a large ovenproof dish with foil and place joint in it. Sprinkle with rosemary, spoon honey over top of meat, then pour the cider around it.

Place in a hot oven (220 C, 425 F, gas 7) for 30 minutes, then reduce to moderate (180 C, 350 F, gas 4), allowing a total of 25 minutes per 450 g/1 lb, plus 20 minutes over. Baste often.

When ready, place on a hot dish, and decorate with sprigs of rosemary. Serve with new potatoes, fresh garden peas and braised leeks. The juice from the meat is sufficient gravy.

Mrs Margaret Williams, Denbigh, Clwyd

SOMERSET LAMB

1 small onion	475 ml/16 fl oz apple juice
25 g/1 oz butter	4 teaspoons clear honey
4 teaspoons oil	1 beef stock cube
4 teaspoons flour	2 carrots, sliced and stamped into
½ teaspoon dry mustard	heart shapes with a tiny
salt and pepper	cocktail cutter
2 225-g/8-oz slices lamb from fillet	4 slices of dessert apple
end of leg	chopped parsley

CHOP onion finely. Fry in the butter and oil. Remove from pan. Sift together flour, mustard, salt and pepper and use to coat the cubed meat. Fry meat to seal in the same pan then remove. Stir remaining flour mixture into pan and brown. Add the apple juice, honey and stock cube and stir until boiling. Replace onion and lamb in the sauce and add the carrot. Cover the pan tightly and simmer for 45 minutes. Five minutes before serving add the slices of apple and turn in the sauce.

Remove meat, carrot and apple with a slotted spoon, place on a hot serving dish and strain the sauce over. Garnish with parsley, and accompany with tiny new potatoes cooked in their skins, and minted garden peas. SERVES 4.

Mrs Doreen Forsyth, Warkworth, Northumberland

STUFFED MARINATED LEG OF LAMB

1 lean leg of lamb, boned	1 teaspoon crushed rosemary
1 tablespoon redcurrant jelly	6 peppercorns
MARINADE	salt to taste
1 onion, finely chopped	STUFFING
1 carrot, finely chopped	50 g/2 oz mushrooms, chopped
1 stick celery, chopped	2 lamb's kidneys, chopped
2 shallots or garlic cloves, finely	50 g/2 oz butter
chopped	1 tablespoon chopped parsley
6 tablespoons oil	1 teaspoon mixed herbs
175 ml/6 fl oz wine vinegar	salt and pepper
600 ml/1 pint red wine and water	2 tablespoons wholemeal
1 bouquet garni	breadcrumbs

FIRST prepare the marinade. Sauté the vegetables in the oil then add the liquids, herbs and seasonings and simmer gently for 30 minutes. Allow to cool then pour it over the lamb in a large deep bowl. Cover the bowl and leave in a cool place, or the bottom of the refrigerator, for 3–4 days, turning occasionally.

Remove the lamb from the marinade, wipe dry and fill with the stuffing. Fry the chopped mushrooms and kidneys gently in the butter and mix in the herbs, seasoning and breadcrumbs. Sew up or skewer the leg of lamb after stuffing and then roast in a covered roaster in a moderately hot oven (190 c, 375 f, gas 5), allowing 30 minutes per 450 g/1 lb, plus 30 minutes over. Take the lid off the roaster to let the joint brown towards the end of the roasting period.

Remove the joint and make a good gravy using the scraps in the tin, the strained marinade and the redcurrant jelly. Thicken with wholemeal flour if a thick gravy is required (it is better with this joint) and serve the lamb with runner or flageolet vert beans. It is very good cold if any is left.

Mrs M. A. Stone, Cheltenham, Gloucestershire

APRICOT BRAISED LAMB

1 shoulder of English lamb, boned and rolled	2 sticks of celery
1 teaspoon salt	25 g/1 oz butter
1 teaspoon paprika	1 64-g/2¼-oz can tomato purée
1 heaped tablespoon flour	12 dried apricots
2 large onions	300 ml/½ pint chicken stock (or
2 large carrots	chicken stock cube and water)

ASK your butcher to bone the joint, and if you ask nicely he might roll and tie it for you! After the meat is rolled and tied, mix together the salt, paprika and flour, and gently dust the joint with it.

Cube the onions, slice the carrots and celery. Melt the fat in a large flameproof casserole and gently brown first the vegetables and then the meat. Sprinkle in the rest of the seasoned flour, stir and add the tomato purée and apricots. Pour over the stock, cover the casserole and simmer gently for 1½ hours, or until the meat is tender.

Serve with fluffy creamed potatoes or piping hot jacket potatoes with a knob of butter. Very tasty colourful dish for any winter's day.

Mrs Judy Griffin, Wheathill, Somerset

GRANNY'S ENGLISH LAMB

2 boned breasts of lamb
225 g/8 oz fresh cranberries or
  redcurrants
75 g/3 oz butter
150 ml/¼ pint hot water

1 packet parsley and thyme
  stuffing mix
1 tablespoon sugar
salt and pepper

WASH and dry the meat, trim off surplus fat. Wash and mince cranberries. Melt butter in hot water and mix in parsley stuffing and cranberries, stir in sugar and seasoning to taste. Divide equally between the breasts of lamb and spread evenly over. Roll up and tie with string. Place in a roasting tin and cook in a moderately hot oven (190 C, 375 F, gas 5) for about 1½ hours, until meat is tender. Serve with hot boiled beetroot on a bed of crisp lettuce and new potatoes garnished with flaked almonds, chopped parsley and tomato rings. SERVES 6.

Mrs Sheila Hey, Gawber, Yorkshire

LEG OF ENGLISH LAMB WITH APPLE AND MINT STUFFING

1.75–2.25-kg/4–5-lb leg of English
  spring lamb, boned
STUFFING
25 g/1 oz butter
50 g/2 oz finely chopped or grated
  onion
175 g/6 oz fresh white
  breadcrumbs
225 g/8 oz apple purée, sweetened
  with 1 tablespoon honey
2 teaspoons freshly chopped mint
  or ¼ teaspoon dried mint
salt and freshly ground black
  pepper

1 beaten egg
GLAZE
1 tablespoon honey
½ teaspoon paprika pepper
1 teaspoon freshly chopped dill or
  ¼ teaspoon dried dill
SAUCE
50 g/2 oz butter
50 g/2 oz flour
600 ml/1 pint milk
75 g/3 oz chopped onion
salt and pepper
2 tablespoons freshly chopped
  parsley

BONE the leg of lamb or ask your friendly butcher to do it for you. Melt the butter for the stuffing over a low heat and place in a bowl with the onion, breadcrumbs, apple purée, mint and seasoning. Bind into a firm mixture with the beaten egg. Pack this stuffing into the pocket left in the lamb. Sew the joint up with a trussing needle, but not too tightly or this may split the joint as it cooks. Weigh the joint again and glaze with the honey mixture. Cook in a moderate oven (180 C, 350 F, gas 4), allowing 35 minutes per 450 g/ 1 lb plus 35 minutes over.

Next prepare the sauce. Melt the butter in a heavy-based pan, add the flour and cook over a gentle heat for 2–3 minutes, being careful not to brown the mixture. Gradually add the warmed milk and stir until smooth. Allow the sauce to simmer for 10 minutes. Meanwhile cook the chopped onion in a little butter to soften it without browning. Adjust consistency of sauce, adding a little more milk if necessary, and season to taste. Add the onion and parsley and serve at once with the easy-to-carve joint. SERVES 6–8.

Mrs Angela Miller, Ganthorpe, Yorkshire

ROAST LOIN OF LAMB WITH CASHEW AND GOOSEBERRY STUFFING

1.5–1.75-kg/3½–4-lb double loin of
   lamb joint, boned
sea salt and black pepper
white wine (optional)
little oil or dripping
STUFFING
1 onion, chopped
25 g/1 oz butter or margarine
100 g/4 oz mushrooms, chopped
1 tablespoon each chopped fresh
   parsley and thyme

50 g/2 oz cashew nuts, chopped
50 g/2 oz gooseberries, chopped
75 g/3 oz fresh white breadcrumbs
1 egg, beaten
TO FINISH
tart gooseberry sauce (made with
   100 g/4 oz green gooseberries,
   1 tablespoon white wine and
   1 dessertspoon sugar; stew
   gently together then sieve)
parsley sprigs

OPEN out the lamb and season the inside lightly. For the stuffing, fry the onion gently in the butter until soft. Add the mushrooms and continue frying for a minute or two. Remove from the heat, stir in the parsley, thyme, cashew nuts and gooseberries. Add the breadcrumbs and sufficient egg to bind, seasoning well. Spread the stuffing over the inside of the lamb. Roll and secure with skewers and/or string. Stand in a greased roasting tin, adding a few tablespoons of white wine (elderflower is delightful). Pour a little oil over joint, or spread with dripping, and season with sea salt and freshly ground black pepper. Roast in a moderately hot oven (200 C, 400 F, gas 6) allowing 30 minutes per 450 g/1 lb and 20 minutes extra. Baste several times during cooking.

Transfer to a serving dish and surround with baby vegetables (carrots, peas, new potatoes). Pour gooseberry sauce over the lamb and garnish with fried parsley sprigs.

Mary Parkinson, Preesall, Lancashire

☆ AUTUMNAL POT ROAST ☆

1 shoulder of British lamb
100 g/4 oz field mushrooms, sliced
1 teaspoon ground allspice
15 g/½ oz butter
1 small onion, thinly sliced
300 ml/½ pint stock, made with
   1 stock cube

1 tablespoon brandy (optional)
275 g/10 oz greengages, cut in half
   and stoned (50 g/2 oz reserved
   for garnish)

BONE lamb and cover cut surface with sliced mushrooms, sprinkle on allspice. Roll up and tie with string.

Melt butter in a large flameproof casserole and brown lamb all over. Remove. Put in onion and soften, pour in stock and brandy and add greengages. Bring to boil and add lamb. Cover and cook in a moderate oven (180 C, 350 F, gas 4) for 1½ hours.

Remove lamb and keep warm. Skim fruity juices, then liquidise and rub through sieve to make sauce. Reheat. Remove string from lamb, place on serving dish surrounded by garnishing greengages. Serve sauce separately.

Jane Hale, Bough Beech, Kent

APRICOT-STUFFED SHOULDER

1 shoulder of spring lamb
STUFFING
450 g/1 lb fresh apricots
1 tablespoon sugar
1 onion, finely chopped

100 g/4 oz mushrooms, chopped
25 g/1 oz butter
1 tablespoon chopped parsley
50 g/2 oz fresh white breadcrumbs
salt and pepper

BONE the shoulder of lamb or ask your butcher to do it for you.

Halve and stone the apricots and poach in a little water with the sugar. When cooked, drain and reserve the juice and six apricot halves. Chop the rest.

Fry the onion and mushrooms in the butter. Mix the chopped apricots with the parsley, breadcrumbs and seasoning then add the onion and mushrooms. Stuff the shoulder with this mixture, roll up and tie with string. Place in a roasting tin, pour over the reserved apricot juice and roast in a moderate oven (180 C, 350 F, gas 4), allowing 35 minutes per 450 g/1 lb, stuffed weight, plus 35 minutes over. Baste occasionally and serve with the apricot halves as garnish.

Mrs F. I. Sample, Crathorne, Cleveland

☆ SEASONAL LAMB ☆

450 g/1 lb boned leg of lamb (fillet end)
225 g/8 oz courgettes
1 tablespoon oil
25 g/1 oz unsalted butter
1 onion, sliced
1 clove garlic, crushed
1 red pepper, sliced
100 g/4 oz button mushrooms, sliced
5 tablespoons dry sherry
4 tablespoons stock
1 tablespoon redcurrant jelly
1 teaspoon chopped mint
½ teaspoon chopped rosemary
100 ml/4 fl oz double cream
salt and freshly ground black pepper
chopped parsley for garnish

CUT the lamb into strips the size of your little finger. Cut the courgettes into sticks and degorge (sprinkle with salt and leave for 20 minutes for the bitter juices to run out). Rinse well and drain thoroughly.

Heat the oil in a pan and brown the lamb over high heat as quickly as possible, the strips should be cooked but not over-cooked. Remove and keep warm. Melt the butter in the pan and cook the onion and garlic until soft and transparent. Add the courgettes and pepper and cook for 5 minutes. Add the mushrooms and cook for a further 2 minutes. Stir in the sherry and stock, deglaze the pan (scrape any sediment from the base of the pan), bring to the boil and reduce by rapid boiling to half its original quantity.

Return the lamb to the pan and add the remaining ingredients. Mix well and season with salt and pepper. Heat through carefully until the lamb is thoroughly heated and serve garnished with chopped parsley. SERVES 4.

Mrs Fox, Gainsborough, Lincolnshire

SUMMERTIME LAMB

1 shoulder of lamb, boned
2 tablespoons plain flour
50 g/2 oz butter
1 bunch spring onions
450 g/1 lb tomatoes
water plus a little wine or cider
  (optional)

1 tablespoon chopped fresh
  marjoram
2 good sprigs rosemary
salt and freshly ground pepper
450 g/1 lb courgettes

CUT the lamb into cubes and toss in the flour. Melt the butter in a flameproof casserole and add the chopped spring onions. Toss in the meat and brown slightly over a gentle heat. Skin the tomatoes, cut into quarters and add. Pour in just enough water to barely cover the meat (adding the wine or cider if used – just a tablespoon or two will make all the difference). Add the marjoram, the rosemary tied in a little muslin, and seasoning to taste. Put on the lid and simmer, either on top of the cooker or in a moderate oven (180 C, 350 F, gas 4), until the lamb is tender, about 1–1½ hours.

Wash and slice the courgettes and add about 20 minutes before the end of cooking time.

The lamb should be succulently cooked in a rich herby, tomato sauce. Serve with new potatoes, buttered baby carrots and fresh peas cooked with mint. SERVES 4–6.

Mrs Barbara Mumford, West Torrington, Lincoln

☆ SATURDAY SPRING LAMB ☆ STIR FRY

1 small leek and 8 plump spring
  onions, trimmed and cut to
  matchstick-sized pieces
1 tablespoon oil
50 g/2 oz butter
1 clove garlic or garlic salt
  (optional)
350 g/12 oz lamb leg fillet, cut into
  very thin strips 3.5 cm/1½ inches
  long

100 g/4 oz button mushrooms,
  thinly sliced
50 g/2 oz cooked peas
soy sauce
salt and pepper

FRY leek and spring onions in half the oil and butter with crushed clove of garlic or some garlic salt until slightly tender. Remove from the pan and set aside. Add lamb strips to the pan with remaining oil and butter and brown, tossing all the time. Lower heat, add mushrooms and cook until tender, about 2–4 minutes. Add peas, then soy sauce and seasoning to taste. Return onion mixture to pan and cook for a further 3–4 minutes, stirring all the time. If there is too much liquid allow to reduce but continue stirring.

Serve on a bed of rice with mixed side salad or, on a cold night, a little curry sauce. SERVES 4.

Mrs C. Parker, Whithorn, Wigtownshire

LAMB WITH APRICOTS AND CORIANDER

1 kg/2 lb boned lamb shoulder	1 tablespoon chopped parsley
olive oil	juice of 1 orange
1 large onion	salt and pepper
1 396-g/14-oz can tomatoes	1 425-g/15-oz can apricots
3 tablespoons tomato purée	225 g/8 oz brown rice
3 bay leaves	1.75 litres/3 pints chicken stock or
¼ teaspoon grated nutmeg	water
¼ teaspoon crushed coriander seeds	strips of orange peel to garnish

TRIM the meat of any excess fat and cut into 2.5-cm/1-inch cubes. Fry over a low heat in a little oil until the meat is evenly browned. Peel and finely chop the onion and add to the meat, cook until transparent. Add the tomatoes, tomato purée, bay leaves, nutmeg, coriander, parsley, orange juice and seasoning. Drain the can of apricots and add the syrup to the meat. Transfer to a casserole dish and cover tightly with foil and a lid. Cook in a moderate oven (180 c, 350 f, gas 4) for 1½ hours.

Remove the cover from the casserole and add the apricots. Return to the oven while preparing the rice. Cook the rice for 35–40 minutes in the stock or water with 2 teaspoons salt. Drain and rinse under hot water.

Spoon the rice on to a warm serving dish and place the lamb in the centre. Arrange the apricots around the edge of the meat and garnish with strips of orange peel. Serve with a salad of lettuce and tomatoes in an orange juice dressing. SERVES 4–6.

Miss Sarah Rawlings, Bradford-on-Avon, Wiltshire

COUNTRY KEBABS

1 kg/2 lb middle cut lamb	12 small flat mushrooms
250 ml/8 fl oz cheap red wine	1 425-g/15-oz can apricot halves
cooking oil	1 spring cabbage
1 bay leaf	2 tablespoons Worcestershire
fresh mint sprigs	sauce
6 small tomatoes	1 tablespoon brown sugar

CUT lamb into 2.5-cm/1-inch cubes, marinate overnight in the red wine, 3 tablespoons oil, the bay leaf and 6 stems bruised mint.

Make up six skewers (metal) in this order: lamb, mint leaf, tomato, lamb, mint leaf, mushroom, lamb, apricot half, lamb, mint leaf, mushroom, lamb. Reserve apricot juice and marinade for later use. Brush everything with oil and grill or barbecue until cooked to your liking (approximately 10–15 minutes on medium heat, turning).

Meanwhile chop cabbage and rinse thoroughly. Drop into boiling water for 1 minute then drain and fry in a little oil in a large pan for about 5 minutes, until cooked. (I find this method leaves cabbage more crisp and wholesome.)

Add juice from apricots to marinade with the Worcestershire sauce and brown sugar. Bring to boil and boil vigorously until reduced by half to three-quarters. Serve kebabs on bed of cabbage and sauce separately. SERVES 6.

Mrs S. A. Crabtree, Alcester, Warwickshire

☆ NEW SEASON LAMB ☆ HOT POT

450 g/1 lb lean lamb (any cut,	1 tablespoon flour
fresh or pre-cooked – both give	600 ml/1 pint stock
equally good results)	3 tomatoes or 1 227-g/8-oz can
1 tablespoon cooking oil	plum tomatoes
2 medium onions	2 medium leeks
2 medium carrots	150 ml/¼ pint red wine
2 sticks celery	450 g/1 lb new potatoes
½ small swede	parsley to garnish
salt and pepper	

CUT lamb into neat pieces. Place with oil in a heavy-based casserole together with chopped onion and carrot. Fry for 5 minutes, turning occasionally. Add chopped celery and swede and continue frying until meat is browned all over or, if using pre-cooked meat, until it is completely heated through. Season to taste. Remove from heat and gently mix in flour. Add half the stock, return to a moderate heat, then add the tomatoes. Simmer for 10 minutes. Slice leeks thinly and add to the casserole with rest of stock. Simmer for about 5 minutes, then stir in wine, cover and cook in a moderate oven (180 c, 350 f, gas 4) for 30 minutes.

Meanwhile scrub and clean potatoes, and boil until almost cooked. Remove casserole from oven, place potatoes on top and return uncovered to oven for a further 20–30 minutes. Garnish with chopped parsley and serve at once. SERVES 4.

Mrs Sally Cuzens, Litton Cheney, Dorset

LAMB SURPRISE

50 g/2 oz butter
1 medium onion, chopped
150 g/5 oz fresh white
    breadcrumbs
2 teaspoons chopped parsley
1 teaspoon chopped mint

grated rind and juice of 1 orange
25 g/1 oz walnuts, finely chopped
salt and pepper
450–900-g/1–2-lb breast of lamb
100 g/4 oz sausagemeat

MELT butter and fry onion until soft, then mix in breadcrumbs, parsley, mint, orange rind and juice, walnuts and seasoning. Meanwhile remove bones from the lamb, spread over the sausage-meat then place the prepared stuffing on top. Roll up and secure it using skewers then tie with string.

Place the meat bones in the bottom of a roasting tin and put meat on top. Cook in a hot oven (220 c, 425 f, gas 7) for 20 minutes then lower heat to moderate (180 c, 350 f, gas 4), allowing 25 minutes per 450 g/1 lb plus 25 minutes over, or until cooked. Make a sauce from the juices in the tin, thickening with a little flour. Serve very hot, tastes delicious on a cold day.

Mrs P. Lewis, Hobarris, Shropshire

ENCASED LAMB WITH HAZELNUTS AND REDCURRANT SAUCE

4 thin lean slices gammon (15–18-cm/6–7-inch rounds, about 50 g/2 oz each)
25 g/1 oz butter
50 g/2 oz finely chopped onion
350 g/12 oz minced lean shoulder of lamb
2 teaspoons chopped lemon thyme
2 teaspoons chopped parsley
25 g/1 oz fresh brown breadcrumbs

salt and freshly ground pepper
6 tablespoons medium sweet English cider
25 g/1 oz chopped hazelnuts
SAUCE
4 tablespoons redcurrant jelly (homemade for preference)
2 tablespoons medium sweet English cider
1 teaspoon arrowroot

REMOVE rind from gammon and lay the slices on a board. Melt butter in a pan and gently fry onion until soft (do not allow to brown). Place minced lamb in a bowl, add lemon thyme and parsley, mix in breadcrumbs and cooked onion. Add a little salt and pepper to taste and blend all ingredients well. Divide lamb mixture into four and place on centre of each piece of gammon, gently flattening the mixture to leave a small edge of gammon all round. Fold in the sides so that the lamb mixture is encased with gammon and resembles a "steak shape", approximately 7.5 × 6.5 cm/3 × 2½ inches. Place the encased lamb, joined side down, in a buttered shallow ovenproof dish. Make three diagonal cuts across each. Spoon over the cider, cover with foil and cook in a moderate oven (180 C, 350 F, gas 4) for 35–40 minutes, until cooked through.

Meanwhile, make the sauce. Melt the redcurrant jelly gently in a pan and add the cider. Blend the arrowroot with a little extra cider until smooth, pour into the pan and heat, stirring until thickened.

When encased lamb is cooked remove foil from dish and drain off juices. Brush each encased lamb with juices and sprinkle over the chopped hazelnuts, gently press down. Return dish to oven for a further 5 minutes to crisp the tops. Transfer encased lamb to a warm serving dish and spoon the redcurrant sauce over each. Any remaining sauce can be served in a sauceboat at the table.

Garnish with sprigs of fresh scarlet redcurrants and parsley and serve with vegetables in season. SERVES 4.

Mrs Joyce Leeming, Burton, Lancashire

STUFFED LAMB ROLLS

1-kg/2-lb breast of lamb	75 g/3 oz fresh breadcrumbs
seasoning	1 teaspoon chopped parsley
butter	1 teaspoon chopped mint
FORCEMEAT	1 teaspoon grated lemon peel
50 g/2 oz chopped bacon	1 beaten egg

FIRST make the forcemeat stuffing. Lightly fry bacon, cool and mix with other ingredients, using enough egg to bind.

Skin and bone the breast of lamb and remove any excess fat. Sprinkle with salt and pepper. Spread with the forcemeat and roll up tightly, secure at intervals with string or skewers and cut into 3–4-cm/1¼–1½-inch lengths. Place in a casserole, stuffing uppermost. Dot with butter and cover with a lid or foil. Cook in a moderate oven (180 c, 350 f, gas 4) for about 1¼–1½ hours. Serve with green peas and new potatoes. SERVES 4.

Miss B. Neal, Inkberrow, Worcester

PORK CASSEROLE

675 g/1½ lb belly pork	1 396-g/14-oz can plum tomatoes
25 g/1 oz butter	150 ml/¼ pint white wine
100 g/4 oz mushrooms, sliced	salt and pepper
½ onion, chopped	1 220-g/7¾-oz can baked beans

SCORE the pork rind and cut off, also trim excess fat from the meat. Just before serving, cook the scored pork rind in a hot oven or under the grill until crisp.

Cut the pork into cubes and brown lightly in the butter. Add the mushrooms and onion, cook for a few minutes then transfer to an ovenproof casserole. Drain the juice from the tomatoes and add to the casserole with the wine and seasoning. Cover and cook in a moderate oven (180 c, 350 f, gas 4) for 1½–2 hours, until tender. Thirty minutes before the end add the tomatoes and baked beans. Accompany the casserole with the crackling, broken into small pieces. SERVES 4.

Mrs F. G. Parrott, Trentham, North Staffordshire

PORK IN TOMATOES

450 g/1 lb belly of pork, cut into pieces	1 425-g/15-oz can tomatoes
1 large onion, chopped	2 teaspoons tomato purée
100 g/4 oz mushrooms, sliced	1 teaspoon dried mixed herbs
margarine to fry	salt and pepper
	cornflour

GRILL belly pork until brown. Fry onion and mushrooms in a little pork fat, add tomatoes, purée, herbs and seasoning. Mix a little cornflour with some cold water and add this to other ingredients to slightly thicken juices. Put everything into a casserole dish, cover and cook in a moderate oven (160 c, 325 f, gas 3) for about 3 hours. SERVES 4.

This dish can be left in a low oven for a whole morning or afternoon and really is delicious. The recipe was handed down to me by my mother.

Mrs Alyson Biggs, Fowey, Cornwall

COUNTRY CASSOULET

The following recipe was given to me by my mother. An excellent family midday dish, it is both warming and filling on a cold winter's day and, what is more, fairly economical. Needless to say it has been adapted from the famous cassoulet of the Languedoc in France.

1 large onion, chopped	225 g/8 oz butter beans, soaked overnight
100 g/4 oz bacon, chopped	
1 tablespoon oil	1 425-g/15-oz can tomatoes
1 kg/2 lb belly pork, boned and skinned	900 ml/1½ pints good stock
	pinch mixed herbs
225 g/8 oz garlic sausage, in the piece and then roughly chopped	freshly ground black pepper
	100 g/4 oz fresh breadcrumbs

FRY onion and bacon in oil in a flameproof casserole. Add the pork which has been cut into fork-sized pieces, and fry for a further 5 minutes. Add the remaining ingredients, except for the breadcrumbs, cover and cook for 1½ hours in a moderate oven (160 c, 325 f, gas 3). Remove from oven, sprinkle the breadcrumbs over and cook uncovered for a further hour. Serve piping, bubbling hot. SERVES 6.

Mrs Fiona Calder, Lowick, Northumberland

RED CABBAGE AND PORK

1 pork belly rasher per person
equal quantities of red cabbage,
cooking apples and onions

dark brown sugar

FRY the pork rashers on both sides until browned. Shred the red cabbage, peel and slice the apples, peel and slice the onions. Layer some cabbage into a casserole, then a layer of apple, sprinkled with a little sugar, then a layer of onion. Continue layers in this order until casserole is full. Add 1 tablespoon water and lay the pork rashers on top. Cover with a lid or foil. Cook in a hot oven (220 C, 425 F, gas 7) for 30 minutes, then reduce to moderate (160 C, 325 F, gas 3) for 1½–2 hours.

Mrs M. Pullen, Winchcombe, Gloucestershire

CRUMBED PORK CASSEROLE

4 large carrots
3 onions
2 turnips
2–3 medium potatoes
2 large cooking apples
salt and pepper

herbs to taste
8–12 belly pork slices
1 egg
breadcrumbs to coat
450 ml/¾ pint chicken stock

PEEL and thinly slice all the vegetables and the apples. Use any other vegetables as available or desired. Place these in layers in a greased casserole dish. Sprinkle with salt, pepper and herbs. Roll pork slices in beaten egg and then press on breadcrumbs. Lay the prepared pork on top of the vegetables. Gently pour the chicken stock down sides of casserole to prevent disturbing crumbed meat.

Cook, uncovered, for 30 minutes in a moderate oven (180 C, 350 F, gas 4) and then a further 1 hour in a cool oven (150 C, 300 F, gas 2). Result: a mouthwatering, aromatic, nourishing meal for a cold evening. SERVES 4.

Mrs Ruth Beavington, Ryarsh, Kent

WEALDEN SPARE-RIB OF PORK

2.25-kg/5-lb joint pork spare-rib
1 medium onion, chopped
salt and freshly ground pepper
450 g/1 lb Bramley cooking
 apples, peeled and sliced

1 tablespoon granulated sugar
50 g/2 oz fresh white breadcrumbs
6–7 leaves fresh sage

HAVE the butcher remove the blade bone from the pork and score the fat. Continue the cut where bone was removed so that the joint opens up like a book.

Stew onion with a little salt and water. Stew apple with sugar and 1 tablespoon water. Combine onion, apple, breadcrumbs, chopped sage and black pepper. Cover bottom half of joint with this mixture, making the layer slightly thicker near the "fold". Replace top layer (creating a meat and stuffing sandwich). Tie and skewer securely.

Roast in a covered casserole or roasting tin for 1¼ hours in a hot oven (230 C, 450 F, gas 8) then remove the lid and cook for a further ¾–1 hour in a cool oven (150 C, 300 F, gas 2). When cooked, remove meat and keep warm. Add about 300 ml/½ pint water to casserole and make gravy by mixing in the meat juices and stuffing remnants. SERVES 8.

Phyllis Highwood, Marden, Kent

SAVOURY PUDDING

Serve before the main course, which must be pork, or to accompany the meat.

225 g/8 oz breadcrumbs, made
 with stale bread
sprinkle of sage
sprinkle of mixed herbs
salt and pepper

4–5 large onions, boiled until
 tender
milk
1 egg
75 g/3 oz shredded suet

PUT the breadcrumbs, sage, herbs and seasoning into a bowl, add the chopped cooked onions and blend together with a little boiled milk. Add the beaten egg and suet. The mixture should be sticky but not too sloppy. Spread into a Swiss roll tin and bake for 1 hour in a moderately hot oven (190 C, 375 F, gas 5) until crispy on top.

Mrs Gillian Douthwaite, Whixley, Yorkshire

TARTED-UP PORK CHOPS

In our family this recipe goes by the rather unglamorous name above, but it can be used just as well with the more humble belly pork strips.

4 pork chops or 675 g/1½ lb pork
  belly strips
oil to fry
1 onion, chopped (optional)
1 clove garlic, crushed (optional)

SAUCE
4 tablespoons tomato ketchup
1 tablespoon brown sugar
1 tablespoon malt or wine vinegar
1 teaspoon dried mustard
2 teaspoons Worcestershire sauce
1 teaspoon mixed herbs

MIX all sauce ingredients with 300 ml/½ pint hot water. Fry pork in a little hot oil to seal and brown. Turn the browned meat into a casserole, add onion and garlic (if used), and pour over the sauce. Cover and cook in a moderate oven (180 c, 350 f, gas 4) for 1–2 hours, longer for the pork belly than the chops. SERVES 4.

Mrs Deborah Benton, Martlesham Heath, Suffolk

PORK CHOPS IN CELERY SAUCE

3 pork chops
oil to fry
½ large head celery, chopped
1 small onion, chopped
75 g/3 oz butter
75 g/3 oz flour

600 ml/1 pint milk
salt and pepper
1 large dessert apple, peeled and
  chopped
brown sugar
chopped parsley

FRY chops in a little oil until lightly browned on both sides. Place in a casserole dish. Meanwhile boil the chopped celery and onion in 300 ml/½ pint water until tender. Melt the butter in a separate saucepan, add flour and then milk and cook, stirring until thickened. Stir in the celery, onion and cooking water and season to taste. Pour over the chops and bake in a moderately hot oven (190 c, 375 f, gas 5) for about 45–50 minutes, until chops are tender. Remove from oven. Sprinkle chopped apple and brown sugar on top and return to oven for a few minutes to brown. Finally garnish with chopped parsley and serve at once with duchesse or creamed potatoes and peas. SERVES 3.

Mrs G. A. Daines, Bunwell, Norfolk

PORK CHOPS WITH HERBS AND LEMON

BRUSH pork chops or steaks with honey. Chop some lemon thyme finely, sprinkle on the chops with the juice of a lemon and leave to soak for 2 hours, turning once. Then grill under a medium heat until cooked. Garnish with a slice of lemon and serve with a tossed green salad and sauté potatoes.

Mrs A. S. Shaw, Matlock, Derbyshire

RAGOÛT OF PORK WITH HERB DUMPLINGS

2 large onions, sliced	¼ teaspoon chilli powder
50 g/2 oz fat and oil	salt and pepper
4 pork loin chops	DUMPLINGS
1 clove garlic	100 g/4 oz self-raising flour
1 green pepper, sliced	pinch salt
2 sticks celery, chopped	50 g/2 oz shredded suet
150 ml/¼ pint red wine	½ teaspoon dried sage or 1 fresh
150 ml/¼ pint stock	leaf, finely chopped
100 g/4 oz mushrooms, sliced	cold water to mix
bay leaf	

FRY onions in fat until tender and place in an ovenproof casserole dish. Fry chops until golden on both sides and place over onions. Crush garlic and cook with sliced pepper and celery until almost tender. Add wine, stock, mushrooms, bay leaf, chilli powder and seasoning. Simmer for 5–10 minutes and pour over chops. Cover and cook in a moderate oven (160 C, 325 F, gas 3) for 1½ hours.

To make dumplings, mix together the flour, salt, suet and herbs with enough water to make a soft dough. Form into eight balls. Add to the casserole and continue cooking for a further 20–30 minutes, until the dumplings are cooked. SERVES 4.

Jean Hayton, Beckwith, Harrogate

PORK AND APPLE SAVOURY

4 pork chops or cutlets	4 dessert apples
sage, salt and pepper	about 300 ml/½ pint stock
4 small onions	4 large potatoes

REMOVE fat and bone from chops, sprinkle with sage, salt and pepper. Place chops in a large ovenproof casserole. Peel and slice onions and apples and put in layers on top of chops. Pour over stock. Peel and slice potatoes very thinly and layer over apples and onion, making a pattern. Cover and cook in a moderate oven (180 c, 350 f, gas 4) for 1½–2 hours. SERVES 4.

Mrs Audrey Forbes, Rudston, North Humberside

TIPSY PORK CHOPS

50 g/2 oz butter	salt and pepper
4 medium potatoes	2 teaspoons tomato purée
2 large onions	barbecue seasoning
4 pork chops	4 tablespoons sweet sherry

HEAT the butter in a flameproof casserole. Peel potatoes, slice and arrange in the casserole. Peel and slice onions over the potatoes, trim pork chops and place on the onions. Season with salt, pepper, tomato purée and barbecue seasoning.

Cover and cook in a cool oven (150 c, 300 f, gas 2) for 2½–3 hours. Pour over sherry 10 minutes before serving. Accompany with carrots, peas and apple sauce. SERVES 4.

Mrs Rhiannon, Llansannan, Clwyd

BAKED PORK CHOPS WITH APPLE AND ONION SAUCE

4 pork chops	300 ml/½ pint stock
25 g/1 oz lard	1 tablespoon chutney
2 medium onions	1 teaspoon tomato purée
2 cooking apples	salt and pepper
25 g/1 oz flour	

FRY chops in a little lard until brown, then place in a shallow ovenproof dish. Peel and slice onions and apples. Fry the onions until golden brown, then add the apples and continue to fry. Add the rest of the lard, stir in flour, add stock and stir until the sauce thickens. Add chutney and tomato purée and season to taste. Spoon sauce over chops and bake uncovered in a moderately hot oven (190 c, 375 f, gas 5) for 40–45 minutes. SERVES 4.

Miss F. J. Leaning, Hascombe, Surrey

PORK COBBLER

675 g/1½ lb shoulder of pork, diced
25 g/1 oz bacon dripping
1 onion, chopped
50 g/2 oz mushrooms, sliced
225 g/8 oz tomatoes, skinned
300 ml/½ pint chicken stock
salt and pepper
parsley to garnish

APPLE SCONE
1 large Bramley cooking apple
225 g/8 oz self-raising flour
½ teaspoon salt
1 teaspoon baking powder
50 g/2 oz butter
50 g/2 oz caster sugar
about 150 ml/¼ pint milk

GENTLY fry diced pork in bacon dripping, add onion and mushrooms. Drain off excess fat and transfer to a casserole dish. Bring skinned tomatoes nearly to boil to soften, then add chicken stock and pour into casserole dish. Season to taste. Cover and cook in a moderate oven (180 C, 350 F, gas 4) for 1½ hours.

Meanwhile, peel and finely chop apple. Sift flour, salt and baking powder into a bowl and rub in butter. Add sugar and apple and mix to a soft dough with milk. Roll out to 1.5-cm/½-inch thickness and shape to fit the casserole dish. Mark into a criss-cross pattern and brush with milk. Bake for a further 15–20 minutes until apple scone is well risen and golden brown. Garnish with parsley and serve with one vegetable of choice. SERVES 4.

Mrs K. Stephens, Callington, Cornwall

PORK HOT POT

675 g/1½ lb lean pork
2 pig's kidneys
1 large onion
salt, pepper and dried mixed
    herbs
450 ml/¾ pint stock

gravy thickening
½ head celery, cut into 2.5-cm/
    1-inch pieces
2 dessert apples, peeled and sliced
450 g/1 lb potatoes, thinly sliced
butter

CUT the pork into cubes and the kidneys into fairly small pieces. Chop the onion, season and add a few mixed herbs. Boil all this slowly in stock for about 30 minutes, or until tender. Add a little gravy thickening. Pour into a large greased ovenproof dish and cover with a layer of celery then a layer of sliced apples (Cox apples are very good for this). Arrange the sliced potatoes on top in rings, slightly overlapping. Dot with a few small knobs of butter and bake in a moderately hot oven (200 C, 400 F, gas 6) until the potatoes are nicely brown, usually about 40 minutes. SERVES 4–6.

Mrs G. Leonard, Shipdham, Norfolk

AUTUMN PORK CASEROLE

450 g/1 lb lean pork, diced
2 tablespoons oil
2 medium onions, sliced
1 tablespoon cornflour
300 ml/½ pint cider
1 stock cube dissolved in 150 ml/
 ¼ pint hot water
2 large cooking apples, peeled,
 cored and diced

100 g/4 oz button mushrooms
100 g/4 oz sweetcorn
1 tablespoon chopped red pepper
1 227-g/8-oz can tomatoes,
 chopped
1 teaspoon chopped fresh thyme
1 clove garlic, crushed
salt and pepper

BROWN pork in hot oil, transfer to an ovenproof casserole. Gently fry onions until almost cooked but not brown, add to pork. Add cornflour to remaining oil to make a roux, stir in cider and stock and bring to the boil, stirring continuously. Add to pork with all other ingredients.

Cover and cook in a cool oven (150 c, 300 f, gas 2) for approximately 2½ hours. Remove casserole lid, increase oven temperature to hot (220 c, 425 f, gas 7) and cook for a further 30 minutes, to reduce sauce a little. SERVES 4.

Mrs S. E. Potts, Hinton St George, Somerset

PORK STROGANOFF

50 g/2 oz margarine
1 onion, sliced
1 clove garlic, crushed
4 rashers streaky bacon, chopped
 finely
¼ teaspoon marjoram

¼ teaspoon caraway seeds
350 g/12 oz pork fillet, cubed
½ teaspoon salt
black pepper
225 g/8 oz mushrooms, sliced
150 ml/¼ pint soured cream

MELT the margarine in a heavy pan or flameproof casserole. Fry the onion until soft then add the garlic, bacon, marjoram and caraway seeds. Cook for 1 minute. Add the pork with the salt and black pepper. Stir briskly until the meat changes colour, then add the mushrooms. Cover and cook very gently for 30 minutes. Add a little stock if the mixture looks too dry. When ready, stir in the soured cream and heat carefully without boiling. Serve on a bed of rice mixed with green peas. SERVES 4.

Mrs E. M. Scott, Whitby, North Yorkshire

SOUTHBROOK PORK

1½ tablespoons oil
25 g/1 oz butter plus 15 g/½ oz
100 g/4 oz mushrooms
1 onion
2 medium Bramley cooking apples
450 g/1 lb pork tenderloin
15 g/½ oz flour
300 ml/½ pint dry cider

100 g/4 oz walnuts, roughly
   chopped
1 teaspoon chopped fresh
   coriander
salt and fresh black pepper
150 ml/¼ pint single cream
   (optional)

HEAT the oil and 25 g/1 oz butter in a flameproof pan. Peel and slice mushrooms and onion. Fry onion for 4 minutes in oil and butter, add mushrooms and fry for a further 2–3 minutes. Remove from pan. Peel apples; core one and slice into rings, slice the other into segments. In a large frying pan gently brown apple rings in 15 g/½ oz butter, keep warm.

Trim pork and cut into 2.5-cm/1-inch cubes. Toss in the flour. Fry pork quickly in the flameproof pan to seal juices. When brown add onion and mushroom mixture and uncooked apple slices. Stir well and gradually add the cider. Bring to boil, stirring continually, then simmer for 3 minutes. Add walnuts, coriander and seasoning. Simmer, covered, for 30–40 minutes, until pork is cooked and tender. If cream is being used, remove dish from heat and stir in now. Top with reheated apple rings.

Serve inside a border of piped creamed potato or on a bed of cooked brown rice. SERVES 4.

Mrs Rosemary Street, Whimple, Devon

PORK IN A RICH CREAM SAUCE

675 g/1½ lb fillet or boned loin of
   pork
2 tablespoons oil
25 g/1 oz butter
1 onion, chopped
1 tablespoon paprika pepper
1 tablespoon flour
1 beef stock cube dissolved in
   300 ml/½ pint water

5 tablespoons sherry
1 teaspoon tomato purée
salt and pepper
175 g/6 oz small button
   mushrooms
1 tablespoon cornflour
150 ml/¼ pint double cream

CUT pork into 3.5-cm/1½-inch pieces. Heat oil in a pan, add the butter, then fry pork pieces quickly until they are just turning brown. Remove meat from pan and drain on kitchen paper. Next fry chopped onion and paprika for 2 minutes. Blend in flour and cook for a further minute. Remove from heat and blend in stock. Add sherry and tomato purée, return to heat and simmer until thick. Season with salt and pepper and add the pork. Cover and simmer for 30–40 minutes, or until pork is tender. Five minutes before the end of the cooking time add mushrooms. Blend cornflour to a smooth paste with 2 tablespoons cold water and add to the pork dish. Heat through, stirring, and just before serving blend in the cream. SERVES 4.

Mrs Sally Anne Mableson, Donington, Lincolnshire

STUFFED PORK TENDERLOIN WITH CIDER AND TOMATO SAUCE

1 pork tenderloin, about 450–675 g/1–1½ lb
1 medium onion, finely chopped
50 g/2 oz butter
100 g/4 oz mushrooms, sliced
1 large eating apple, peeled, cored and chopped
2 tomatoes, skinned and chopped
50 g/2 oz fresh breadcrumbs
black pepper, salt and dried mixed herbs
1 beaten egg
4 bacon rashers, rind removed
1 tablespoon flour
1 tablespoon tomato purée
300 ml/½ pint cider

WITH a very sharp knife slice tenderloin through the centre lengthways. (I let my butcher do this for me!) Beat a little to flatten.

Fry onion in butter until soft. Add mushrooms and cook a little before adding apple and tomatoes. Fry together for a few minutes. Add to breadcrumbs, seasoning and herbs and mix well with the beaten egg. Spread over one half of tenderloin, put other half on top and shape like a large sausage. Wrap bacon all round to keep in shape. Place in a roasting tin and cook in a moderate oven (180 c, 350 F, gas 4) for about 1 hour.

Remove from tin and keep hot on a serving dish. Make a sauce with the juices in tin, the flour, tomato purée and cider, stirring until thickened and boiling. Pour over the meat to serve. SERVES 4.

Mrs E. Capstick, Picts Cross, Herefordshire

☆　GINGER PORK　☆

900 g/2 lb lean pork, shoulder or
　leg steak
vegetable oil
2 large onions
450–600 ml/¾–1 pint bone stock or
　water (not stock cubes)

2 tablespoons brown sugar
3 tablespoons cider vinegar
1 teaspoon ground ginger
salt and black pepper
a little finely chopped fresh sage
6 gingernut biscuits

CUBE pork and quickly brown in oil to seal juices. Slice onions thickly and fry lightly. Place all ingredients except biscuits in lidded flameproof casserole, bring to boil on top of stove, then cook for 2 hours in a moderate oven (180 C, 350 F, gas 4). Crumble biscuits finely, stir into casserole 30 minutes before end of cooking time.

Mrs P. Bland, Foxhill, Wiltshire

P.S. PORK

450 g/1 lb pork mince
100 g/4 oz mushrooms, chopped
1 red pepper, deseeded and
　chopped
5 heaped tablespoons desiccated
　coconut
225 g/8 oz cottage cheese

4 tablespoons tomato purée
a little stock or water
salt and pepper
225 g/8 oz tomatoes, peeled and
　quartered
225 g/8 oz peas (frozen or tinned)

BROWN the mince thoroughly in a non-stick pan. (If the mince is lean, add a little cooking oil; otherwise not.) After 5 minutes, add the mushrooms and red pepper. Cook for a further 4–5 minutes, stirring occasionally, then stir in the coconut. Add the cottage cheese, tomato purée and enough stock or water to make a moist, but not water-logged, mixture. Stir thoroughly and season to taste. Bring to the boil, cover and simmer gently for 10 minutes. Stir in the tomatoes and simmer for 5 minutes more. Finally add the peas and cook for a further 2–3 minutes. Serve with boiled rice or potatoes. SERVES 4.

David Harbourne, London SW19

PORK AND APPLE DISH

1 large onion
450 g/1 lb cooking apples, stewed
  and sweetened to taste
675 g/1½ lb minced pork
1 tablespoon chopped fresh or 1
teaspoon dried marjoram

175 g/6 oz bacon rashers, cut into
  strips
2–3 tomatoes (optional)
100 g/4 oz mushrooms (optional)

GREASE an 18 × 25-cm/7 × 10-inch ovenproof dish. Cover the base
with sliced or chopped onion and spread over the stewed apple.
Mix together the pork and marjoram and spread over the apple.
Finally put the strips of bacon over the pork. Sliced tomatoes and
mushrooms can be spread on top of bacon at this stage, if liked.

Cover with foil and cook in a moderate oven (180 C, 350 F, gas 4)
for 1¼ hours, removing foil for the last 15 minutes to crisp the
bacon. Serve with baked jacket potatoes and seasonal vegetables.
SERVES 6.

Mrs E. S. Ullyott, Middleton-on-the-Wolds, North Humberside

I. I. SPECIAL

450 g/ lb potatoes
pinch salt
25 g/1 oz margarine

450 g/1 lb cooking apples
450 g/1 lb sausagemeat
1 medium orange

PEEL and boil potatoes with a pinch of salt. Mash and add
margarine. Peel, core and slice apples and cook gently in a very
little water until soft. Line a pie dish with sausagemeat and add a
layer of apple. Peel the orange, separate into segments and place on
top of the apple. Cover with mashed potato and cook in a
moderately hot oven (200 C, 400 F, gas 6) for 35–40 minutes. It is
delicious served with a fresh green salad. SERVES 4.

This was a very popular dish at home that my mother cooked
and named after herself. SERVES 4.

Mrs G. Batstone, Whiteparish, Wiltshire

SAVOURY COTTAGE PIE

450 g/1 lb potatoes
450 g/1 lb pork sausagemeat
1 large onion, sliced

1 medium cooking apple
300 ml/½ pint beef stock

BOIL and mash potatoes. Fry sausagemeat gently but thoroughly (no need to use any extra fat if sausagemeat is kept stirred). Remove sausagemeat from pan, add onion and fry gently.

Using a 1.15-litre/2-pint pie dish, peel and slice apple on to the base, cover with the sausagemeat and then the fried onion. Make up stock (the potato water is fine for this, with a stock cube). Pour over contents of dish and finally top with mashed potato. Cook in a moderate oven (180 c, 350 f, gas 4) until golden brown, about 25–30 minutes. Cooked cabbage is an ideal accompaniment to this dish. SERVES 4.

Mrs D. L. Hopkins, Shadoxhurst, Kent

SAUSAGE AND BEAN SUPPER

225 g/8 oz haricot beans
1 large onion, chopped
225 g/8 oz streaky bacon, diced
1 large cooking apple, peeled and
    chopped
1 396-g/14-oz can tomatoes

1 tablespoon tomato purée
freshly ground black pepper
1 teaspoon made mustard
1 teaspoon mixed dried herbs
450 g/1 lb sausagemeat
flour

SOAK beans overnight, then strain reserving 150 ml/¼ pint water. Fry onion, bacon and apple for 3 or 4 minutes until soft, then stir in tomatoes, purée, pepper, mustard and herbs. Add the beans and reserved liquid and put into a heavy casserole.

Shape sausagemeat into balls, toss in a little flour, add to casserole, cover and cook for 1½ hours in a moderate oven (180 c, 350 f, gas 4); remove the lid for the last 30 minutes.

Delicious on its own, or with a green vegetable and granary bread. SERVES 4.

Mrs M. Hull, Southminster, Essex

SAUSAGE AND KIDNEY

Here is a recipe which vividly brings to mind our winter journey from Hampshire to Shropshire in the 1930's in order to spend Christmas with our grandparents at Whitchurch. As soon as we reached Prees Heath, about 5 miles from our destination, we used to say that we could smell Grandma's Sausage and Kidney – which would have been slowly cooking overnight in the bake-house oven. It was always absolutely superb. The recipe has been handed down through the family, and so it is with nostalgia that I give it below.

450 g/1 lb good pork sausages, pricked
1 large onion, chopped
2 lamb's kidneys, thinly sliced
½ teaspoon dried sage
½ teaspoon dried thyme
salt and freshly ground black pepper
1 Oxo cube

PLACE sausages, onion and kidney in an ovenproof dish. Add herbs, salt and pepper. Dissolve the Oxo cube in sufficient hot water to cover contents of dish and pour over. Cover with lid or foil and cook in a cool oven (150 C, 300 F, gas 2) for about 6 hours, or overnight in a slow cooker. Cool and skim off fat.

Reheat next day for about 30 minutes or so in a moderate oven (160 C, 325 F, gas 3). Serve with mashed or jacket potatoes (necessary for soaking up the delicious gravy). SERVES 4.

Mrs Josephine Keat, Bishop's Waltham, Southampton

SAUSAGES IN CIDER

450 g/1 lb onions
2 tablespoons vegetable oil
450 g/1 lb pork sausages
2 large cooking apples
225 g/8 oz mushrooms
salt and pepper
a good 300 ml/½ pint cider
mixed herbs

FRY sliced onions in the oil in a large frying pan until soft. Cook sausages. Peel, core and slice apples, and peel and slice mushrooms. Add apples and mushrooms to the onion. Season and pour in cider. Bring to boil. Place sausages in ovenproof dish and sprinkle with mixed herbs. Pour over the frying pan mixture, cover and cook in a moderate oven (180 C, 350 F, gas 4) for 25 minutes. Eat with plenty of bread and butter.

Mrs Maureen Dinsdale, Leyburn, Yorkshire

FARMHOUSE SAUSAGE CASSEROLE

2 medium onions
675 g/1½ lb farmhouse sausages
fat to fry
225 g/8 oz parsnips
225 g/8 oz carrots
1 425-g/15-oz can tomatoes

300 ml/½ pint stock, thickened
  with a little cornflour
sprinkling of mixed herbs
black pepper
1–2 teaspoons Worcestershire
  sauce
dash of Tabasco sauce

SLICE the onions and fry over a moderate heat with the sausages until brown. Cut the sausages into thirds and place in a casserole with the onions, sliced parsnips and carrots and lightly chopped tomatoes. Add the stock and season to taste with mixed herbs, freshly ground black pepper, Worcestershire sauce and Tabasco (this really adds the winter warmth). Cover and cook for about 1 hour in a moderately hot oven (190 C, 375 F, gas 5), stirring occasionally.

Serve piping hot with jacket potatoes and garlic butter.

Mrs I. E. Sykes, Market Weighton, Yorkshire

SUSSEX SAUSAGE CASSEROLE

450 g/1 lb sausages
40 g/1½ oz butter
1 large onion, sliced
1 tablespoon flour
1 cooking apple, peeled, cored and
  quartered
3 tomatoes, quartered

4 rashers streaky bacon, derinded
  and diced
½ green pepper, sliced
1 clove of garlic, crushed
½ bottle red wine
salt, pepper and mixed herbs
100 g/4 oz button mushrooms

GRILL sausages until brown. Melt butter in a flameproof casserole over a low heat and fry onion until golden. Add flour, stir continuously until blended. Remove casserole from heat and add sausages, apple, tomatoes, bacon, green pepper and garlic. Pour in the wine, making sure the sausages are well covered; if not add a little more! Season with salt, pepper and mixed herbs. Cover and cook in a moderately hot oven (190 C, 375 F, gas 5) for 45 minutes, after which remove from oven and add the mushrooms. Cook for a further 15 minutes.

Serve with new potatoes and fresh vegetables. SERVES 4.

M. Lampson, Maresfield, Sussex

☆ HAMPSHIRE GOOSE ☆

4 potatoes
4 onions
4 apples
a good handful of fresh sage (less
    if dried)

salt and pepper
8 thick sausages, lightly browned
    (or cold cooked ham or pork)
white stock
100 g/4 oz grated Cheddar cheese

PEEL vegetables and keep in cold salted water. Peel and core apples and put with the vegetables. Pick over the sage, remove coarse stalks and chop the leaves finely.

Slice a layer of potato into a greased casserole dish and over this layer slices of apple and onion, sprinkling with sage and seasoning. Continue like this for half the vegetables and apples then place the sausages (or cold meat) in a row down the centre of the dish. Layer as before, ending with a layer of potato. Add stock slowly to just below last layer of potato.

Cook in a moderate oven (180C, 350F, gas 4) for about 45 minutes. Remove from the oven, top with grated cheese and cook for a further 5 minutes. SERVES 4.

Anne Newton, Guildford, Surrey

LOGGER'S WARMING CASSEROLE

8–12 turkey sausages
2 onions, diced finely
2 carrots, grated
SAUCE
1 tablespoon sugar

1 tablespoon flour
4 tablespoons tomato ketchup
2 teaspoons curry powder
1 teaspoon salt

USE turkey sausages; they swell up rather than shrink and don't exude fat. Put sausages in casserole and spread prepared vegetables evenly over top.

Mix together the sauce ingredients in a small bowl and add 450 ml/¾ pint boiling water, stirring briskly. Pour over sausages. Cover with lid and cook in a moderate oven (180C, 350F, gas 4) for 1½–2 hours. Serve with mashed or baked potatoes and a green vegetable. SERVES 4–6.

J. Streather, Rushden, Hertfordshire

SAUSAGES IN CURRY SAUCE

2 onions, finely chopped
225 g/8 oz mushrooms, chopped
50 g/2 oz butter
225 g/8 oz streaky bacon, cut into small pieces
1 kg/2 lb good-quality pork sausages

50 g/2 oz plain flour
300 ml/½ pint chicken stock
1 425-g/15-oz can tomatoes
4 heaped teaspoons medium curry powder
pinch dried mixed herbs
salt and pepper

FRY onions and mushrooms in butter until soft. Transfer to a casserole with a slotted spoon. Cook bacon gently in the same pan and add to the onion mixture. Brown sausages on both sides, then lay on top of the other ingredients in the casserole. Stir flour into the remaining pan juices. Cook for 1–2 minutes, remove from the heat and gradually stir in the chicken stock. Return to heat to thicken the sauce, stirring. Add the can of tomatoes and roughly chop up the tomatoes. When the sauce is bubbling, mix in the curry powder, stirring all the time. Cook for 2–3 minutes. Add mixed herbs and season with salt and pepper. Pour curry sauce over sausages in casserole. Cover and cook in a moderate oven (180 C, 350 F, gas 4) for 1 hour.

Garnish with fresh parsley and serve with mashed potatoes and a green vegetable. I have found this to be a very popular dish with shooting gentlemen, especially on a frosty day. SERVES 6.

Mrs Christine Gooderham, Croxton, Norfolk

WINTER BACON WARMER

INTO an earthenware dish about 9 cm/3½ inches deep, well greased with butter, slice some "falling" potatoes into small chunks rather than thin even pieces. On top put a layer of sliced onions, a sprinkle of freshly chopped fresh sage and cover with thickish pieces of home-cured bacon. Pepper it, but go carefully with salt, because of the bacon. Next put a good thick layer of soaked butter beans, and repeat the layers, finishing with bacon. Half-fill the dish with good stock, cover and bake in a moderate oven (180 C, 350 F, gas 4) for about 1½ hours, uncovering for the last 15 minutes to crisp the bacon.

Serve with boiled beetroot lightly turned in oil and vinegar. This dish has warmed up my family for many winters – handed down from my Lancashire origins. It's guaranteed to give one a glow!

Mrs Margaret Croston, Christleton, Cheshire

LAYERED SAUSAGE BAKE

675 g/1½ lb potatoes
1 medium onion
¼ teaspoon dried rosemary
25 g/1 oz plain flour
1 teaspoon salt
pepper
1 beef stock cube
450 g/1 lb beef sausages
1 small tomato
sprigs of parsley

PEEL and thinly slice potatoes and onion. Crush rosemary on a plate with a spoon. Mix in flour, salt and a shake of pepper. Arrange layers of potato and onion in a shallow 1.5-litre/2½-pint ovenproof dish. Sprinkle with seasoned flour. Repeat using remaining potato, onion and flour, finishing with a layer of potato. Dissolve beef stock cube in 300 ml/½ pint boiling water and pour over potatoes. Cover dish with lid. Bake in centre of a moderately hot oven (190 C, 375 F, gas 5) for 40–45 minutes, until vegetables are just tender. Remove lid from dish and arrange sausages on top of potato. Return to oven and bake uncovered for a further 30–35 minutes until sausages are dark golden brown. Cut tomato into wedges and arrange in between sausages with sprigs of parsley. SERVES 4.

Evy McCracken, Castlewellan, County Down

SAUSAGE HOT POT

450 g/1 lb pork sausagemeat or
sausages
1 large onion
4 large potatoes
2 Oxo cubes dissolved in 600 ml/
1 pint water

FLATTEN the sausagemeat with a large knife on a board. (If using sausages remove skins first.) Slice the onion thinly, slice the potatoes. Fill a pie dish or similar with layers of the ingredients, starting with potato slices, then onion and then the sausagemeat, ending up with two layers of potato slices on the top. Pour the Oxo gravy over until the liquid fills the dish and just shows around the edge. Cook in a moderately hot oven (200 C, 400 F, gas 6) for 2 hours. If the potatoes begin to get too brown on the top either reduce the heat slightly or discard the top layer before serving. SERVES 4.

D. L. Miller, Piltdown, Sussex

BACON BEANY
(BLANKS AND PRIZES)

450 g/1 lb unsmoked streaky
bacon
675 g/1½ lb shelled broad beans

600 ml/1 pint milk
salt and pepper
3 tablespoons plain flour

DERIND bacon and cut into 2.5-cm/1-inch cubes. Place in a large saucepan, just cover with water and simmer gently for 20 minutes. Add the beans and enough milk to cover by about 1 cm/½ inch. Simmer a further 20 minutes. Taste for salt as the bacon may have salt enough, and add a good seasoning of pepper. Blend the flour with the remaining milk, stir into beans and bacon and simmer for 3 minutes, until thickened.

Serve on a shallow dish, surrounded by small English potatoes sprinkled lightly with parsley. SERVES 4.

This recipe has been in my husband's family for generations.

Mrs Mary Ryman, Narborough, Leicestershire

BACON CHOPS WITH CREAMED
MUSHROOMS

225 g/8 oz button mushrooms
50 g/2 oz butter
salt, pepper and garlic salt
1 tablespoon cornflour
150 ml/¼ pint single cream

½ wineglass sherry
4 bacon chops or thick slices back
bacon
chopped parsley

FRY the mushrooms lightly in the melted butter. Shake salt and pepper into the pan and, for those who like the flavour, a sprinkling of garlic salt would be excellent. Blend the cornflour with a little of the cream, stir remaining cream into the mushrooms and simmer gently. Gradually stir in the cornflour cream, stirring until it thickens, add sherry and simmer for a further 5 minutes. Keep the sauce hot and cover to prevent a skin forming; if a thinner sauce is required add more cream.

Meanwhile trim bacon chops and grill or fry. Arrange on a heated dish, spoon over the creamed mushrooms and garnish with chopped parsley. Serve with buttered green peas, new potatoes and a fresh salad. SERVES 4.

Mrs Barbara Houseman, Darley, North Yorkshire

GLAZED FRUIT GAMMON

1 small gammon joint, soaked
overnight
40–50 g/1½–2 oz butter or
margarine
2 cooking apples, peeled, cored,
sliced into rings and brushed
with a little lemon juice

1 227-g/8-oz can pineapple rings
salt and pepper
6 tablespoons pineapple or apricot
jam
chopped parsley

DOT the gammon joint all over with butter and bake in a moderate oven (180 C, 350 F, gas 4) until tender, allowing 25 minutes per 450 g/1 lb and 25 minutes over. Remove from the oven and cut into thick slices. Reassemble the gammon, sandwiching the slices alternately with apple and pineapple rings. Season, place in a shallow ovenproof dish and surround with remaining fruit. Melt the jam and pour over gammon and fruit. Return to oven for a further 10–15 minutes. Arrange in a serving dish and sprinkle with parsley. Very tasty.

Mrs K. Macrae, Munlochy, Ross-shire

STUFFED LIVER ROAST

1 whole calf's liver, with a
"pocket" cut large enough to
hold stuffing
8 rashers of smoked bacon, rinds
removed

STUFFING
3 tablespoons chopped onion
chopped rinds from the bacon
50 g/2 oz fresh breadcrumbs
2 tablespoons chopped parsley
beaten egg to bind
salt and pepper

MIX the stuffing ingredients together and fill the liver "pocket". Wrap the bacon rashers around the liver until it is completely covered and tie in place. Cook in a covered roasting tin in a moderately hot oven (200 C, 400 F, gas 6) for 1½ hours. Remove string and carve as a joint. Serve with fresh salad.

Mrs Rhiannon Evans, Llandrillo, Clwyd

HAYNES LANDRACE AU GRATIN

1-kg/2-lb bacon joint, home-
   produced if possible
4 shallots
450 g/1 lb whole baby carrots
450 g/1 lb French beans, cut into
   2.5-cm/1-inch lengths
450 g/1 lb peas, shelled
4 baby courgettes
4 hard-boiled eggs

SAUCE
50 g/2 oz butter
50 g/2 oz flour
300 ml/½ pint milk
100 g/4 oz grated Cheddar cheese
1 twist ground black pepper
GARNISH
25 g/1 oz grated Cheddar cheese
4 small tomatoes
parsley sprigs

SOAK the bacon joint in water for about 4 hours then boil in fresh water to cover for 1¼–1½ hours, adding the prepared shallots and carrots for last 20 minutes. Remove vegetables and allow bacon to cool. Reserve cooking stock.

Lightly boil French beans and peas. Slice courgettes. Halve eggs. Dice cold bacon. Arrange bacon, eggs and vegetables in layers in an ovenproof dish.

Melt the butter, stir in the flour and then the milk to make a sauce. Add the cheese, pepper and sufficient bacon stock to make required consistency. Pour over the vegetable mixture and sprinkle with remaining grated cheese. Bake in a moderate oven (180 C, 350 F, gas 4) for 35 minutes, or until golden. Garnish with sliced tomatoes and parsley and serve with buttered broad beans and new potatoes.

Sally Osgerby, Muckton, Lincolnshire

BACON CASSEROLE

3 medium onions
350 g/12 oz collar bacon, cut into
   thin rashers

450 g/1 lb potatoes
pepper
about 450 ml/¾ pint milk

THINLY slice onions and place in the bottom of a casserole dish. Derind bacon and make into rolls, place these on the onions. Peel and thinly slice potatoes and cover bacon in neat overlapping layers, adding pepper at each layer. Pour in enough milk to come three-quarters way up dish and place bacon rinds on top of potatoes. Cover and bake for 1 hour in a cool oven (150 C, 300 F, gas 2). Remove lid and bacon rinds and bake for a further half hour until potatoes are brown and most of the liquid absorbed. Serve with Brussels sprouts or cabbage. SERVES 4.

Mrs R. Meikle, Black Dog, Devon

OSLO SAUCE

This recipe can be used with steaks, pork chops, lamb chops or pork sausages.

4 steaks or chops
1 onion, chopped
1 stick celery, chopped
1 tablespoon vinegar
1 tablespoon brown sugar
2 tablespoons tomato purée

1 teaspoon Worcestershire sauce
1 teaspoon curry powder (optional)
1 stock cube and 300 ml/½ pint water
2 teaspoons cornflour

FRY meat lightly on both sides to seal, then place in a casserole and sprinkle with chopped onion and celery.

Mix all the remaining ingredients together very thoroughly; you may have to warm it slightly to ensure a smooth mixture. Pour over the meat, cover and cook in a moderate oven (160 C, 325 F, gas 3) for 2 hours.

Mrs Phyllis Wilde, Brailes, Oxfordshire

DUMPLING PUDDING

175 g/6 oz self-raising flour
75 g/3 oz shredded suet
½ teaspoon salt
1 small finely chopped or grated onion

pinch of sage, thyme or other herbs (depending on the flavour of the stew the pudding is to be served with)
5–6 tablespoons cold water

MIX all ingredients together with cold water to make a fairly soft dough. Place in a small greased pudding basin, cover with buttered greaseproof paper folded with a pleat, and tie with string. Place in a saucepan of boiling water, to come halfway up the sides of the basin, and steam for 1½ hours.

Serve in slices with beef stew, lamb hot-pot etc., instead of dumplings. This pudding will simmer away quite happily if the dinner has to be postponed for any reason (unlike dumplings!)

Mrs E. Eyre, Sibsey, Lincolnshire

POULTRY AND GAME

CHICKEN POT ROAST

1 1.5-kg/3-lb chicken
25 g/1 oz butter
1 large onion, chopped
1 tablespoon flour
300 ml/½ pint stock mixture
  (chicken stock and dry
  vermouth or dry cider,
  according to taste)
2 tablespoons tomato purée

225 g/8 oz tomatoes, skinned and
  chopped
2 teaspoons chopped parsley
salt and pepper
225–350 g/8–12 oz carrots, sliced
225–350 g/8–12 oz courgettes,
  sliced
1 bay leaf

BROWN the chicken to an even colour in the melted butter then remove from the pan. Brown the onion in the remaining butter until soft then add the flour and cook for a few minutes. Add the stock mixture, tomato purée and tomatoes (½ teaspoon sugar can be added if the tomatoes are bitter), and bring to the boil, stirring. Simmer until thickened, add the parsley and seasoning to taste.

Lay the prepared vegetables in the base of a large casserole and season with salt and pepper. Place the browned chicken on the vegetables and pour over the tomato sauce (a little more liquid can be added if required). Add the bay leaf, cover and cook in a moderate oven (180 c, 350 f, gas 4) for 1½–2 hours, until tender.

Mrs E. M. Elliott, Frampton, Dorset

LEMON CHICKEN

1 small onion	1 large or 2 small lemons
1 clove garlic	4 streaky bacon rashers
1 chicken, about 1.75 kg/4 lb	1.15 litres/2 pints chicken stock
mixed herbs	salt and pepper

ROUGHLY chop onion and garlic and place inside chicken with herbs. Thinly slice lemon and lay half the slices over the base of a good-sized casserole dish. Place chicken on lemon slices, put bacon rashers on chicken breast and then place the rest of the lemon slices all over the chicken. Add the stock and seasoning. Cover and cook as slowly as possible in a cool oven (150 C, 300 F, gas 2) for about 2½–3 hours. When cooked remove bacon and lemon slices and brown the bird briefly in a hot oven (220 C, 425 F, gas 7).

Serve either hot or cold. If hot: dice bacon rashers and add to thickened stock for gravy. If cold: remove chicken from stock and place on serving dish. Dry bacon on separate dish and dice. Prepare a crisp green salad of Cos lettuce. Dice some cubes of white bread and deep fry until crisp then cool. Roughly chop some hazelnuts. Toss the lettuce with French dressing and turn in with it the chopped bacon pieces, hazelnuts and croûtons. Serve the salad with the chicken and keep the stock for a light soup.

Nicola Brazier, Uley, Gloucestershire

FOWL RICE PUDDING

3–4 streaky bacon rashers	4 onions, sliced
1 boiling chicken	600 ml/1 pint milk
bay leaf, parsley and tarragon	salt and pepper
knob of butter	grated nutmeg
225 g/8 oz rice	

LAY the bacon rashers over the chicken and pop the herbs inside the bird with a knob of butter. Place in an ovenproof casserole, sitting on a bed of rice. Add the onions and pour over the milk, season well and sprinkle with nutmeg.

Cover and cook in a cool oven (150 C, 300 F, gas 2) for several hours or even all day. Look at twice and add a further 600 ml/1 pint milk if necessary. Transfer to a large platter to serve.

Mrs C. H. Liddell, Andover, Hampshire

SAIGHTON CHICKEN

1 1.5-kg/3-lb chicken, jointed
100 g/4 oz butter
50 g/2 oz bacon, diced
1 medium onion, chopped
1 carrot, chopped
50 g/2 oz flour
600 ml/1 pint beef stock

2 tablespoons tomato purée
4–5 tablespoons sherry
salt and pepper
100 g/4 oz mushrooms, sliced
2 tablespoons double cream
chopped parsley

FRY the chicken joints in half the butter until browned all over. Place in a casserole dish. In same pan melt the remaining butter and gently fry together the bacon, onion and carrot for about 5 minutes. Stir in the flour to form a roux. Add the beef stock slowly, stirring until the sauce thickens. Blend in the tomato purée, sherry and seasoning.

Pour this sauce over the chicken, cover with a tight-fitting lid and cook in a moderate oven (160 C, 325 F, gas 3) for 1½ hours. Add the mushrooms and cook for a further 10 minutes. Swirl in the cream to serve and sprinkle with chopped parsley. SERVES 4.

Mrs S. Pickering, Saighton, Cheshire

AUTUMN CHICKEN STEW

75 g/3 oz butter
1 large onion, roughly chopped
1 green chilli, finely chopped
1 cm/½ inch fresh root ginger, peeled and finely grated
450 g/1 lb boneless chicken pieces
1 425-g/15-oz can tomatoes
1 heaped teaspoon turmeric powder
½ green pepper, chopped
1 teaspoon salt (or to taste)
300 ml/½ pint water (or more if necessary)

1 chicken stock cube
2 medium potatoes, cut into 2.5-cm/1-inch cubes
1 15-cm/6-inch piece marrow, cut into 2.5-cm/1-inch cubes
2 courgettes, sliced
1 medium aubergine, cut into 2.5-cm/1-inch cubes
1 113-g/4-oz packet frozen mixed vegetables
1 teaspoon garam masala
1 tablespoon tomato purée
sprig fresh coriander

MELT butter in a flameproof casserole and add onion, chilli and ginger. Cook over medium low heat until onions are opaque. Add chicken and seal on all sides. Stir in tomatoes, turmeric, green pepper, salt, water and stock cube. Bring to boil, cover and simmer gently for 15 minutes. Add potatoes, marrow, courgettes and aubergine, bring back to boil and simmer, covered, for 30 minutes. Add frozen mixed vegetables, garam masala and purée and simmer for 10 minutes more. Just before serving stir in chopped coriander. Serve with rice. SERVES 4.

Miss Sally-Ann Davies, Southall, Middlesex

DEVILLED CHICKEN WITH SAVOURY TOPPING

50 g/2 oz butter or margarine
4 chicken joints, skinned and boned
1 tablespoon flour, seasoned with salt and pepper
1 onion, chopped
½ teaspoon grated nutmeg
1–2 tablespoons tomato ketchup
1 teaspoon Worcestershire sauce

1 tablespoon sugar
300 ml/½ pint chicken stock
SAVOURY TOPPING
50 g/2 oz butter or margarine
100 g/4 oz self-raising flour
pinch salt
1–2 tablespoons milk
1 teaspoon made mustard
100 g/4 oz Cheddar cheese, grated

MELT the fat in a frying pan. Coat the chicken joints with seasoned flour and cook in a pan with the onion for a few minutes, until the chicken is nicely browned. Turn into a round casserole dish. Blend the nutmeg, tomato ketchup, Worcestershire sauce, sugar and stock and pour over the chicken and onion. Cover and cook in a moderate oven (160 C, 325 F, gas 3) for 45 minutes, or until chicken is tender.

Meanwhile make the savoury topping. Rub fat into sifted flour and salt until mixture resembles fine breadcrumbs. Bind with milk and mustard to make a soft dough. Knead lightly and roll out to a rectangle, about 5 mm/¼ inch thick. Scatter with the grated cheese and roll up like a Swiss roll, starting with a long side. Cut dough into 1-cm/½-inch wide slices, dipping the knife in flour if it sticks. Place slices on top of the casserole, overlapping them around the edge. Return the casserole, uncovered, to a moderately hot oven (200 C, 400 F, gas 6) for 10–15 minutes, until topping is well risen and golden brown. Serve with creamed potatoes and sprouts. SERVES 4.

Mrs Jean Hayton, Beckwith, North Yorkshire

LAZY CHICKEN

6–8 chicken joints (wings are very
  tasty and cheaper)
flour seasoned with salt, pepper
  and 1 teaspoon dried mixed
  herbs
25–50 g/1–2 oz butter
150 ml/¼ pint white wine or cider

½ green pepper
½ onion
2 large tomatoes
100 g/4 oz mushrooms
300 ml/½ pint pouring white sauce
  (20 g/¾ oz butter, 20 g/¾ oz flour
  and 300 ml/½ pint milk)

DIP the chicken joints in seasoned flour and coat well. Melt the
butter in a flameproof casserole and fry the joints gently on each
side until golden brown. Pour in the wine or cider.

Chop or slice the pepper, onion, tomatoes and mushrooms and
add all to the casserole. Make a white sauce in the usual way and
add to the chicken. Carefully mix all the ingredients together and
stir for a few seconds. Season to taste.

Simmer on top of the cooker for 5–10 minutes then cover and
cook in a moderately hot oven (190 c, 375 f, gas 5) for about 1 hour,
until tender.

Served with simply a crisp salad, this dish is a meal in itself.
SERVES 4–6.

Mrs Angela Pears, Penistone, Yorkshire

CHICKEN AND HONKY DORY SAUCE

Named by my two children.

2 tablespoons cooking oil
4 chicken portions, skinned
1 large onion, chopped
2 garlic cloves, crushed
1 green pepper, chopped
225 g/8 oz button mushrooms
25 g/1 oz flour
300 ml/½ pint chicken stock
1 396-g/14-oz can tomatoes,
  liquidised or mashed

½ teaspoon dried tarragon
1½ teaspoons dried mixed herbs or
  1 bouquet garni
1 tablespoon chopped parsley
½ teaspoon crushed rosemary
salt and pepper

HEAT oil in a pan and fry chicken portions until lightly brown on
both sides. Transfer to a large casserole dish, then lightly fry onion,
garlic, green pepper and mushrooms. Add to the chicken in the

casserole. Mix flour with a little chicken stock to a smooth paste and add to pan with rest of stock. Stir in tomatoes, all the herbs and seasoning to taste. Cook gently, stirring all the time, until sauce starts to thicken. Pour over chicken, cover with lid or foil and cook in a moderate oven (180 C, 350 F, gas 4) for about 1 hour, until chicken is cooked.

Serve with a fresh green salad and rice or noodles. SERVES 4.

Mrs B. Dunne, Lathom, Lancashire

☆ AUTUMN CHICKEN ☆ CASSEROLE

2 sticks celery
1 onion
1 medium marrow
450 g/1 lb tomatoes
1 green pepper
4 chicken joints
seasoned flour to coat
sprinkling mixed herbs
butter to fry

chicken stock
salt and pepper
TOPPING
225 g/8 oz self-raising flour
pinch salt
pinch mixed herbs
55 g/2 oz margarine
7 tablespoons milk

CHOP celery and onion. Peel, deseed and cube marrow. Skin and chop tomatoes. Deseed and slice pepper. Place all vegetables in a large casserole dish.

Coat chicken joints with seasoned flour and herbs and fry lightly in butter until golden brown on all sides. Place on top of the vegetables. Top up with chicken stock or water to just cover the vegetables and season well. Cover and cook in a moderately hot oven (190 C, 375 F, gas 5) for about 1½–2 hours, until chicken is cooked and vegetables tender. Transfer chicken joints to a plate and keep warm.

Make topping. Mix flour, salt and herbs in a bowl and rub in margarine. Stir in enough milk to make a soft dough. Roll out to 1-cm/½-inch thickness and cut into 5-cm/2-inch rounds. Place on top of vegetables, slightly overlapping each other, and bake at 200 C, 400 F, gas 6 for 15 minutes, or until well risen and golden brown. Serve with chicken joints and boiled potatoes. SERVES 4.

Mrs K. Medley, Bamford, via Sheffield

MEXICAN CHICKEN

4 chicken joints	1 tablespoon tarragon vinegar
75 g/3 oz butter	5 tablespoons white wine
4 small whole onions	1 green pepper, deseeded and
25 g/1 oz flour	sliced
2 tablespoons tomato purée	salt and pepper
300 ml/½ pint chicken stock	100 g/4 oz seedless raisins
4 cloves	12 stoned green olives (optional)
1 clove garlic, crushed	

LIGHTLY fry the chicken in the melted butter. Transfer to a large ovenproof casserole. Toss the onions in the butter and add to the chicken. Remove pan from heat and blend in the flour then the tomato purée. Gradually add stock, stirring to keep free from lumps. Replace over heat, stirring until thickened. Pour over chicken. Add cloves, garlic, vinegar, wine and green pepper slices. Season with salt and pepper, cover and cook in a moderate oven (180 c, 350 f, gas 4) for 1–1½ hours, adding raisins and olives for the last 15 minutes. SERVES 4.

Mrs A. Griffin, Minety, Wiltshire

CHICKEN SURPRISE PARCELS

1 1.5-kg/3½-lb chicken, or 4	1 green pepper
chicken portions	1 onion (optional)
1 439-g/13½-oz can pineapple slices	salt and pepper
1 red pepper	

CUT chicken into four portions with game cutters or a very sharp knife, and remove the skin if preferred. Place each portion on a piece of foil, large enough to make a parcel. Place the foil in a deep baking tin and pour an equal amount of pineapple juice over each chicken portion. Wash, deseed and cut peppers into narrow strips, place over the chicken. Add a little chopped onion and seasoning to taste. Seal the parcels.

Bake in a moderate oven (180 c, 350 f, gas 4) for about 1 hour (don't let the juices dry up). Open up parcels, add the pineapple slices, reseal and return to oven for a further 10 minutes (until pineapple nice and hot).

Serve with green peas and baked jacket potatoes. I wash the potatoes and wrap them in foil to cook along with the chicken. Delicious. SERVES 4.

Mrs E. Paterson, Brechin, Angus

CREAMED CHICKEN AND LEEKS

1 1.5-kg/3½-lb chicken, jointed
450 g/1 lb leeks
50 g/2 oz butter
salt and pepper

450 ml/¾ pint milk
cornflour to thicken
chopped parsley to garnish

PLACE the chicken portions in a casserole. Add the leeks chopped into 2.5-cm/1-inch pieces, dot with the butter and season. Cover and cook in a moderately hot oven (190 C, 375 F, gas 5) until chicken is tender, about 1 hour.

Pour the juices into a saucepan; if there seems to be too much fat, spoon this off. Add the milk and bring to the boil. Make a paste of cornflour and cold water and add this gradually to the sauce, stirring until required thickness is obtained. Cook for a few minutes and season to taste.

Pour over the chicken and leeks in the casserole and serve garnished with chopped parsley.

Mrs M. L. Rose, Martley, Worcester

CHICKEN FRICASSÉE '85

6 chicken portions
300 ml/½ pint chicken stock
salt and pepper
50 g/2 oz mushrooms, sliced
100 g/4 oz bacon, chopped
50 g/2 oz butter
25 g/1 oz cornflour

600 ml/1 pint milk
1 egg
2 tablespoons single cream
225–275 g/8–10 oz cooked creamed
  potatoes
50 g/2 oz Lancashire cheese

SIMMER chicken portions in stock and seasoning for 45 minutes. Add mushrooms and bacon and simmer for a further 15 minutes. Keep hot.

Make béchamel sauce in usual way; melt butter, stir in cornflour and gradually add milk, stirring continuously. Remove from heat and add previously blended egg and cream, season lightly then return to a low heat to cook for 1 minute.

Pipe creamed potatoes around a heated serving dish, arrange chicken portions, mushrooms and bacon in the centre and pour over the warm sauce. Sprinkle with the grated cheese and toast until just colourful under the grill.

Serve with hot buttered carrots and cauliflower florets or courgettes. SERVES 6.

Mrs Evelyn Mycock, Hodthorpe, Nottinghamshire

FAVOURITE CHICKEN CASSEROLE

4 chicken breasts or portions
1 packet sage and onion stuffing
  mix
450 g/1 lb broccoli
50 g/2 oz butter
25 g/1 oz flour
450 ml/¾ pint stock, or 1 stock
  cube and water

100 ml/4 fl oz whipped or soured
  cream
3 tablespoons sherry
salt and pepper
100 g/4 oz Cheddar cheese, grated

COAT chicken pieces with stuffing mix. Place in a shallow oven-proof dish and cover tightly with foil. Bake in a moderately hot oven (200 C, 400 F, gas 6) for 40 minutes, or until tender.

Cook broccoli in boiling salted water until just tender. Drain and keep warm.

Melt butter in a saucepan and blend in flour. Remove from heat and slowly stir in stock. Cook and stir over a low heat until thickened. Fold in cream and sherry and season to taste. Place broccoli in a shallow flameproof dish and pour over half the sauce. Arrange the chicken pieces on top. Add half the grated cheese to remaining sauce and pour over the chicken. Sprinkle the rest of the cheese on top and place under the grill until sauce bubbles and is lightly browned. Serve with new potatoes and buttered baby carrots. SERVES 4.

This casserole is so handy because it can be prepared in advance. Just store in the refrigerator and, when needed, heat through in a moderately hot oven (190 C, 375 F, gas 5) for about half an hour.

Mrs E. Matthews, Bangor, County Down

☆ SPINACH CHICKEN ☆

4 chicken breasts
1 onion
50 g/2 oz bacon
25 g/1 oz butter
450 g/1 lb fresh spinach
salt and freshly ground black
  pepper

grated nutmeg
1 tablespoon chopped tarragon
a little well-seasoned flour
1 beaten egg
dry white breadcrumbs
2 tablespoons oil
50 g/2 oz butter

REMOVE the skin from the chicken breasts. Cut each breast nearly in half (horizontally), open out and place between two sheets of wet greaseproof paper. Gently beat with a rolling pin to flatten each breast.

Chop the onion finely and dice the bacon. Fry both gently in the 25 g/1 oz butter until cooked but not coloured.

Discarding the stalks, wash the spinach thoroughly and place into a pan without water. Add a pinch of salt. Cover and cook, shaking the pan occasionally, for 5–7 minutes; the spinach will reduce by about two-thirds. Drain very thoroughly by squeezing between two plates. Turn onto a board and chop roughly. Add the spinach to the onion mixture, season with salt, pepper and nutmeg and add the tarragon. Allow to cool.

When cool, divide the spinach mixture between the chicken breasts. Fold the breasts over the stuffing to make parcels. Dip each chicken parcel in seasoned flour, then beaten egg and finally coat in breadcrumbs. Leave to set in the fridge for 20 minutes.

Heat the oil and butter in a frying pan, add the chicken parcels and fry for 5–8 minutes on each side. Serve immediately. Delicious with parsley butter, new potatoes, grilled tomatoes, mushrooms and French beans. SERVES 4.

Mrs T. Bryant, Horncastle, Lincolnshire

CHICKEN WITH BACON AND CELERY

3 rashers streaky bacon, chopped
3 sticks celery, chopped
25 g/1 oz butter
25 g/1 oz flour
300 ml/$\frac{1}{2}$ pint milk
150 ml/$\frac{1}{4}$ pint soured cream
1 teaspoon dried mixed herbs
salt and pepper
450–675 g/1–1$\frac{1}{2}$ lb cooked chicken, diced
4 rashers back bacon
watercress sprigs

IN a heavy-based pan or flameproof casserole, fry the chopped bacon and celery in the butter for a few minutes. Stir in the flour then blend in the milk and soured cream to make a sauce. Bring to the boil, stirring, then season with the herbs and salt and pepper, and add the diced chicken meat. Cover and simmer for 15 minutes, to heat through; stir frequently to prevent catching.

Meanwhile, grill the bacon rashers. Serve the chicken and sauce on a bed of rice, top with the bacon rashers and garnish with watercress. SERVES 4.

Irene Stewart, Ballantrae, Ayrshire

CHICKEN GALANTINE

350–450 g/12–16 oz raw chicken
450 g/1 lb cooked ham
100 g/4 oz fresh white
  breadcrumbs
2 eggs, beaten

150 ml/¼ pint double cream
pinch of grated nutmeg
salt and pepper
6–8 rashers streaky bacon, rind
  removed

MINCE the chicken and ham, or chop into small pieces. Add the breadcrumbs, eggs, cream, nutmeg and seasoning, and mix well. Line a 1-kg/2-lb loaf tin with the bacon rashers, put in the chicken mixture and cover securely with greased foil. Cook in a moderately hot oven (190 C, 375 F, gas 5) for 1–1¼ hours. Serve hot or cold.

Mrs Peggy Carter, Marlborough, Wiltshire

☆ CHICKEN AND MUSHROOM ☆ CHEESECAKE

BASE
75 g/3 oz butter
100 g/4 oz crushed Krackerwheat
  biscuits or cream crackers
4 tablespoons dry sage and onion
  stuffing mix
FILLING
275 g/10 oz sieved cottage cheese
3 eggs, separated
25 g/1 oz flour
150 ml/¼ pint soured cream
50 g/2 oz mushrooms, sliced and
  sautéed

50 g/2 oz bacon, cooked and
  chopped
175 g/6 oz cooked chicken
2 tablespoons chopped parsley
salt and pepper
TOPPING
25 g/1 oz butter
1 small onion, thinly sliced
50 g/2 oz mushrooms, sliced
150 ml/¼ pint soured cream
1 tablespoon chopped parsley

To make base, melt butter and stir in crushed biscuits and stuffing. Press firmly into a greased 20-cm/8-inch loose-bottomed cake tin.

For filling, beat all ingredients except egg whites in a large bowl, season. Whisk egg whites until stiff and fold into the cheese mixture. Spoon into cake tin and smooth level. Bake in a moderate oven (160 C, 325 F, gas 3) for 1¼ hours, until firm but springy.

Melt butter for topping and fry onions and mushrooms until soft and lightly coloured. Stir in cream. Gently remove cheesecake from tin and place on a serving dish. Spoon over the cream mixture and sprinkle with parsley. Serve with salad or fresh vegetables.

Mrs S. Dearlove, Cockayne Hatley, Bedfordshire

SAVOURY TURKEY BALLS

1 turkey leg, including thigh
  (uncooked)
1 rasher of bacon, lean part only
25 g/1 oz vegetable fat
½ teaspoon pepper
½ teaspoon salt
a few bacon rinds

1 medium onion
75 g/3 oz brown rice
25 g/1 oz white pudding rice
2 teaspoons freshly chopped
  parsley
1 432-g/15¼-oz can tomato soup

REMOVE skin from the turkey and cut off all the meat. Mince with the lean bacon.

Melt the vegetable fat in a heavy pan or flameproof casserole. Stir in minced meats and season with the pepper and salt. Cook very gently for about 30 minutes, keeping lid tightly fixed. Stir occasionally to avoid burning and, if it seems too dry, add a little water to moisten.

Separately fry any fat from the bacon rasher together with the bacon rinds. Remove from pan. Add finely chopped onion and cook gently until soft but not brown.

Put the brown rice into 900 ml/1½ pints boiling salted water and cook without lid until fairly soft, about 30–40 minutes. Put the white pudding rice into 300 ml/½ pint boiling water and cook until soft, about 15 minutes.

To the cooked minced turkey add the onion, parsley, strained brown rice and strained white rice, with enough of the cooking liquid to make a stiff but pliable mixture. Divide mixture into balls, roll as tightly and smoothly as possible and place in a deep ovenproof dish.

When ready to cook pour over the can of tomato soup and place in a moderately hot oven (200 C, 400 F, gas 6) for 30 minutes. SERVES 4.

Mrs Valerie Anderson, Bedale, Yorkshire

PHEASANT AUX MARRONS

2 hen pheasants
1 tablespoon flour
MARINADE
2 tablespoons olive oil
2 tablespoons red wine
100 g/4 oz mushrooms, chopped
salt and pepper

STUFFING
225 g/8 oz chestnuts
50 g/2 oz shredded suet
100 g/4 oz fresh breadcrumbs
100 g/4 oz sausagemeat
1 large onion, grated
1 small egg
GARNISH
cooked chestnuts

MIX the oil and wine together, add the mushrooms and seasoning. Pour over the pheasants, cover and marinate for 1–2 hours.

Prepare the stuffing. Boil, peel and pound or chop the chestnuts. Mix the suet, breadcrumbs, sausagemeat and grated onion together. Add the chestnuts, season and bind with the beaten egg.

Drain the wine marinade from the pheasants, stuff the birds and place in a casserole. Pour over the wine mixture, cover and cook in a moderately hot oven (200 c, 400 f, gas 6) for 1½ hours. Baste frequently.

Drain the juices from the casserole dish and heat in a saucepan, thickening with 1 tablespoon flour slaked with 1 tablespoon water. Place the pheasants on a serving dish and surround with chestnuts. Serve with Brussels sprouts and game chips. SERVES 6.

Mrs Lucy Cooper, Horham, Norfolk

☆ PHEASANT IN CIDER ☆

1 pheasant, plucked and drawn
1 orange, quartered
5 large cabbage leaves
4 rashers fatty bacon
¼ teaspoon salt

¼ teaspoon ground black pepper
¼ teaspoon grated nutmeg
300 ml/½ pint cider
3 bay leaves

STUFF pheasant with the quartered orange and two cabbage leaves. Wrap in bacon and the remaining cabbage leaves and tie up with string. Place pheasant in a casserole, sprinkle with salt, pepper and nutmeg, pour over cider and add the bay leaves. Cover and leave for 1 hour.

Baste with cider, cover with lid and cook in a moderate oven (180 c, 350 f, gas 4) for 2½ hours, basting every 45 minutes. Serve with roast potatoes and vegetables

Mrs A. Hudd, Bourton, Wiltshire

PEASANT'S PHEASANT

175 g/6 oz butter
450 g/1 lb mushrooms
salt and pepper
1 brace of pheasants

40 g/1½ oz flour
750 ml/1¼ pints stock
1 wineglass sherry

MELT half the butter and cook sliced mushrooms gently for 10 minutes. Season and cool.

Stuff the pheasants with three-quarters of the mushrooms. Brown the birds in the rest of the butter and place in a large casserole. Blend flour into pan juices and gradually work in stock and sherry, stirring. Season and pour over birds to cover them. Cover and cook for 1¼ hours in a moderate oven (160 C, 325 F, gas 3).

Just before serving add remaining mushrooms. Serve with an accompaniment of redcurrant jelly.

Geraldine Haworth, Radlett, Hertfordshire

PHEASANT À LA MARSHALLS

1 brace pheasants, jointed
50 g/2 oz butter
2 medium dessert apples, peeled
  and sliced
1 medium onion, chopped
3 sticks celery, chopped

1 tablespoon flour
300 ml/½ pint cider
300 ml/½ pint chicken stock
salt and pepper
150 ml/¼ pint double cream
chopped parsley

BROWN pheasant joints in butter in flameproof casserole. Remove from casserole and put in apples, onion and celery. Sauté gently for 5 minutes. Stir in the flour and gradually add cider and stock. Bring to boil, season, then liquidise in a blender until smooth. Return joints to casserole and pour over the sauce. Cover and cook in a moderate oven (180 C, 350 F, gas 4) for 1½ hours. Stir in cream just before serving and dust with parsley.

Mrs J. Lywood, Kirdford, West Sussex

☆ PHEASANT CASSEROLE ☆

2 young pheasants
2 rashers bacon, chopped
1 tablespoon flour
salt and pepper
300 ml/½ pint red wine
2 onions, chopped
1 carrot, chopped

1 clove garlic, crushed
2 shallots, chopped
bouquet garni
1 tablespoon brandy
4 tablespoons sherry
225 g/8 oz mushroom caps

BROWN the pheasants on both sides with the bacon in a flameproof casserole. Sprinkle on flour, salt and pepper and blend with the wine. Fry onions and add to the pheasants with carrot, garlic, shallots and bouquet garni. Add enough water to cover, then cover the casserole and simmer in a moderate oven (160 C, 325 F, gas 3) for about 3 hours, until the sauce is dark brown. Half an hour before serving add brandy, sherry and mushroom caps and remove bouquet garni.

Serve with baked potatoes and greens or a salad.

Mrs C. A. Briggs, Bishampton, Worcestershire

AUTUMN PHEASANT CASSEROLE

salt and black pepper
1 cock pheasant
300 ml/½ pint chicken stock
225 g/8 oz carrots, sliced
mixed herbs
Worcestershire sauce

cloves garlic
1 large measure of port
few grapes, halved and pipped
2 tablespoons redcurrant jelly
cornflour to thicken

RUB salt into skin of pheasant and roast in a moderate oven (180 C, 350 F, gas 4) for 20 minutes per 450 g/1 lb. Reserve the juices from the cooked bird and pour into a large casserole dish with the stock. Strip meat from cooked bird.

Place the meat, carrots, black pepper, herbs, Worcestershire sauce, garlic to taste and port in the casserole dish with the stock. Cover and cook for 30 minutes in a moderate oven (180 C, 350 F, gas 4).

Remove from oven and add the grapes. Stir in the redcurrant jelly and thicken with a little cornflour mixed with cold water if necessary. SERVES 4.

Nicola Fitzhugh, Stanwick, Northamptonshire

POTTED PHEASANT

75 g/3 oz butter per bird	black pepper
2–3 pheasants (well hung)	nutmeg or mace

MELT the butter in a large flameproof casserole and turn the birds in this one at a time, then pack them all in together. Season well with freshly ground black pepper and grated nutmeg or mace, the butter providing the salt. Cover and cook in a moderate oven (180 C, 350 F, gas 4), or on top of the stove over a low heat, until tender, about 1½–2 hours.

When cooked, strain off the pan juices into a small bowl, and as soon as the birds are cool enough to handle, skin them and remove the meat in as large pieces as possible, taking out any shot or splinters. Pack the meat into a straight-sided dish, first a layer of small pieces, then the large pieces laying in one direction, then the rest of the small bits. The skin and bones go back in the saucepan with giblets and water added, for stock.

Spoon the butter from the casserole juices into the filled dish and press down well with a wooden spoon. The butter should fill all the spaces, if not add a little more melted butter. Cover with buttered paper or foil and weight down firmly with kitchen scale weights. Put in a cold larder until the next day. The gravy from the casserole juices must not go into the dish but should be preserved as it is to turn the stock into a wonderful game soup.

Next day, remove paper or foil, and unless the dish is to be eaten at once, seal it with a little more butter if needed.

This is an old-fashioned recipe which will keep a week or two in the larder; most useful in the shooting season. You could serve it as a starter to dinner party guests with hot toast, but a slice with a plain jacket potato and some celery is in itself a meal fit for a king.

Mrs E. Hollingsworth, Cotton, Suffolk

FIELD FARE OR GAME WITH MUSHROOMS

1 brace of partridge or 1 cock
    pheasant (duck or small chicken
    may be used depending on
    availability and economics)
oil or tasty dripping
2 large onions, chopped
450 g/1 lb giant puff ball (white
    inside) or field mushrooms

salt and pepper
300 ml/½ pint stock
150 ml/¼ pint dry white wine
cornflour and water paste to
    thicken

REMOVE flesh from bird, dice and gently fry in oil or dripping for 5–10 minutes, stirring frequently to ensure even cooking. Add the onions, mushrooms and seasoning and cook over a low heat until the mushrooms have shrunk and turned golden brown and the onion is soft. Pour on the stock and wine and thicken to taste with the cornflour. Cover and simmer for 10–15 minutes, until meat is cooked.

Serve on a bed of brown rice with buttered courgettes and a tomato and chive salad. Wild blackberries and thick cream are the perfect sweet to follow. SERVES 4.

Mrs I. Adams, Uttoxeter, Staffordshire

GROUSE DELICACY

2 young grouse
6 rashers of fat bacon
100 g/4 oz butter

juice of 1 lemon
salt and pepper
300 ml/½ pint port or claret

WRAP the birds in the bacon rashers and put a walnut-sized knob of butter mixed with the lemon juice, salt and pepper into the body of each before placing in the roasting pan. Add the rest of the butter to the pan and cook in a moderately hot oven (200 c, 400 f, gas 6) for 20 minutes. Then add the port or claret, baste well and return to the oven for 10–20 minutes, until cooked. Remove the birds from the pan, take off the bacon and keep warm. Reduce the gravy by fast boiling on top of the cooker and serve separately.

Serve the grouse with game chips, bread sauce and a bowl of peeled and seeded grapes in their own juice. SERVES 4.

E. A. Walling, Cockerham, Lancashire

BRAISED PIGEON WITH WHISKY AND RAISINS

50 g/2 oz butter or margarine
1 medium onion, finely chopped
6 rashers bacon, rind removed
  and roughly chopped
2 pigeons
25 g/1 oz plain flour
600 ml/1 pint chicken liver stock

2–3 tablespoons whisky
50 g/2 oz raisins
bouquet garni
salt and pepper
2 slices crustless bread
watercress sprigs

HEAT the fat in a large, deep flameproof casserole then gently cook the onion without colouring. Add the bacon and cook. Add the pigeons, sauté until lightly coloured. Remove the pigeons and leave on one side. Mix in the flour to form a roux, add the stock a little at a time, stirring to make a thin sauce. (The whole quantity of stock may not be needed, but keep the liquid in case the dish needs topping up during cooking.) Stir in the whisky and raisins, then return the pigeons to the casserole dish; they should be just covered with the liquids. Add the bouquet garni, making sure that it is well immersed in the liquid, then season to taste. Bring to the boil, cover and simmer for 2½ hours, or until tender.

When cooked, remove bouquet garni, then arrange on a salver. Place toasted bread triangles and watercress sprigs around the edge of the salver to garnish. SERVES 4.

Sarah Hall, Bramley, Hampshire

VENISON CASSEROLE

ROLL bite-sized pieces of venison in flour seasoned lightly with finely chopped sage, rosemary and marjoram. Fry slowly in butter until brown. Line a large casserole with thin slices of country cured ham and in goes part of the venison, a layer of small potato balls, a layer of onion rings then more venison. Repeat the process, ending with a layer of venison. Then comes enough claret to cover. In a moderate oven (180 C, 350 F, gas 4) this soon cooks away and is replaced by a modicum of cream. Cooked for a total of 2½ hours this is a good one-dish meal in itself. The cook serves it with a salad of cucumber and raw button mushrooms in a heavy garlic-laced dressing. For a second course there can be slices of fine Stilton, toasted French bread and a trifle of sound chutney.

Mrs E. S. Nicholson, Lochinver, Sutherland

RABBIT MARENGO

50 g/2 oz butter
1 tablespoon olive or corn oil
4 joints roasting rabbit, about
675 g/1½ lb in weight
1 large onion, grated
1 clove garlic, finely chopped
150 ml/¼ pint dry white wine
150 ml/¼ pint stock

1 396-g/14-oz can tomatoes
225 g/8 oz mushrooms, sliced
¾ teaspoon salt
¾ teaspoon sugar
1 tablespoon brandy
1 tablespoon finely chopped
parsley

PUT butter and oil into a 2.5-litre/4½-pint flameproof casserole and stand over medium heat. When both are hot and start to sizzle, reduce heat to low. Add rabbit joints, fry gently until pale gold then remove to a plate. Add onion to remaining fat and fry gently. Replace rabbit, add garlic mixed with wine and stock, tomatoes, mushrooms, salt and sugar. Slowly bring to boil, reduce heat to minimum, cover and simmer for about 1¼–1½ hours, or until rabbit is tender.

Transfer rabbit to a warm platter, add brandy to liquor in pan and boil briskly for 5 minutes. Replace rabbit, sprinkle with parsley and serve with creamed potatoes and a green vegetable. SERVES 4.

Mrs Molly Wurr, Burstwick, North Humberside

RABBIT IN RED WINE SAUCE

1 rabbit
1 carrot
1 onion
1 piece celery
1 bay leaf
oil

salt and pepper
1 wineglass red wine (elderberry,
damson or grape may be used)
300 ml/½ pint thick fresh cream
100 g/4 oz mushrooms, sliced
1 teaspoon cornflour

CUT the rabbit into joints, dry well. Clean the carrot, onion and celery. Wash and tie in muslin with the bay leaf.

Heat a little oil in a flameproof casserole and brown the meat. Sprinkle salt and pepper over the browned pieces. Add the wine, cream and mushrooms and the bundle of vegetables. Cover and cook in a moderate oven (180C, 350F, gas 4) for 1–1½ hours, until tender. If juice is too light thicken with a little cornflour and water paste. Remove vegetable bundle before serving.

Mrs J. Hawker, Ardens Grafton, Warwickshire

POMMY RABBIT

cooking oil
1 heaped tablespoon flour
salt and pepper
1 heaped teaspoon dried thyme
1 rabbit, jointed

4 large potatoes, sliced and
  blanched in boiling water
4 large cooking apples, peeled and
  sliced
1 large onion, chopped
½ bottle cider

RUB oil round a deep casserole. Mix the flour, salt, pepper and thyme in a large plastic bag. Immerse rabbit pieces in this mixture and shake well. Heat a little oil in a pan and fry pieces until sealed. Transfer to casserole. Arrange layers of sliced potato and apple over the rabbit and distribute chopped onion evenly. Add more salt, pepper and thyme to taste. Pour over the cider, cover and cook in a moderate oven (180 c, 350 f, gas 4) for about 1½–2 hours, until tender.

Mrs A. Hargreaves, East Farndon, Leicestershire

RABBIT FEAST

1 rabbit, jointed
2 tablespoons dripping
100 g/4 oz bacon, chopped
2 onions, chopped
1 tablespoon flour
1.15 litres/2 pints stock

salt and pepper
bouquet garni
1 kg/2 lb potatoes
selection of root vegetables
100 g/4 oz fresh or frozen peas
  (optional)

BROWN the rabbit joints on all sides in the dripping. Place in a casserole dish. Fry the bacon and add to the casserole. Fry the onions gently until golden brown, mix in the flour and stir over a low heat for 2 minutes. Carefully add the stock, stirring all the time, until it thickens. Remove from the heat and season well. Pour over the rabbit and add the bouquet garni. Cover the casserole and cook in a moderate oven (160 c, 325 f, gas 3) for 2 hours, or until the meat is tender.

When tender, remove the rabbit and carefully take all the meat off the bones. Place the meat in a large saucepan with the stock, bacon and onions from the casserole. Add the peeled and diced potatoes and a selection of chopped root vegetables: carrots, swedes, turnips. Check seasoning, bring to the boil, cover and simmer for 1 hour. If using peas, add 15 minutes before serving.

Serve with hot crusty rolls of bread.

Mrs P. S. Buckle, Solva, Dyfed

☆ SPRING RABBIT AND ☆ CHICKEN LOAF

1 small rabbit
2 chicken joints
1 onion, quartered
bouquet garni
900 ml/1½ pints stock or water
1 egg

100 g/4 oz fresh breadcrumbs
1 small bunch spring onions
½ teaspoon made mustard
pinch ground nutmeg
pinch ground allspice

COOK meat and onion with bouquet garni in stock until meat falls from the bones (easiest in pressure cooker). Remove meat from stock, discard bones and mince or cut the meat finely. Reduce stock well, add meat, beaten egg, breadcrumbs, finely cut spring onions using all the green, mustard and spices, and mix well.

Place in a well-greased loaf tin and cover with greaseproof paper. Bake in a moderate oven (180 C, 350 F, gas 4) for 1½ hours. Remove from oven, press under a heavy weight until cold then remove from tin.

Serve with lettuce, raw carrots and hard-boiled egg rings or salad.

Conan Fryer, Froxfield, Hampshire

CASSEROLE OF RABBIT OR HARE

2 large onions
25 g/1 oz dripping
1 rabbit or hare, jointed
flour, salt and pepper

225 g/8 oz carrots
300 ml/½ pint stout or brown ale
300 ml/½ pint stock (made with
    chicken stock cube)

PEEL and slice onions, fry in pan with the dripping. When softened put in base of casserole. Wash and dry meat joints, dip in seasoned flour and cook quickly in frying pan to seal. Place these when browned on top of onions. Slice carrots fairly thickly and place between joints. Make a roux in the remaining fat in the pan, with as much of the seasoned flour as it will take, and into this pour the stout or ale and stock. Bring to the boil, stirring continuously. Pour whole over contents of casserole, cover and cook for about 2 hours, in a moderate oven (180 C, 350 F, gas 4) for rabbit and moderately hot (190 C, 375 F, gas 5) for hare. Delicious.

Patricia Godfrey, Ickleton, Essex

PRUNES AND APPLES HARE

450 ml/¾ pint red wine	450 g/1 lb dried prunes
2 tablespoons brandy	175 g/6 oz bacon pieces
4 tablespoons vinegar	15 g/½ oz margarine
bouquet garni	3 tablespoons flour
2 onions, chopped	1 tablespoon olive oil
1 clove garlic, crushed	1 kg/2 lb dessert apples
salt and freshly ground pepper	50 g/2 oz butter
1 3–4-kg/6½–9-lb hare	

PREPARE a marinade with the wine, brandy, vinegar, bouquet garni, onions, garlic, salt and pepper. Joint the hare and marinate for 24 hours, turning from time to time. The liver and blood of the hare should be put in a bowl with a teaspoon of vinegar. Soak the prunes overnight in warm water.

In a large flameproof casserole cook the bacon pieces in the margarine. Dry the pieces of hare on kitchen paper and brown them with the bacon. Remove the hare and bacon, add the flour to the casserole and cook until brown. Dilute little by little with the marinade, stirring all the time. Return the hare and bacon to the casserole. There must be sufficient sauce to cover all the pieces, if not add a little more wine or water. Cover and simmer gently for 3 hours. Stir in the olive oil and prunes and cook for a further 15 minutes.

Cook the liver for a few minutes in a frying pan without fat. Finely chop the liver and mix it with the blood. Add the mixture little by little to the sauce, mixing all the time before boiling.

While the hare is cooking prepare the apples. Peel and cut into thin slices, melt the butter in a frying pan and cook the apples for 10 minutes, mixing gently. Cover and leave to cook over a low heat for a further 10 minutes.

Serve the hare in the sauce with the apples. SERVES 8.

Catherine McGuffie, Rowington Green, Warwickshire

CANES FARM RABBIT CASSEROLE

2 large onions, chopped
1 clove garlic, crushed
fat to fry
1–1.25 kg/2–2½ lb rabbit pieces
300 ml/½ pint stock
150 ml/¼ pint white wine
2 large carrots, sliced

2 tomatoes, chopped
2 sage leaves
1 tablespoon chopped fresh or
 1 teaspoon dried marjoram
1 teaspoon salt
ground black pepper
chopped parsley to garnish

FRY onion and garlic in a little fat until soft, add rabbit pieces and brown quickly. Drain and place in a casserole. Mix together stock and wine and pour over meat, add carrots and tomatoes, herbs and seasoning.

Cover and cook in a moderate oven (180 C, 350 F, gas 4) for 2–2½ hours, until tender. Remove sage leaves, sprinkle with chopped parsley and serve with jacket potatoes and more carrots.

Mrs A. Burchnall, Burstall, Suffolk

CURRIED RABBIT

1 rabbit, jointed
dripping
2–3 teaspoons curry powder
 mixed with a little flour
1 large onion, finely chopped

1 large cooking apple, chopped
pinch of salt
stock or water to cover
150 ml/¼ pint milk

DIP the rabbit joints into some melted dripping and then coat with the curry powder and flour mixture. Melt a little dripping in a flameproof casserole and fry the onion for about 5 minutes. Add the rabbit and fry for a further 15 minutes, turning from time to time. Add the apple and salt and cover with water or stock. Cover and cook in moderate oven (180 C, 350 F, gas 4) for about 2½–3 hours.

Arrange rabbit joints on a warm serving dish. Stir the milk into the curry juices and heat through carefully for a few minutes. Pour over the meat and serve with rice.

Mrs J. M. Haward, Mistley, Essex

SAVOURY PIES AND PASTIES

HAM AND CHEESE FLAN

PASTRY
100 g/4 oz plain flour
50 g/2 oz fat
pinch of salt
1 egg yolk
cold water to mix
FILLING
25 g/1 oz butter

20 g/¾ oz flour
450 ml/¾ pint milk
1 teaspoon grated onion
1 egg, separated
little made mustard
salt and pepper
100 g/4 oz chopped ham
50 g/2 oz grated cheese

MAKE the pastry in the usual way, binding with the egg yolk and just sufficient cold water. Roll out to fit an 18-cm/7-inch flan dish, or flan ring placed on a baking tray, and bake blind in a moderately hot oven (200 c, 400 F, gas 6) for 10–15 minutes.

Meanwhile prepare the filling. Melt the butter in a pan, stir in the flour and mix well. Stir in milk and grated onion and cook for 5 minutes. Cool slightly, then add beaten egg yolk, mustard and seasoning. Fold in stiffly whisked egg white and chopped ham. Pour mixture into cooked flan case, then sprinkle grated cheese on top. Bake in a moderate oven (180 c, 350 F, gas 4) for 30 minutes.

Mrs G. M. Bromwell, Crickhowell, Powys

☆ CHEESY FARMHOUSE ☆ FLAN

PASTRY
175 g/6 oz plain flour
pinch each salt, cayenne and dry
mustard
100 g/4 oz cream cheese
150 g/5 oz butter
50 g/2 oz Cheddar cheese, grated
FILLING
225 g/8 oz lean bacon
2 good-sized leeks
25 g/1 oz margarine

1 heaped tablespoon flour
200 ml/7 fl oz rich white stock
150 ml/¼ pint single cream
salt and pepper
TOPPING
1 root celeriac, peeled and sliced
450 g/1 lb potatoes, peeled
a little milk
knob butter
grated cheese

To make pastry, sieve flour with salt, cayenne and mustard. Using two knives, cut the cream cheese and butter into the flour until the mixture resembles coarse breadcrumbs. Add the grated cheese and work the mixture together into a firm ball. Chill overnight.

To prepare filling, cut bacon into strips and fry gently for a few minutes. Slice leeks and cook in salted water until tender. Drain well.

Put celeriac and potatoes in a pan and cook in salted water for 30 minutes, drain and keep hot.

Roll out pastry and use to line a 20–23-cm/8–9-inch flan dish. Prick lightly and bake blind in a moderately hot oven (200 c, 400 f, gas 6) for 15 minutes, until golden.

Melt margarine, stir in flour and cook for 2–3 minutes. Remove from heat and blend in stock. Bring to the boil, stirring, and simmer for a few minutes. Reserve 3 tablespoons cream for potatoes, stir rest into sauce, add leeks and bacon and season well.

Purée potatoes and celeriac, adding milk, butter, reserved cream and seasoning to give a fluffy consistency. Spoon hot leek filling into pastry case, pile potato purée over top and dust liberally with grated cheese. Grill until bubbling and brown or finish off in the oven.

Miss Rosalind Gray, Billingshurst, Sussex

SAVOURY TOMATO QUICHE

175 g/6 oz prepared shortcrust
　pastry (175 g/6 oz flour etc.)
FILLING
450 g/1 lb tomatoes
1 medium onion
1 clove garlic
15 g/½ oz butter
3 sprigs parsley, chopped

3 sprigs thyme, chopped, or 3
　teaspoons dried thyme
2 tablespoons tomato purée
2 eggs
100 g/4 oz grated cheese
salt and pepper
50 g/2 oz field mushrooms, sliced

ROLL out pastry to line a 20-cm/8-inch flan dish. Plunge tomatoes
into boiling water, remove skins and seeds and chop coarsely.
Chop onion, crush garlic. Melt butter in a heavy-based pan, add
tomatoes, onion, garlic, parsley, thyme and purée and cook gently
for 30 minutes. Draw pan off heat and cool slightly. Beat in eggs,
cheese and seasoning. Pour into pastry case and top with mushrooms. Cook in a moderately hot oven (190 c, 375 f, gas 5) for about
30–40 minutes. Serve hot, decorated with a sprig of parsley.

Mrs Sheila Jerrard, Oldhamstocks, East Lothian

☆ CAULIFLOWER SOUFFLÉ ☆ FLAN

225 g/8 oz prepared shortcrust
　pastry (225 g/8 oz flour etc)
FILLING
1 small cauliflower, cut into florets
25 g/1 oz butter
25 g/1 oz flour
300 ml/½ pint milk

½ chicken stock cube
black pepper and salt
150 ml/¼ pint cream
1 large egg, separated
50 g/2 oz grated Cheddar cheese
1 tablespoon fresh breadcrumbs
butter to dot

ROLL out the pastry to line a 23-cm/9-inch flan ring placed on a
baking tray, and bake blind in a moderately hot oven (200 c, 400 f,
gas 6) for 10 minutes.

Cook cauliflower florets until tender but firm. Drain. Make a
roux with butter and flour and cook for 2–3 minutes. Add milk,
stock cube and black pepper to taste. Boil, stirring all the time.
Simmer until thickened, remove from heat, add cream, egg yolk
and salt to taste. Whisk egg white then fold into sauce.

Place florets in flan, cover with sauce and sprinkle cheese and
breadcrumbs on top. Dot with butter and bake in a moderately hot
oven (190 c, 375 f, gas 5) for 25 minutes. Serve immediately.

Mrs Elizabeth Sneath, Pinchbeck, Lincolnshire

SAVOURY SPINACH FLAN

PASTRY
45 g/1½ oz margarine
45 g/1½ oz lard
175 g/6 oz plain flour
pinch salt
cold water to mix

FILLING
knob of butter
1 medium onion
3 rashers streaky bacon
225 g/8 oz fresh spinach
3 eggs
100 g/4 oz strong cheese
1 tomato

RUB margarine and lard into flour and salt until it resembles fine breadcrumbs. Mix lightly to a dough with as little water as possible. Use to line an 18-cm/7-inch flan dish.

Melt the knob of butter, add chopped onion and chopped streaky bacon and fry together until onion is translucent.

Strip the spinach from the coarse centre ribs if necessary, wash and put in a saucepan with a tight-fitting lid with no more water than that left from washing. Simmer gently until cooked with the lid on firmly. Drain thoroughly and chop small.

Lightly beat the eggs, add grated cheese, onion and bacon mixture and spinach. Mix thoroughly together and put into flan case. Slice the tomato and decorate flan with the rings. Bake in a moderately hot oven (200 C, 400 F, gas 6) for 40 minutes.

Served with potatoes and fresh tomatoes and watercress, this is the almost perfectly balanced meal. It should of course be followed by bramble and apple pie with lashings of cream!

Miss A. M. Brown, Bignall End, Staffordshire

WHOLEMEAL VEGETABLE PIE

PASTRY
225 g/8 oz wholemeal flour
110 g/4 oz margarine
pinch of salt
water and milk to mix
FILLING
1 cauliflower, broken into florets
450 g/1 lb fresh peas
450 g/1 lb new carrots, sliced
1 bunch spring onions, chopped
SAUCE
25 g/1 oz butter

25 g/1 oz flour
600 ml/1 pint milk
100 g/4 oz Cheshire cheese, grated
salt and pepper
CRUMBLE TOPPING
25 g/1 oz margarine
50 g/2 oz wholemeal flour
50 g/2 oz rolled oats
15 g/½ oz sunflower seeds
2 teaspoons freshly chopped mixed
    herbs (parsley, chives, sage,
    thyme, rosemary)

MAKE the pastry in the usual way, using equal amounts of water and milk to mix. Roll out to line a deep 20-cm/8-inch pie dish. Bake blind in a moderately hot oven (190 c, 375 f, gas 5) for 20–25 minutes, but do not let brown or overcook.

Meanwhile lightly cook the cauliflower, peas and carrots in a minimum of boiling salted water, until just tender. Drain thoroughly, arrange in the pie dish and sprinkle over the chopped spring onions.

Melt the butter for the sauce, stir in the flour and gradually add the milk (thinning with the vegetable water if desired). Stir in the cheese and season to taste. Pour over the vegetables and top with the crumble mixture; rub the margarine into the flour, add the oats, sunflower seeds and fresh herbs.

Cook in a moderate oven (180 c, 350 f, gas 4) for 30–35 minutes, until the crumble is golden brown.

Mrs R. Culshaw, Mawdesley, Lancashire

☆ VEGETABLE HARVEST PIE ☆

PASTRY
100 g/4 oz plain wholemeal flour
100 g/4 oz self-raising white flour
¼ teaspoon salt
½ teaspoon dry mustard
100 g/4 oz margarine or lard
100 g/4 oz grated hard cheese
cold water to mix

FILLING
1 large onion
1 medium potato
1 large carrot
1 stalk celery
1 small beetroot
2 courgettes or 1 large slice of marrow
a few runner or French beans
50 g/2 oz fresh or frozen peas
1 turnip
1 or 2 tomatoes
a little cabbage or cauliflower
200 ml/7 fl oz vegetable stock or water
1 teaspoon yeast extract
1 teaspoon dried herbs
1 rounded tablespoon cornflour

FIRST make the pastry. Sieve dry ingredients together, rub in fat, add cheese and mix to a dough with a little water.

Prepare and slice vegetables, put into the boiling vegetable stock or water and simmer for 5 minutes. Stir in the yeast extract and herbs and thicken with the cornflour mixed to a thin cream with a little water. Season to taste.

Pour vegetables with sauce into a greased, warmed, deep pie dish. Cover with pastry, flute edges and make a small steam vent. Bake for about 45–60 minutes in a moderately hot oven (190 c, 375 f, gas 5).

Mrs Margaret Jenks, Newtown, Shropshire

SEAFOOD QUICHES

PASTRY
350 g/ 12 oz plain flour
pinch of salt
225 g/8 oz butter
1 egg yolk
a little water
FILLING
175 g/6 oz smoked salmon

600 ml/ 1 pint prawns, shelled
1 tablespoon lemon juice
4 large eggs, beaten
150 ml/¼ pint single cream
450 ml/¾ pint milk
salt and pepper
chopped parsley

SIFT the flour and salt into a bowl. Rub in the butter until the mixture resembles fine breadcrumbs. Blend the egg yolk and water together and stir into the rubbed-in ingredients. Knead the pastry lightly on a floured surface, divide into six and roll into pieces large enough to line six 13-cm/5-inch shallow flan cases. Lay the pastry in the cases, prick the bases and crimp the edges.

Using scissors, snip tiny pieces of smoked salmon into a bowl. Add the prawns and sprinkle with lemon juice. Beat the eggs, cream and milk and season well.

Divide the salmon and prawns between the flan cases and pour the egg mixture over each. Bake in a moderately hot oven (200 c, 400 f, gas 6) for 15 minutes then reduce to moderate (160 c, 325 f, gas 3) for a further 20 minutes. Sprinkle with parsley and serve warm or cold. SERVES 6.

Caroline Millman, Chulmleigh, North Devon

COCKLE PIE

1 kg/2 lb fresh cockles (in their
    shells)
350 g/ 12 oz prepared shortcrust
    pastry (350 g/ 12 oz flour etc.)
450 g/1 lb bacon, sliced

6–8 tablespoons chopped chives
1 beaten egg
pepper
milk to brush

SIMMER the shellfish in 300 ml/½ pint water for 15 minutes. Drain, reserving liquid, and remove fish from shells.

Roll out pastry and use most of it to line the sides and base of a 2.25-litre/4-pint pie dish. Put in even layers of bacon, cockles and chives and continue in layers until all is used up. Mix the strained cooking liquid with the egg, add pepper to taste and pour into the pie. Make a lattice top with remaining pastry, brush lightly with milk and bake in a moderately hot oven (200 c, 400 f, gas 6) for 35 minutes. SERVES 4.

Mrs Rhiannon Evans, Llandrillo, Clwyd

SALMON AND SPINACH FLAKE

225 g/8 oz flaky pastry
175 g/6 oz salmon or salmon trout,
  cooked and flaked
450 g/1 lb fresh spinach, cooked,
  well drained and puréed
15 g/½ oz butter

1 small bunch spring onions,
  chopped
2 eggs
scant 150 ml/¼ pint milk or thin
  cream
salt and pepper

PREPARE flaky pastry in advance and chill, or defrost frozen pastry. Prepare fish and spinach. Butter a deep 20-cm/8-inch flan dish and a pie funnel.

Melt the 15 g/½ oz butter over a low heat and sweat onions until transparent. Beat egg and add milk or cream. Fold onions, salmon and spinach into egg mixture and season to taste. Pour into flan dish, distribute evenly and position pie funnel in the centre. Roll out pastry to make a lid, place over funnel and seal edges. Cook in a hot oven (220 C, 425 F, gas 7) for 15 minutes, then reduce to (180 C, 350 F, gas 4) until fully cooked.

Serve with parsley new potatoes, peas and a tomato and cucumber salad.

Unity Lawler, Heysham, Lancashire

☆ GRANDMA'S FARMHOUSE ☆ PIE

1 kg/2 lb best Scotch rump steak
1 large swede (after first frost)
stock
salt and pepper
225 g/8 oz shortcrust or suet
  pastry (225 g/8 oz flour etc)

225 g–450 g/8–16 oz Devonshire
  clotted cream or thick double
  cream

CUT beef and swede into 2.5-cm/1-inch or 5-cm/2-inch cubes. Place in a pie dish with enough stock to cover the swede, season. Cover with a thick lid of pastry, cut a steam vent and cook for 1–1½ hours in a moderate oven (180 C, 350 F, gas 4).

Remove from oven, lift off pastry and keep to one side. Spread cream over meat and swede and replace pastry – return to the oven and heat through. Delicious eaten with or without vegetables.

Mr Francis Parkhouse, Torrs Park, North Devon

PUFF-TOPPED BEEF AND WINE PIE

675 g/1½ lb chuck steak, cubed
25 g/1 oz seasoned flour
3 tablespoons oil
1 onion, chopped
225 g/8 oz mushrooms, sliced
150 ml/¼ pint red wine
300 ml/½ pint beef stock
salt and freshly ground pepper
1 tablespoon chopped parsley
1 teaspoon dried basil
1 368-g/13-oz packet frozen puff
  pastry, thawed
beaten egg to glaze

TOSS meat in seasoned flour. Heat oil in pan and fry meat until sealed. Remove meat, fry onion and mushrooms until soft. Tip in any remaining flour and cook for 2 minutes. Remove from heat, add wine and stock. Return to heat and bring to boil, stirring all the time. Season and add herbs. Return the meat to the sauce. Cover and allow to simmer for 2–2½ hours. Transfer the beef in sauce to a 1.15-litre/2-pint pie dish. Allow to cool.

Roll out pastry thinly and using a 6-cm/2½-inch cutter cut out 18–20 circles. Cut out centres of these with a 2.5-cm/1-inch cutter. Top the pie with the pastry rings and glaze with beaten egg. Bake in a hot oven (220 C, 425 F, gas 7) for 15 minutes, then reduce to moderate (180 C, 350 F, gas 4) for a further 15 minutes. SERVES 4.

Mrs A. H. Wraith, Garthorpe, South Humberside

MINCE AND YOGURT PIE

PASTRY
450 g/1 lb plain flour
100 g/4 oz butter
100 g/4 oz lard
salt
cold water to mix
FILLING
450 g/1 lb minced lamb or beef
2 medium onions, chopped
2 cloves garlic, crushed
2 sticks celery, chopped
225 g/8 oz carrots, chopped
25 g/1 oz butter
salt and pepper
300 ml/½ pint natural yogurt

MAKE pastry in the usual way and, retaining enough for lid, roll out remainder to line a 25-cm/10-inch round flan case.

Gently fry mince, onions, garlic, celery and carrots in the butter, until cooked. Add salt, pepper and yogurt and mix well. Tip into the flan case and cover with pastry lid. Make a steam vent in the lid and cook the pie in a moderate oven (180 C, 350 F, gas 4) for about 45 minutes. Serve with new potatoes and a salad. SERVES 4.

Mrs G. Stobart, Tregony, Cornwall

MUM'S SURPRISE

225 g/8 oz flaky or shortcrust
  pastry, rolled to an oblong not
  more than 2.5 mm/$\frac{1}{10}$ inch thick
watercress or parsley for garnish
FILLING
350 g/12 oz minced beef pre-
  cooked with chopped onion and
  seasoned, or sausagemeat mixed
  with finely chopped onion,
  seasoning and a beaten egg to
  bind

SAUCE
450 ml/$\frac{3}{4}$ pint stock or gravy from
  the mince
150 ml/$\frac{1}{4}$ pint natural yogurt
salt and pepper

SPREAD the meat filling over the pastry to the edges. Roll up from the long side and seal the long edge carefully. Cut the roll into 5-cm/2-inch lengths and place in an ovenproof baking dish, turning each piece of roll on its side. Mix the sauce ingredients together, pour over the pastry rolls and bake in a hot oven (220 c, 425 f, gas 7) for 15–25 minutes, until the pastry is a nice golden brown. Garnish with parsley or watercress sprigs to serve.

M. J. Mister, Dorchester, Dorset

CORNED BEEF PIE

350 g/12 oz corned beef
100 g/4 oz carrots, sliced
50 g/2 oz onion, chopped
1 small red pepper, deseeded and
  chopped
1 small green pepper, deseeded
  and chopped

stock
cornflour to thicken
salt and pepper
225 g/8 oz prepared puff pastry

CUT corned beef roughly into cubes and place in a pie dish. Cook carrots, onion and peppers in enough beef stock to cover. When just tender spoon vegetables over corned beef. Thicken the cooking stock with cornflour and season to taste. Pour over the vegetables and corned beef and cover with the pastry.

Cook in a hot oven (220 c, 425 f, gas 7) for 20–25 minutes until pastry is golden brown. Serve with minted potatoes and Brussels sprouts.

Mrs Mary Holland, Moiviaive, Dumfries-shire

☆ CHIBBLE PASTY ☆

PASTRY
225 g/8 oz self-raising flour
110 g/4 oz fat (margarine and lard)
pinch salt
cold water to mix
beaten egg or milk to brush

FILLING
225 g/8 oz streaky bacon rashers
3 bunches spring onions
1 egg
salt and pepper

LINE an 18-cm/7-inch flan or pie tin with pastry, leaving enough for lid. Remove rind from bacon and line pastry case with the rashers. Chop spring onions and place on top of bacon. Beat egg with a little salt and pepper and pour over bacon and onions. Put pastry lid on top, crimp edges and make a vent for steam. Brush top with egg or milk. Cook for approximately 1 hour in a moderate oven (180 C, 350 F, gas 4).

Delicious served with green salad for a family supper.

Mrs I. Tucker, Chelfham, North Devon

BRAMLEY PORK PIE

FILLING
575 g/1¼ lb lean pork (pork steaks)
pepper and salt
1 teaspoon chopped fresh sage
175 g/6 oz onions
225 g/8 oz carrots
2 medium Bramley cooking apples
½ ham stock cube
butter to dot

150 ml/¼ pint strong dry cider
SHORTCRUST PASTRY
150 g/5 oz wholemeal flour
¼ teaspoon salt
150 g/5 oz unsalted butter, cut
    into small pieces
4 tablespoons iced water
milk or beaten egg to brush

CUT pork into 1.5-cm/¾-inch cubes, season with pepper and salt and sprinkle with the chopped sage. Chop the onions and thinly slice the carrots. Core and peel apples, then cut into quarters, finely slice and place in a bowl of water until required.

Lightly grease a 20-cm/8-inch pie dish and layer the filling as follows: half the onions; half the carrots; sprinkle the half stock cube over vegetables; layer of apple; half the pork; layer of apple; half the pork; layer of apple; half the onions; half the carrots. Dot with a little butter, pour over the cider, cover with foil and cook in a moderate oven (180 C, 350 F, gas 4) for approximately 1 hour. Remove from oven and cool slightly.

Meanwhile make the pastry. Mix flour and salt in mixing bowl and work in butter quickly. Add 2 tablespoons iced water and use fork to mix thoroughly, then add just enough water to make dough into a firm ball. Wrap in cling film and chill in refrigerator for at least 30 minutes.

To finish, roll out pastry until a 1-cm/½-inch margin is allowed all round the pie dish, so that it can be turned under at the edges. Crimp edges and make a small slit in the centre, decorate top and finally brush with milk or beaten egg.

Cook pie for a further 20–25 minutes in a hot oven (220 c, 425 f, gas 7).

Colin Izzard, Camberley, Surrey

SOMERSET PORK PIE

FILLING

1.75 kg/4 lb pork (hand and
  spring), boned and cubed
50 g/2 oz flour
salt and ground black pepper
275 g/10 oz button onions
5 tablespoons oil
300 ml/½ pint chicken stock
300 ml/½ pint dry cider

PASTRY

225 g/8 oz self-raising flour
110 g/4 oz shredded suet
pinch of salt
1 teaspoon finely grated zest of
  orange
7 tablespoons fresh orange juice
beaten egg or milk to glaze

TOSS meat in the mixed flour and seasoning. Fry onions in oil in large pan until golden. Remove with slotted spoon to plate. Add pork to pan and fry until browned. Return onions and stir in stock and cider. Bring to boil, cover and cook gently for 1 hour, or until meat is tender. Transfer to a 1.5-litre/2½-pint pie dish and leave to cool.

Meanwhile make the pastry. Mix together flour, suet, salt and grated orange zest. Stir in orange juice (if necessary adding a little cold water) to form a soft, but not sticky, dough. Knead very lightly on floured surface then roll out to fit the pie dish. Dampen dish edges and place over pastry lid. Seal and flute edges and decorate with pastry leaves made from the trimmings. Make a small air vent, brush the pastry with egg or milk and lightly sprinkle with salt.

Bake in a moderately hot oven (200 c, 400 f, gas 6) for 40–45 minutes until pastry is golden. Serve with jacket potatoes, carrots and Brussels sprouts. SERVES 6.

Mrs Betty Cozens, Henlade, Somerset

SAUSAGEMEAT, APPLE AND ONION PIE

225 g/8 oz shortcrust pastry (225 g/
  8 oz plain flour 50 g/2 oz lard,
  50 g/2 oz margarine)
2 large onions, sliced
2 large cooking apples, peeled and
  sliced

3 tablespoons demerara sugar
1 egg, beaten
450 g/1 lb sausagemeat

ROLL out the pastry to line a 25-cm/10-inch round pie dish, crimp edges. Layer onions and apples in dish, sprinkling sugar over apple layers and finishing with a layer of onions. Mix beaten egg and sausagemeat together, turn onto a floured board and pat into a round to exactly cover top of pie. Place carefully on top of onion layer. Use leftover pastry trimmings to make pastry leaves to decorate edges of pie. Bake in a moderately hot oven (190 c, 375 f, gas 5) for ¾–1 hour. Serve hot.

Miss Anne Ruddy, Brightling, East Sussex

KNUCKLE PASTIES

2 small gammon knuckles
1 bay leaf
1 small knuckle of veal
¼ teaspoon grated lemon rind
salt, pepper and herbs to taste

3 hard-boiled eggs
350 g/12 oz flaky or rough puff
  pastry, chilled
milk or beaten egg to brush

SIMMER gammon with bay leaf and veal in water to cover for about 1½–2 hours, until meat leaves the bone. Lift out of liquid, add lemon rind, herbs and seasoning and simmer for a short time. Leave to cool. Cut meat into small pieces, also eggs, and moisten with some of the cooling stock.

Roll out pastry thinly and cut into circles with a saucer. Place a generous amount of filling on one side, damp edges with water and fold over. Brush each with milk or beaten egg and make two slits on top. Place on a dampened baking tray and bake in a hot oven (220 c, 425 f, gas 7) for 15–20 minutes. May be served hot with autumn vegetables or cold with salad.

Mrs B. Brinkler, Hill Ridware, Staffordshire

TOPSY TURVY CHICKEN PIE

TAKE a 20-cm/8-inch solid-based flan dish. Arrange prettily on the bottom (this will eventually be the top!): 2 sliced hard-boiled eggs; 4 slices lean streaky bacon, derinded, flattened with a knife, cut in half and rolled; ½ cup frozen peas and ½ cup frozen sweetcorn kernels, mixed together and carefully sprinkled over the egg and bacon pattern; approximately 350 g/12 oz skinned and diced cooked chicken, or enough to fill up the flan dish. Make up 300 ml/ ½ pint aspic and pour enough over the filled flan to come halfway up the dish. Cover the flan with 175 g/6 oz shortcrust pastry, making a hole in the middle for steam to escape and also to take the funnel for topping up the aspic. Bake in a moderate oven (180 c, 350 F, gas 4) for 30–40 minutes. Remove from oven and whilst cooling keep topping up with the remaining aspic. Put in fridge to set overnight.

To serve, loosen sides with a carefully wielded knife. Place flan dish in very shallow hot water and turn out on to a serving plate or board. Decorate, if liked, with piped mayonnaise.

Mrs Heather Sargent, Burstow, Surrey

FARMER'S CHICKEN PIE

3 rashers bacon, derinded	900 ml/1½ pints water
1.25-g/2½ lb chicken joints, skinned	1–2 tablespoons cornflour
	100 g/4 oz mushrooms, roughly chopped
1½ tablespoons chopped parsley	
2 teaspoons made mustard	225 g/8 oz prepared shortcrust
1 large onion, chopped	pastry (225 g/8 oz flour etc.)
1 bay leaf	milk to brush

CUT bacon into thin strips. Place chicken joints, bacon, parsley, mustard, onion, bay leaf and water in a large saucepan. Bring to boil, place a tightly fitting lid on pan and simmer for 35–40 minutes. Remove chicken from stock, carefully take all meat from joints and cut into even-sized pieces. Place in an ovenproof dish. Blend cornflour with a little cold water and gradually add to boiling stock until a coating consistency is obtained. Remove bay leaf from stock, add mushrooms then pour over chicken.

Roll out the pastry to cover the dish. Brush with a little milk and cut a small air vent in lid. Bake for about 30 minutes in a moderately hot oven (200 c, 400 F, gas 6).

Mrs C. Robinson, Silsden, Yorkshire

CHICKEN AND SAUSAGEMEAT PIE

PASTRY
450 g/1 lb plain flour
pinch salt
225 g/8 oz lard
a little cold water
milk to brush

FILLING
1 1.75-kg/4-lb chicken
6 peppercorns
1 teaspoon dried mixed herbs
1 onion
15 g/½ oz gelatine
salt and pepper
450 g/1 lb sausagemeat

COOK the chicken until tender in water with the giblets, peppercorns, herbs and quartered onion; I use the type of steamer that has a side steam vent, this method gives you an excellent stock, otherwise poach gently in a covered pan.

While the chicken is cooking prepare the pie tin and pastry. Use a round loose-bottomed cake tin for the pie, 19–20 cm/7½–8 inches in diameter and 7.5 cm/3 inches deep. Brush the inside of the tin with melted fat or oil. Line the base with a circle of greaseproof paper and the side with a band of paper; brush these with melted fat or oil.

Mix the flour and salt, rub in fat until a crumbly mixture is formed. Mix to a rough dough with a little water and turn out onto a floured board. Put one-third aside for the lid, roll out the rest to 5 mm/¼ inch thickness and shape this into the prepared tin. Press well into the sides with your knuckles, trim off around the top of tin.

When the chicken is tender remove flesh from bones, discarding skin, and cut into slices. Drain off the stock, measure 450 ml/¾ pint and dissolve 15 g/½ oz gelatine in this while it is still hot. Season to taste and cool until jellied.

Put half the chicken slices into the pastry-lined tin, season with salt and pepper and a little of the jellied stock. Press the sausagemeat into a round to fit the tin exactly and place on top of the chicken, then the rest of the chicken on top of that. Take care to mix light and dark meat evenly. Sprinkle with salt and pepper and fill almost to the top with jellied stock. Roll out the rest of the pastry to fit the top of the pie. Dampen the edges and place the lid on top, press down securely, ease pastry from side of tin with a knife and pinch edges. Make a steam vent in the centre of the lid and brush pastry with milk.

Bake the pie in a hot oven (220 C, 425 F, gas 7) for 15 minutes, then cover the top with brown paper or foil and cook for a further

30 minutes at 190 c, 375 f, gas 5. Remove from the oven and fill up with remaining jellied stock through steam vent in lid. Cool completely and serve with a green salad.

Mrs R. M. Shipley, Felixkirk, North Yorkshire

GAME PIE

1 rabbit	4 tablespoons cornflour
1 pheasant	900 g/2 lb flaky or rough puff
1 pigeon	pastry
1 brace partridge	beaten egg
350 g/12 oz streaky bacon	parsley
350 g/12 oz mushrooms	
1 chicken stock cube dissolved in	
1.15 litres/2 pints water	

PREPARE game in the usual manner. Derind and bone bacon, clean mushrooms and leave whole.

Place all the above together with giblets in a large roasting tin or casserole and pour over the stock. Cover tightly with foil or foil and a lid. Cook in a moderate oven (160 c, 325 f, gas 3) for 2 hours, or until meat is cooked and flesh comes easily away from bones.

When meat is cooked let it cool. Pull all meat from bones and break into pieces. Cut bacon into pieces and slice mushrooms. Discard giblets. Pack all into a 23 × 33-cm/13 × 9-inch pie dish. Measure the cooking liquid and make up to 1.15 litres/2 pints with water. Strain into a saucepan and thicken with the cornflour, mixed first to a paste with a little cold water. Add a little of this thickened liquor to the meat and reserve rest to serve separately with pie.

Roll out pastry to size of pie dish. Dampen edge of dish, cover with pastry. Flute edges and decorate centre with leaves from pastry scraps. Using a skewer, make a hole in centre of pastry to let steam escape and brush pie with beaten egg. Place on a baking sheet and bake in a hot oven (220 c, 425 f, gas 7) for about 30 minutes until pastry is well browned. Garnish with parsley and serve hot.

Mrs Angela Smith, Margaretting, Essex

HARE PIE

675–900 g/1½–2 lb cubed hare meat	1 finely chopped clove of garlic
2 tablespoons flour	100 g/4 oz butter
½ teaspoon grated nutmeg	150 ml/¼ pint stock
salt and black pepper	1 glass port
1 finely chopped onion	pastry
2 finely chopped shallots	beaten egg to brush

Toss the meat in the flour seasoned with nutmeg, salt and pepper. Fry the onion, shallots and garlic gently in 25 g/1 oz butter. Put the meat, onion mixture, remaining butter and stock in a casserole. Cover with a lid lined with foil and cook in a moderate oven (160 c, 325 f, gas 3) for approximately 3 hours.

Remove from oven, test for tenderness and return to oven for a further half hour if necessary. Add the port, stir well and taste to adjust seasoning.

Pour into a pie dish with a pie funnel in the centre. Allow to cool then cover with your favourite pastry. Brush with egg and bake in a moderately hot oven (190 c, 375 f, gas 5) for about 30–35 minutes, until the pastry is cooked and the meat thoroughly heated through. (For puff pastry cook for 20–25 minutes at 220 c, 425 f, gas 7.)

Serve hot with forcemeat balls, redcurrant or crab apple jelly, a green vegetable and possibly sauté potatoes. Hare pie is also delicious served cold with a winter salad and jacket potatoes.

Mrs Frances Evans, Craven Arms, Shropshire

SUPPER DISHES

STUFFED LEEKS

450 g/1 lb leeks, trimmed
6 rashers streaky bacon, derinded
  and finely chopped
100 g/4 oz field mushrooms, finely
  chopped

50 g/2 oz fresh white breadcrumbs
75 g/3 oz Cheddar cheese, grated
salt and freshly ground pepper

COVER the leeks with cold water, bring to the boil, cover and cook for 1 minute. Drain and slice lengthwise, leaving the two halves attached, and place in an ovenproof dish.

Cook the bacon in a pan with no added fat. When it is crispy, add the mushrooms and cook for 2–3 minutes. Remove the pan from the heat, add half the breadcrumbs and half the cheese. Season this mixture well and spoon it on to the leeks. Mix the remaining breadcrumbs and cheese and sprinkle on top of the leeks. Cook in a moderately hot oven (200 c, 400 F, gas 6) for 15 minutes, or until golden brown and crispy.

Makes a good lunch or supper dish, served with hot French bread and garlic butter.

Miss Caroline Rowe, Beckenham, Kent

SIMPLE SUPPER

1 large onion, chopped
2 tablespoons cooking oil
crushed garlic to taste
450 g/1 lb field mushrooms,
  chopped

1 heaped tablespoon finely
  chopped parsley
salt and pepper
250 ml/8 fl oz thick-set natural
  yogurt

HEAT a heavy pan, then gently sauté chopped onion in the oil. Add garlic, mushrooms, parsley and seasoning, stirring constantly until mushrooms are softening and beginning to brown. Remove from the heat and allow to cool slightly. Stir in the yogurt and gently reheat. Serve immediately with hot crusty bread. Serves 2 for supper or 4 as a starter.

Mrs H. Mummery, Coldred, Kent

COURGETTE, ONION AND TOMATO BAKE

1 medium onion
knob of margarine
4 tomatoes
2 medium courgettes

600 ml/1 pint cheese sauce
salt and pepper
grated cheese and dried
  breadcrumbs to sprinkle

PEEL and slice onion. Cook until tender in a little margarine. Plunge tomatoes into boiling water, peel and slice. Slice courgettes thickly.

Layer courgettes, onion and tomato then cheese sauce. Season well and repeat layers. Finish with grated cheese and dried breadcrumbs and bake in a moderate oven (180 C, 350 F, gas 4) for 30 minutes.

Mrs M. J. Edwards, Westbury, Shropshire

ONION CHEESE

FRY two pounds of sliced onions very slowly in butter or oil until soft. Into this grate several ounces of Cheddar Cheese, as much as can be spared. Season to taste and thicken if desired with a little cornflour.

Served with hot crusty bread it makes a tasty meal and quite filling, enough for perhaps four.

Mrs A. L. Kemp, Sewards End, Essex

☆ STUFFED MARROW RINGS ☆

1 marrow
450 g/1 lb pork sausagemeat
1 onion, chopped small

few leaves sage, chopped small
pepper and salt
streaky bacon rashers

CLEAN and prepare marrow, removing seeds and cutting into rings 2.5 cm/1 inch thick. Blend together the remaining ingredients, except bacon, and use to fill the rings. Lay flat in a well-greased baking dish, cover with bacon rashers and cook in moderate oven (180 c, 350 f, gas 4) for 45 minutes.

This may be served as a main dish with vegetables, making gravy from the juices in pan, or as a tasty supper dish with bread and butter.

Mrs R. J. Williams, Llangoran, Gwent

WINTER WARMER

1 large or 2 small Spanish onions, sliced
6 medium potatoes, sliced
1 swede, diced
6 carrots, sliced
salt and pepper
450 g/1 lb mature Cheddar cheese, grated

2 teaspoons made mustard
2 egg whites
175–225 g/6–8 oz streaky bacon rashers
100 g/4 oz button mushrooms
butter to fry

SIMMER the prepared vegetables in lightly salted water until just tender. Strain then mash in a large mixing bowl with the cheese and mustard. Whisk the egg whites until they stand in stiff peaks and then beat all together with a mixer until well blended. Season liberally with pepper. Place in a greased open pie dish and bake in a moderately hot oven (190 c, 375 f, gas 5) until you have a lovely browned top, about 40 minutes.

Meanwhile, halve and fry the bacon rashers with the mushrooms in a little butter. Season to taste and wrap each mushroom in a piece of bacon. Skewer with wooden cocktail sticks and serve around the edge of the hot vegetable pie – it looks good, smells good and tastes good.

Mrs F. Langford, Northend, Oxfordshire

MELTING MILKY HOT-POT

1 kg/2 lb potatoes
2 large onions
½ teaspoon salt
pepper

450 ml/¾ pint milk
100 g/4 oz cheese

PEEL and slice the potatoes fairly thinly. Peel and slice the onions. Arrange in layers in a large casserole dish, add salt and liberally sprinkle with pepper. Pour over the milk, cover and bake in a cool oven (150 C, 300 F, gas 2) for 2–2¼ hours, or until the potatoes are soft. Cut the cheese into slices, place over the vegetables and return to the oven, uncovered, for a further 10–15 minutes.

Serve with wholemeal bread. SERVES 4–6.

Mrs Sarah Davies, Glanaman, Dyfed

BACON AND POTATO PUFF

salt and pepper
4 large potatoes, cooked and
    mashed
1 large egg, separated
½ small teaspoon dry mustard

2 tablespoons milk
175 g/6 oz cooked minced bacon
2 tomatoes, skinned and chopped
little melted butter

LIGHTLY grease a small pie dish. Season mashed potatoes then fold in the stiffly whisked egg white. Beat together the egg yolk, mustard and milk, add to the bacon and tomatoes and stir until evenly blended. Season to taste and spread over the base of the pie dish. Cover smoothly with potato and brush with melted butter. Bake in a hot oven (220 C, 425 F, gas 7) for 35–45 minutes, until golden brown. Serve hot with vegetables.

Sara Howard, Rollesby, Norfolk

POTATO AND HAM SOUFFLÉ

2 large potatoes
25 g/1 oz butter
3 eggs
225 g/8 oz cooked ham, finely
    chopped

1–2 tablespoons chopped parsley
salt and pepper

COOK potatoes in boiling, salted water. Drain well and mash with butter. Separate eggs and add yolks to potatoes. Whip with an electric beater until very creamy and smooth, adding a little milk if necessary. Mix in the ham and parsley and season well.

Whisk egg whites until very stiff and fold into potato mixture. Turn into a greased soufflé dish and bake in a moderate oven (180 C, 350 F, gas 4) for about 25–30 minutes.

Helen Clark, Weston, Bath

CRISPY CHEESE AND BACON DISH

90 g/3½ oz butter
1 large onion, chopped
350 g/12 oz marrow, cut into
    cubes
350 g/12 oz lean bacon, chopped
175 g/6 oz mushrooms, sliced
225 g/8 oz cauliflower florets
40 g/1½ oz flour

450 ml/¾ pint milk
salt and pepper
100 g/4 oz Cheddar cheese, grated
4 tomatoes, sliced
3 large thick slices bread, cubed
225 g/8 oz Brie cheese, cubed
a little butter
chopped parsley

MELT 50 g/2 oz of the butter in frying pan until hot. Add onion and marrow and fry gently for 7–8 minutes. Remove from the pan and add bacon and mushrooms, cook for 3–4 minutes. Cook cauliflower in boiling salted water until just tender, drain.

Melt remaining butter, add flour and cook for 2–3 minutes. Gradually stir in milk, add seasonings and bring to the boil. Remove from the heat and stir in grated Cheddar cheese.

In a gratin dish layer half the marrow, bacon and cauliflower mixtures. Pour over half the sauce. Cover with 2 sliced tomatoes. Repeat the layers, ending with tomatoes. Top evenly with the cubes of bread and Brie. Dot with butter and place in a moderately hot oven (200 C, 400 F, gas 6) for 35–40 minutes, reducing heat after 30 minutes if top is getting too brown. Sprinkle with chopped parsley and serve.

Mrs M. Ward, Loxwood, Sussex

BEAN GUNGE

1 medium onion
fat to fry
3 rashers streaky bacon
4–6 sausages
1 447-g/15¾-oz can baked beans

1 tablespoon dried tomato soup
   mix
1 tablespoon tomato sauce
salt and pepper

FINELY chop the onion and fry in a little fat in a saucepan. Chop the bacon, thickly slice the sausages and add to the pan. Cook for a few minutes until lightly browned. Stir in the baked beans.

Put the tomato soup mix and tomato sauce in a measuring jug and make up to 150 ml/¼ pint with cold water. Season and add to the pan. Bring all to the boil, cover and simmer gently for 20 minutes, or until sausage is cooked through. SERVES 4.

Miss J. C. Doidge, Whitchurch, Devon

BACON AND PEA HOT POT

225 g/8 oz yellow split peas
100 g/4 oz red lentils
175–225 g/6–8 oz carrots, sliced
1 medium onion, chopped
2 medium potatoes, sliced

175–225 g/6–8 oz bacon pieces,
   rind removed
salt, pepper and paprika
   (optional)
900 ml/1½ pints water

PLACE peas and lentils, then carrots, onion and potatoes in a large flameproof casserole with a tight-fitting lid. Put the bacon pieces on top, add seasoning to taste (allow for bacon pieces being salty) and pour over the water. Cover and simmer gently for about 2 hours. Check that it does not dry out, add a little more water if necessary.

Mix with a fork just before serving and adjust seasoning if necessary. SERVES 4–6.

Mrs W. M. McIntyre, How Mill, Cumbria

GUERNSEY BEAN JAR

450 g/1 lb haricot beans, soaked
  overnight
450 g/1 lb onions, chopped
450 g/1 lb carrots, grated or diced

1 large potato, diced
1 pig's trotter or beef shin bone
thyme, sage and parsley to taste
salt and pepper

PLACE above ingredients in an earthenware jar. Add water to cover and place in a hot oven (220 c, 425 f, gas 7). Bring to the boil then reduce to cool (150 c, 300 f, gas 2). Cover the bean jar and simmer for 6 hours, adding more water when necessary.

Mrs W. Le Tissier, Guernsey, Channel Islands

DORMERS

225 g/8 oz cooked lamb or mutton
50 g/2 oz suet
75 g/3 oz rice, boiled
salt and pepper

1 egg, beaten
breadcrumbs to coat
dripping or oil to fry

CHOP the meat, suet and rice finely. Mix well together and add a liberal seasoning of salt and pepper. Roll into sausage shapes, coat with egg and breadcrumbs and fry in hot dripping or oil for about 15 minutes until golden. Serve in a dish with gravy poured around them.

Janet Thompson, Paddock Wood, Kent

TOMATO AND ONION SAVOURY

100 g/4 oz butter
6 ripe medium tomatoes
2 medium onions

salt and pepper
1 teaspoon flour

PUT the butter in a small saucepan to melt slowly. Skin the tomatoes, cut into quarters and add to the butter. Cut the onions into small pieces and add to the pan with seasoning to taste. Cook slowly until tender. Mix the flour to a smooth paste with a little water, stir into the savoury. When it begins to thicken and bubbles, it is ready to eat. Very tasty on toast.

Mrs Mary Powell, Llan-Tacyllyn, Powys

MONDAY CURRY

1 onion
1 apple
2 tablespoons oil
½–1 tablespoon curry powder
1 tablespoon flour
450 ml/¾ pint stock

1 tablespoon chutney
50 g/2 oz sultanas
225 g/8 oz cooked, diced meat
   (beef or chicken)
pinch of salt

PEEL and chop onion and apple and fry in oil. Add curry powder and flour and fry gently for 1 minute. Blend in stock and bring to boil, stirring. Add chutney and sultanas and simmer for 30 minutes. Add the meat and salt and heat through gently for 15 minutes.

I find this recipe useful after having a roast chicken or beef. A small amount of leftover meat finishes up substantial enough for a family supper. Serve with rice and, if hungry, jacket potatoes. SERVES 4.

Mrs J. Marshall, Fulstow, Lincolnshire

CHEESE AND BEEFBURGER PIE

4 beefburgers
25 g/1 oz butter or margarine
1 large onion, chopped
1 green pepper, chopped
100 g/4 oz mushrooms, chopped
about 3 tablespoons water
1 tablespoon tomato purée

½ stock cube
salt and pepper
100–175 g/4–6 oz Cheddar cheese,
   grated
450–675 g/1–1½ lb potatoes, cooked
   and creamed

LIGHTLY grill beefburgers and chop into bite-sized pieces. Melt butter and lightly fry onion, pepper and mushrooms for a few minutes. Mix in the beefburger pieces. Mix together water, tomato purée and stock cube, add to beefburger mixture. Simmer for 2–3 minutes and season to taste. Put into an ovenproof dish and sprinkle 25–50 g/1–2 oz grated cheese over the top.

Mix the remaining cheese with the hot creamed potatoes and pipe over beefburger mixture. Brown under grill then pop into a moderate oven (180 c, 350 f, gas 4) for a few minutes to ensure that all cheese is melted. SERVES 4.

Mrs Linda Beasty, South Newbald, Yorkshire

CORNED BEEF SURPRISE

INTO a large greased baking tin put 8 medium thick slices of corned beef. On top of this arrange a layer of cooked sliced onions, a layer of cooked carrots and a layer of thinly sliced apples. Salt and pepper each layer then pour over enough beef stock to just cover. Finally smooth over lots of creamy mashed potato. Cook in a moderately hot oven (200 C, 400 F, gas 6) for 25–30 minutes, until crispy and brown. Sprinkle the top with grated cheese to serve.

Mrs H. P. French, Lilley, Bedfordshire

MACARONI FIRESIDE SUPPER

100 g/4 oz quick-cook macaroni
25 g/1 oz butter or margarine
1 tablespoon cornflour
300 ml/½ pint milk
salt and pepper
3 hard-boiled eggs
50 g/2 oz ham
50 g/2 oz strong cheese

COOK the macaroni in plenty of boiling salted water in a large pan for 6 minutes, or according to packet instructions. Drain well.

Melt the butter, mix in the cornflour and then gradually add the milk, stirring to make a thick sauce. Season well and mix in the macaroni. Slice the eggs thickly, cut the ham into 2.5-cm/1-inch wide strips and grate the cheese.

Lightly grease a shallow ovenproof dish and layer into it: macaroni; ham; macaroni; eggs; macaroni. Sprinkle cheese over the top and bake in a moderately hot oven (200 C, 400 F, gas 6) for about 20 minutes. Serve with crusty bread and fresh tomatoes. SERVES 2.

Mrs C. Gatenby, Rudston, North Humberside

SPANISH PANCAKES

PANCAKES
100 g/4 oz plain flour
pinch salt
1 egg
300 ml/½ pint milk
oil for frying
FILLING
1 Spanish onion, chopped

1 clove garlic, crushed (optional)
butter for frying
1 396-g/14-oz can tomatoes
100 g/4 oz mushrooms, sliced
1 teaspoon dried mixed herbs
salt and black pepper
225 g/8 oz sausages
6 rashers bacon

PREPARE pancake batter a few hours in advance or leave in fridge overnight. Sieve flour and salt into a bowl. Add beaten egg and half the milk. Beat until smooth. Stir in the rest of milk and put into refrigerator.

Fry chopped onion and garlic in a little butter until soft. Add tomatoes, mushrooms, herbs and seasoning and cook for a few minutes.

Meanwhile, grill sausages and bacon. Cut into bite-sized pieces and add to the tomato mixture. Keep warm.

Make pancakes using the batter mixture. Divide filling between the pancakes and roll up each one. Serve with a tossed green salad.

Mrs S. McCormick, Woodford Green, Essex

PICNIC FARE

SAUSAGE LOAF

450 g/1 lb pork sausagemeat
1 large onion, finely chopped
6 rashers streaky bacon, finely
  chopped
1 tablespoon finely chopped
  parsley

2 tablespoons rolled oats
salt and pepper
about 150 ml/¼ pint good stock or
  gravy
5–6 hard-boiled eggs

In a large bowl mix together the sausagemeat, onion, bacon, parsley and oats. Season and add enough stock to bind it all into a nice smooth mixture, not too thick and not too runny. Place half the mixture in an ovenproof dish, arrange the halved eggs over the top, cut side down, and cover with the remaining sausage mixture.

Bake in a moderately hot oven (190 c, 375 f, gas 5) for about 45–60 minutes, until the top is a nice golden brown. Leave to cool.

Ideal for the busy farmers who have cold picnic lunches in the fields.

Miss Vera Becuar, Blackboys, Sussex

BEEF AND PORK LOAF

175 g/6 oz streaky bacon rashers, rind removed	1 tablespoon chopped parsley
450 g/1 lb lean minced beef	1 teaspoon dried mixed herbs
450 g/1 lb pork sausagemeat	salt and pepper
2 eggs, lightly beaten	2 cloves garlic, crushed (optional)
1 medium onion, finely chopped	dash of Worcestershire sauce
	1 beef stock cube, crumbled

STRETCH the bacon rashers and use to line a 1-kg/2-lb loaf tin. Mix remaining ingredients well together and press into lined tin. Cover with foil, place on a baking tray and cook for about 2 hours, beginning in a moderately hot oven (200 C, 400 F, gas 6) for 30 minutes and decreasing gradually to a cool oven (150 C, 300 F, gas 2) for the remaining time.

When cooked pour off surplus fat, cool slightly and turn out, bacon uppermost. Very nice eaten hot and especially good sliced cold.

Mrs Grace Pearce, Sandygate, Devon

MOCK CRAB

225 g/8 oz tomatoes	1 egg, beaten
50 g/2 oz grated cheese	pepper and salt
knob of butter	

SKIN, deseed and chop tomatoes and cook gently in a pan for 5–10 minutes. Add grated cheese and butter and lastly egg. Season with pepper and salt. Good for sandwiches.

Miss M. Rider, Ryther, North Yorkshire

EGG AND TOMATO PATTY

PASTRY	1 teaspoon chopped parsley
85 g/3 oz lard	½ teaspoon dried mixed herbs
175 g/6 oz plain flour	pinch of salt
cold water to mix	1 teaspoon flour
FILLING	1 tablespoon milk
25 g/1 oz margarine	2 eggs
1 large tomato, skinned, deseeded and chopped	

RUB fat for pastry into the flour until mixture resembles bread-crumbs then add enough water to bind together. Roll out to line an

18-cm/7-inch flan tin and bake blind in a moderately hot oven (190 c, 375 f, gas 5) for 20–25 minutes, until cooked.

Melt margarine, add tomato, parsley, herbs and salt and cook for a few minutes. Stir in flour, then milk and lastly lightly beaten eggs. Stir until almost set but do not overcook. Turn into flan case. Does not require further cooking. Serve warm or cold.

This filling is also very good in sandwiches

Miss M. K. Hume, Goodnestone, Kent

☆ PICNIC SURPRISE ☆

PASTRY
75 g/3 oz lard
225 g/8 oz plain flour
1 teaspoon baking powder
pinch salt
FILLING
225 g/8 oz sausagemeat (pork or beef)

oil or fat for frying
2 large onions
salt and pepper
2 small eggs
2 tablespoons milk
1 teaspoon dried sage

RUB fat well into flour, add baking powder, salt, mix with a little water to a stiff dough. Roll out half the dough to line a deep 20-cm/8-inch pie dish.

Fry sausagemeat in a little oil or fat, leave to cool. Chop onions finely and cook in a very little water with a shake of salt and pepper. Cool. Beat eggs with milk, season.

Put half onion into the lined pie dish and sprinkle with half the sage. Cover with the sausagemeat, then the remaining onion and sage. Pour over the eggs. Roll out rest of pastry to make a lid, wet edges, cut vents or prick with a fork. Make fancy leaves with pastry off-cuts. Brush with milk and bake in a moderate oven (180 c, 350 f, gas 4) for 45–60 minutes. SERVES 6.

Mrs Betsy Jackson, Austwick, Lancashire

CURRIED VOLS-AU-VENT

1 onion, finely chopped
2 tablespoons oil
450 g/1 lb minced beef
1 tablespoon curry powder or
   paste (or more to taste)

100 g/4 oz cooked potatoes, diced
25 g/1 oz cooked peas (optional)
6 large or 12 small vol-au-vent
   cases (cooked)

FRY onion gently in oil, add mince and brown thoroughly. When cooked, add curry, potatoes and peas. Fill vol-au-vent cases and bake in a moderately hot oven (190 C, 375 F, gas 5) for about 20–30 minutes.

Can be served hot or cold. When cold ideal for picnics. If small vol-au-vent cases are used this makes a very good savoury with drinks.

Mrs O. Sanderson, Grafty Green, Kent

PICNIC CHICKEN

1 1.75-kg/4-lb chicken
½ teaspoon salt
2 sprigs tarragon
25 g/1 oz butter
250 ml/8 fl oz water
1 lettuce (Cos for preference)
50 g/2 oz walnut pieces
SAUCE
1 tablespoon made mustard

1 teaspoon sugar
½ teaspoon each salt and pepper
6 tablespoons oil
2 tablespoons wine vinegar
3 tablespoons single cream
4 tablespoons chicken stock
1 213-g/7½-oz can cherries, drained
   and stoned

RUB chicken with salt. Put tarragon and half the butter inside chicken and rub remaining butter over bird. Place in a roasting tin and pour the water round. Cook in a moderate oven (180 C, 350 F, gas 4) for 1½–2 hours until tender, basting often. The juices from the bird should be clear when cooked. Cut the chicken into portions, cool and refrigerate.

Meanwhile, make the sauce for the chicken. Place mustard, sugar, salt and pepper in large screw-topped jar. Add oil and vinegar, shake well and add cream. Shake to mix and add chicken stock and cherries.

Serve the chicken on a bed of lettuce, pour the sauce over and decorate with walnuts.

This is ideal for a picnic as both chicken and sauce can be carried separately and served when required. Lovely with wholemeal bread.

Mrs A. Bell, Lowry Hill, Carlisle

PLOUGHMAN'S PIE

450 g/1 lb shortcrust pastry to line and cover a 1.15-litre/2-pint pie dish (wholewheat or 50–50% wholewheat and white plain flour)

FILLING

450 g/1 lb cooked mutton or lamb, diced

100 g/4 oz stringless runner beans, boiled for 2 minutes

2 medium cooking apples, peeled, cored, chopped and tossed in brown sugar, cinnamon and nutmeg

50 g/2 oz whole wheat, boiled or steamed until tender

salt and pepper

COMBINE filling ingredients and place in pie dish lined with pastry. Cover with pastry lid, make a small hole for steam to escape and decorate with a "wheatsheaf" made from pastry scraps. Bake for 40 minutes in a moderately hot oven (190 c, 375 f, gas 5).

Serve cold or lukewarm for lunch in the fields with brown bread and tomatoes, or hot in the evening with potatoes and baby turnips.

Mrs Chrissie Cullymore, Kelston, Bath

STICKY GINGERBREAD

175 g/6 oz dark brown sugar

2 tablespoons black treacle

2 tablespoons golden syrup

2 eggs

150 g/5 oz lard

250 ml/8 fl oz water

275 g/10 oz self-raising flour

pinch salt

1 teaspoon bicarbonate of soda

1 teaspoon grated nutmeg

1 teaspoon ground cinnamon

2 teaspoons ground ginger

BEAT together sugar, treacle, syrup and eggs. Heat lard and water to boil. Meanwhile, sift and mix dry ingredients.

Stir dry ingredients into treacle mixture. Stir in lard and water slowly, then mix very well. Bake in a greased, lined 1-kg/2-lb loaf tin, for 30 minutes in a moderate oven (160 c, 325 f, gas 3) then 30 minutes in a cool oven (150 c, 300 f, gas 2), or until cooked.

The recipe came from my husband's grandmother, who was Scottish; the reason, perhaps, for the more economical lard and water instead of the usual butter and milk. This gingerbread is always a success, moist but not heavy.

Mrs Anne Padfield, Theydon Mount, Essex

GOOSEBERRY FLAN

225 g/8 oz prepared shortcrust
  pastry (225 /8 oz flour etc)
FILLING
450 g/1 lb gooseberries, topped,
  tailed and washed
juice and grated rind of 1 small
  lemon
100 g/4 oz castor sugar
1 tablespoon cornflour

1 tablespoon water
8 sponge fingers, crushed
TOPPING
75 g/3 oz ground almonds
75 g/3 oz ground rice
50 g/2 oz icing sugar
2 eggs
½ teaspoon almond essence
beaten egg to glaze

ROLL out pastry to line a 20-cm/8-inch greased flan ring placed on a baking tray. Bake blind for 20 minutes in a moderately hot oven (190 C, 375 F, gas 5).

Gently cook gooseberries, lemon rind, juice and sugar until tender. Mix cornflour with water, stir into fruit and cook until thickened. Stir in the sponge fingers, cool then pour into flan case.

Mix together all topping ingredients. Put in a piping bag fitted with a 5-mm/¼-inch star nozzle and pipe a lattice over the cold flan. Brush lattice with egg and lightly brown under a hot grill for 5 minutes or so. Serve sliced.

Mrs Rita Robinson, Yaddlethorpe, South Humberside

RHUBARB AND LEMON COOLER

4 sticks of rhubarb
2 lemons

4.5 litres/8 pints water
450 g/1 lb sugar

WASH and chop the rhubarb, wash and slice the lemons and place together in large bowl. Boil the water and pour it over the fruit. Stir in the sugar until dissolved. Cool, cover and leave overnight. Strain, serve chilled.

This is the perfect drink for cooling down haymakers and harvesters and a must for outings and picnics.

Mrs J. Freeman, Bishopswood, Herefordshire

SALADS

LEE SALAD

1 lettuce
1 grapefruit
2 oranges
2 apples
2 pears
juice of 1 large lemon

½ head celery
100 g/4 oz grapes
50 g/2 oz chopped walnuts
French dressing flavoured with
    fresh chopped mint
salt and pepper

TRIM any discoloured leaves from lettuce, wash, drain, pat dry.
Place leaves on base and around salad bowl.

Peel grapefruit and oranges, remove each segment and place in a
bowl, drain off any juice. Wash, core and slice apples and pears,
sprinkle with lemon juice and add to grapefruit and orange
segments. Add scrubbed and chopped celery. Cut each grape in
half to remove pips. Reserve a few for decoration and mix
remainder into bowl with 25 g/1 oz walnuts. Toss all this in mint
French dressing, turn into salad bowl and garnish with reserved
grapes and walnuts. SERVES 4–6.

Mrs Aline Lee, Kirkconnel, Dumfries-shire

RICE AND NUT SALAD

50 g/2 oz brown long-grain rice   15 g/½ oz walnut pieces, chopped
50 g/2 oz fresh or frozen peas

BOIL rice in salted water for 30–45 minutes until just tender, or cook at high pressure in a pressure cooker for 15 minutes. Drain and rinse with cold water. Cook peas and cool. Mix all ingredients together.

The rice and nut salad may be served as it is, or tossed in your favourite salad cream or dressing. Serve with other salad vegetables such as tomatoes, radishes and lettuce, to accompany cubed or grated cheese, hard-boiled eggs or cold meats. SERVES 2.

Mrs V. Hoare, Staverton, Devon

CAULI CRISP

1 medium cauliflower   few splashes Worcestershire sauce
5 tablespoons salad cream   chopped parsley to garnish
5 tablespoons tomato ketchup

CUT cauli florets from stalk and then into bite-sized pieces. Soak/rinse in cold salted water. Mix remaining ingredients together, adjusting to taste. Drain cauli and mix into the sauce. Place in dish and garnish with chopped parsley. SERVES 6.

NB Increase sauce mixture depending on size of cauliflower. The florets need to be well coated with the sauce.

Mrs Gill Falkingham, Howden, North Humberside

CRUNCHY POTATO SALAD

6 medium potatoes   MAYONNAISE
2 sticks celery   1 egg
½ large Spanish onion (or   ½ teaspoon dry mustard
    according to taste)   2 teaspoons vinegar
salt and pepper   salt and pepper
     300 ml/½ pint corn or olive oil

BOIL potatoes, cool and cut into cubes. Slice celery, finely chop onion and add to potatoes. Season to taste.

Make mayonnaise by liquidising or beating together egg, mustard, vinegar and seasoning; still liquidising pour the oil slowly and steadily into mixture.

Add potatoes, onion and celery to mayonnaise and turn into a serving dish.

This recipe was passed down from my mother many years ago. I have often taken this salad on picnics in a food flask. SERVES 4.

Miss W. J. Crooks, Morley, Derbyshire

COTTAGE CHEESE FRUIT SALAD

prepared lettuce
1 large tomato per person, cut in 6
cucumber, sliced
carrot, grated
potato salad
portion of cottage cheese per
  person

peach slices, drained, 5 slices per
  person
chopped green pepper to sprinkle
cress to sprinkle

ARRANGE the lettuce leaves over one half of each plate, top with tomato wedges and cucumber slices. Over the remaining half plate make two small mounds of grated carrot and potato salad, then a third mound of cottage cheese. Arrange the peach slices round the cottage cheese and sprinkle chopped green pepper over. Finally sprinkle cress over the green salad.

Mrs H. Crane, Yaxham, Norfolk

A FAMILY SALAD

1 lettuce
225 g/8 oz tomatoes, quartered
4 hard-boiled eggs, quartered
¼ cucumber, sliced

1 stick celery
1 carrot
100 g/4 oz red or white cheese
1 box cress

CUT up lettuce with scissors and arrange over a serving platter. Top with tomato, eggs and cucumber. Cut up celery in small pieces, grate carrot and grate cheese. Sprinkle over salad with the cress.

Delicious for a family. SERVES 4.

Mrs J. Dawson, Baycliff, Cumbria

SAUSAGE TWIST SALAD

225 g/8 oz small pork and beef
  sausages
225 g/8 oz pasta twists
1 283-g/10 oz can kidney beans

1 198-g/7-oz can sweetcorn
salad cream
pinch of dried mixed herbs
freshly ground pepper and salt

GRILL the sausages and allow to cool. Cook the pasta in a pan of boiling salted water until soft. Drain and cool.

Now drain the kidney beans and sweetcorn. Chop the cooled sausages into small chunks and combine all the ingredients with salad cream. Season with a pinch of mixed herbs, salt and freshly ground pepper. Serve with some crusty wholemeal bread and butter. SERVES 4.

Mrs Carole Ford, Warminster, Wiltshire

SUPREME SUMMER SALAD

225 g/8 oz fresh broad beans
  (weight without pods)
225 g/8 oz fresh runner beans, cut
  into 1-cm/½-inch lengths
225 g/8 oz new potatoes, scrubbed
  and cut into 1-cm/½-inch cubes
150 g/5 oz fresh garden peas
  (weight without pods)
4 spring onions
6 radishes
¾ cucumber

1 lettuce
450 g/1 lb unsmoked bacon from
  cooked joint
2 large tomatoes
chopped fresh parsley to garnish
DRESSING
3 tablespoons mayonnaise
1 tablespoon lemon juice
¼ teaspoon ready made mustard
3 tablespoons salad cream
salt and pepper

COOK broad beans, runner beans, potatoes and peas in boiling salted water until just tender, do not overcook. Drain and leave to cool.

Wash and trim spring onions, cut into 1-cm/½-inch lengths. Wash and trim radishes and slice thinly. Wash cucumber, reserve two-thirds; cube remaining one-third into 1-cm/½-inch dice (leave skin on). Wash and drain lettuce.

Arrange lettuce leaves on an oval platter, darker leaves on platter edge and lighter ones inside. Place two slices of the bacon at each end of platter, slightly overlapping edges. Cube remaining ham.

Make dressing: add small amount of mayonnaise to lemon juice and mustard and mix well until blended. Add remaining ingredients for dressing and mix well. Season to taste. Add the cooled vegetables, spring onions, radish, cucumber cubes and bacon cubes to mayonnaise dressing, toss until well coated. Pile mixed salad on to centre of lettuce.

Slice remaining cucumber and arrange slices around edge of mixed salad, overlapping edges. Reserve four cucumber slices. Slice tomatoes and arrange across centre of mixed salad overlapping edges. Make four cucumber twists and arrange two each side of tomato slices. Garnish with chopped parsley sprinkled over salad.

Serve with warm crusty bread, homemade if possible, and butter. SERVES 4.

Mrs A. Pascoe, Helston, Cornwall

QUICK TOSSED SALAD

1 large lettuce	3 firm tomatoes, quartered
100 g/4 oz chopped spring onions	grated cheese to taste
100 g/4 oz chopped celery	homemade salad dressing
2 hard-boiled eggs, quartered	salt and pepper

WASH and dry lettuce and shred leaves. Place all ingredients in a large salad bowl. Toss well in dressing and season to taste. Ready to serve. SERVES 4.

Mrs D. McCord, Cookstown, Co Tyrone

SPRING SALAD FOR FARM HANDS

1 kg/2 lb potatoes, cooked and sliced	1 kg/2 lb tomatoes, sliced
1 kg/2 lb carrots, cooked and sliced	1 dozen eggs, hard-boiled and halved
6–8 medium beetroot, cooked	3 large lettuces
celery sticks for 6, chopped	good helping of spring onions

THIS mixed salad was served to our farm hands 30 years ago, enjoyed by 6 to 8 men at midday, with bread buns, buttered with fresh farm butter, and washed down with a mug of cider. Accompany the salad with a homemade apple chutney.

Mrs G. E. Hammond, Stoke Hammond, Buckinghamshire

☆ GARDENER'S SALAD ☆

The vegetables mentioned here are just a suggestion. You may replace them with other fresh vegetables or add extra ones as you wish.

225 g/8 oz broad beans, shelled	salt and black pepper
225 g/8 oz new carrots, sliced	4 spring onions, chopped
225 g/8 oz new potatoes	4 hard-boiled eggs, quartered
4 tablespoons French dressing	225 g/8 oz cold cooked chicken,
4 tablespoons natural yogurt	diced

COOK the beans, carrots and potatoes in separate pans of boiling, salted water until just tender.

Mix together the French dressing, yogurt and seasoning. Dice the potatoes and toss them in the yogurt mixture while they are still warm. Leave to cool, then add the remaining ingredients and mix well. Transfer to a salad bowl and serve chilled. SERVES 4.

Miss R. A. Page, Sibton, Suffolk

CHICKEN, CELERY AND WALNUT SALAD

REMOVE the meat from a cooked chicken and cut into small pieces. Place on lettuce leaves with 1-cm/½-inch lengths of celery. Sprinkle with salt, add a few drops of vinegar and cover with a thick mayonnaise dressing.

Slightly brown 10–12 walnuts in the oven with a sprinkling of salt and butter. Chop the walnuts, season lightly with salt and pepper, add a little oil and vinegar and leave to stand for about an hour before adding to salad.

Serve very cold. SERVES 4–6.

Mrs J. M. Sykes, Cawood, North Yorkshire

CHICKEN SURPRISE SALAD

225 g/8 oz frozen peas
15 g/½ oz powdered gelatine
1 295-g/10½-oz can consommé
675 g/1½ lb cooked chicken, diced
450 g/1 lb cooked new potatoes,
  diced

300 ml/½ pint homemade or a good
  mayonnaise
freshly ground black pepper and
  salt to taste
chives

COOK the peas and allow to cool. Melt gelatine in the consommé.
Take one-third of the consommé and mix in the peas. Pour this
into a ring mould or soufflé dish and put in the freezer for a few
minutes to set. Mix the chicken, potatoes and mayonnaise with the
remaining consommé. Season to taste and add a few chopped
chives if liked. Put on top of the set peas and leave in the fridge
until set.

Turn out on to a plate; if using a ring mould fill with chopped
lettuce, or sit the mould on to some lettuce. Sliced cucumber,
tomatoes and watercress go well with this, or just a plain salad.
SERVES 6.

Mrs A. Wilson, Holt Pound, Surrey

ADSTONE SUMMER CHICKEN

1 425-g/15-oz can sliced peaches,
  drained
1 green pepper, deseeded
½ cucumber
100 g/4 oz green grapes, halved
  and pipped
450 g/1 lb cooked chicken meat,
  cut into 3.5-cm/1½-inch pieces

black pepper and onion salt
150 ml/¼ pint double or
  whipping cream
150 ml/¼ pint mayonnaise or salad
  cream
pinch of ground mace
lettuce leaves
pinch of paprika pepper

CUT peaches and green pepper into 2.5-cm/1-inch pieces. Cut
cucumber into dice. Mix all fruit and vegetables together with
chicken pieces, season to taste with black pepper and onion salt.

Whip cream until stiff, mix with mayonnaise and add mace.
Toss chicken mixture into cream mayonnaise until well coated.
Line a shallow silver or glass bowl with washed lettuce leaves and
pile chicken into centre. Sprinkle with paprika and chill well.

This is delicious served with fresh crusty bread and butter and a
simple green salad outside on a summer's day. SERVES 4–6.

Mrs L. J. Underwood, Adstone, Northamptonshire

CHICKEN AND GRAPE SALAD

1 apple
100 g/4 oz cooked chicken
50 g/2 oz black grapes
15 g/½ oz black olives
3 spring onions

100 g/4 oz cooked diced potatoes
salt and pepper
2 tablespoons mayonnaise
½ lettuce

PEEL apple and dice. Dice chicken. Halve grapes and pip. Halve olives and stone. Chop spring onions.

In a large bowl combine all ingredients, retaining half the grapes for decoration. Spoon over mayonnaise and toss until well coated.

Serve on a bed of lettuce and arrange remaining grapes on top. SERVES 2.

Mrs M. Pugh, Llanidloes, Powys

DRESSED SUMMER CHICKEN

1 grapefruit
½ melon
1 green pepper
225 g/8 oz diced cooked chicken
lettuce, cucumber and watercress

DRESSING
150 ml/¼ pint natural yogurt
1 teaspoon lemon juice
1 tablespoon finely chopped spring
  onions
pinch of dry mustard
salt and pepper

CHOP grapefruit flesh, scoop out melon balls and slice green pepper. Mix with the chicken and toss in prepared dressing.

Serve on bed of lettuce, garnished with cucumber and watercress. SERVES 2–3.

Mrs F. Robinson, Killinchy, Co. Down

FRENCH STYLE SPRING SALAD

6–8 medium tomatoes
1 225-g/8-oz packet frozen
  sweetcorn, thawed
1 avocado pear
450 g/1 lb fresh prawns
1 lettuce

FRENCH DRESSING
1 tablespoon white wine vinegar
½ teaspoon white pepper
½ teaspoon salt
3 tablespoons olive oil

FIRST make the dressing. Mix vinegar with seasonings, add oil and stir well.

Cut each tomato into four (they must be firm or the seeds will spill out), and mix with the sweetcorn. Peel the avocado pear, chop and add to the tomatoes and sweetcorn. Shell the prawns and mix with other ingredients.

Pile on a bed of lettuce and pour the French dressing over the salad. Serve with chilled Chablis wine. SERVES 6.

Mrs Lucy Cooper, Horham, Norfolk

TUNA AND APPLE SALAD

1 lettuce	1 small green pepper, seeded and
3 medium dessert apples, peeled	chopped
and chopped	100 g/4 oz cottage cheese
juice of ½ lemon	salt and pepper
1 198-g/7-oz can tuna fish,	½ lemon and parsley to garnish
drained and flaked	

WASH lettuce and leave to drain. Sprinkle chopped apple with lemon juice to prevent fruit going brown. Mix together tuna, green pepper, apple with lemon juice and cottage cheese. Season to taste.

Serve on a bed of lettuce garnished with lemon slices or wedges and parsley. SERVES 3.

Mrs Margaret Mackenzie, Kilmory, Isle of Arran

☆ SCOTTISH PLATTER ☆

175 g/6 oz smoked haddock	DRESSING
little milk	150 ml/¼ pint double cream
175 g/6 oz smoked gammon	1 tablespoon milk
1 crisp lettuce	¼ teaspoon salt
3 tomatoes	¼ teaspoon dry mustard
1 red apple	1 tablespoon wine vinegar
1 fresh peach	

POACH haddock in milk, bone and flake. Cube gammon and fry. Drain.

Make a bed of crisp lettuce on a flat platter. Arrange sliced tomatoes, cubed red apple (unskinned) and cubed peach on lettuce with haddock and gammon piled in centre.

Whip dressing ingredients together, gradually adding vinegar and serve separately. SERVES 3–4.

Nancy Graham, Maddiston, Falkirk

BUCKLING AND POTATO SALAD

3 buckling	salt and pepper
225 g/8 oz cooked potatoes	GARNISH
225 g/8 oz red apples	2 tomatoes
DRESSING	2 hard-boiled eggs
4 tablespoons olive oil	sprigs of dill or fennel
3 tablespoons lemon juice	

SLICE buckling along back-bone. Skin and fillet then blanch in boiling water for 3 minutes. Break fish into large pieces and place in serving bowl. Cut the potatoes into cubes and add to bowl. Wash and core apples and chop into fine chunks, add to cooled fish and potatoes.

Mix together the oil, lemon juice and seasoning to make a dressing. Pour over the salad, toss carefully and leave for 15 minutes for the flavours to develop.

Wash tomatoes and cut into eighths. Slice eggs and arrange with the tomatoes and herbs around the salad. Serve with hot crusty bread. SERVES 4.

B. Cross, Upware, Cambridgeshire

SALAD DRESSING

225 g/8 oz flour	750 ml/1¼ pints milk
225 g/8 oz sugar	250 ml/8 fl oz water
1 tablespoon dry mustard	250 ml/8 fl oz vinegar
½ teaspoon salt	1 egg yolk

MIX dry ingredients in a large saucepan. Gradually stir in milk and water over a low heat. Very, very slowly add vinegar and finally egg yolk.

Continue stirring over a gentle heat until mixture is thick and begins to bubble at sides; do not boil. Cool and store.

This is a superb accompaniment to salads, delicious in sandwiches or on its own with potatoes.

Mrs Jean Black, Silverton, Devon

VEGETABLE DISHES

CALLCANNON

8 medium potatoes	450 g/1 lb carrots
675 g/1½ lb cabbage or spring greens	1 large onion
	50 g/2 oz butter
225 g/8 oz parsnips	salt and pepper

PEEL and quarter potatoes, separate cabbage leaves (or prepare spring greens if used), scrape and slice parsnips and carrots, dice onion.

Boil all vegetables together in large saucepan until tender. Strain and mash vegetables, adding the butter, and season with salt and pepper.

Can be served as a vegetarian dish, but is also excellent when accompanied by hot or cold meat e.g. boiled bacon, fried bacon rashers, chicken or sausages. Leftovers can be fried and served as a tasty snack. SERVES 6.

Mrs S. Winters, Oxhey, Hertfordshire

LUXURY CARROTS

450 g/1 lb young carrots
grated rind and juice of 1 lemon
50 g/2 oz butter

50 g/2 oz sugar
2 teaspoons chopped mint

WASH and scrape the carrots, cut into even-sized pieces. Put into a saucepan and just cover with slightly salted boiling water, add the lemon rind and cook for 10 minutes.

Drain off the water, then add the lemon juice, butter and sugar. Stir gently and simmer until just tender and it has a glazed appearance. Stir in the mint. Arrange in a hot dish and spoon over any juice. SERVES 4.

Mrs P. Neal, Inkberrow, Worcestershire

CREAMY POTATOES

4 medium potatoes
salt and pepper

50 g/2 oz butter
175 ml/6 fl oz double cream

SLICE potatoes thinly and arrange in layers in ovenproof dish. After each layer, shake with salt and pepper. Finish with the butter dotted over the top layer and pour over the cream.

Bake in a moderately hot oven (190 c, 375 f, gas 5) for 30–40 minutes, or until a golden brown layer has formed on the top of dish.

Absolutely delicious served with roast meats and also very simple to prepare. SERVES 2–4.

Janet House, Puriton, Somerset

FLUFFY CAULIFLOWER BAKE

1 small cauliflower
2 slices bread, crusts removed and
   cut into cubes
butter
50 g/2 oz streaky bacon rashers,
   chopped

2 eggs
50 g/2 oz grated Cheddar cheese
300 ml/½ pint milk
salt and pepper

COOK cauliflower in salted boiling water until just tender, drain. Fry bread cubes in butter on both sides, then fry bacon. Beat eggs, add cheese, milk and seasoning to taste.

Butter four or six individual soufflé dishes and divide cauliflower equally between them, or put into one large dish. Add the bacon pieces and croûtons and pour on egg mixture. Bake in a moderately hot oven (190 C, 375 F, gas 5) for 15–20 minutes, slightly longer for the large dish, until golden brown and firm to the touch. Serve hot. SERVES 4–6.

Mrs Margaret Harbord, Goodrich, Herefordshire

SCALLOPED TOMATOES

225 g/8 oz tomatoes
1 small onion
50 g/2 oz fresh breadcrumbs

salt and pepper
25 g/1 oz butter
a few browned crumbs

DIP the tomatoes for a minute into boiling water, after which the skin will peel off quite easily. Cut them into slices. Chop the onion very finely.

Put a layer of crumbs in a small well greased pie dish, then a layer of tomato, sprinkle over a little of the onion, season with salt and pepper and dot with butter. Repeat the layers until the dish is full. Finish off with a layer of crumbs, piling all well up in the middle of the dish, and sprinkle a few browned crumbs over the top. Bake for about 30 minutes in a cool oven (150 C, 300 F, gas 2). SERVES 2–3.

Mrs S. Dales, Askham Bryan, Yorkshire

CHEESE, MARROW
AND TOMATO BAKE

1 marrow
450–675 g/1–1½ lb tomatoes
1 onion

margarine
salt, pepper and mixed herbs
100 g/4 oz grated Cheddar cheese

FILL an ovenproof dish with alternate layers of peeled and sliced marrow, sliced tomato and extremely thinly sliced onion. Scatter amongst them a few shavings of margarine and season well. Add some mixed herbs if desired.

Cover with lid or foil and bake in a moderate oven (180 C, 350 F, gas 4) for 45 minutes.

Remove lid, scatter with grated cheese to cover the top, dot with margarine and bake for a further 15–20 minutes, or brown under grill if time is short.

NB This is an extremely economical dish; diced ham or chicken or sausages may be added if desired. Preparation time is minimal for the busy farmer's wife. SERVES 4.

Mrs P. M. Puzey, Longcot, Oxfordshire

COURGETTE AND MUSHROOM
DISH

4 medium courgettes
225–350 g/8–12 oz large
  mushrooms
4 tablespoons fresh breadcrumbs
1 egg
2 heaped teaspoons chopped
  chives
2 heaped teaspoons chopped
  parsley
1 small onion, chopped

1 clove garlic, crushed
about 3 tablespoons cream
SAUCE
40 g/1½ oz flour
40 g/1½ oz butter
40 g/1½ oz cheese
about 300 ml/½ pint milk
salt and pepper
40–50 g/1½–2 oz grated cheese for
  topping

CUT ends off courgettes and cook in boiling water for 5–10 minutes, depending on size. Cut in half lengthways and scoop out a little of the flesh. Take stalks off mushrooms. Arrange the eight courgette halves like the spokes of a wheel in a round ovenproof dish and put mushrooms between spokes (or arrange how you like).

Mix courgette flesh, chopped mushroom stalks, breadcrumbs, beaten egg, herbs, onion and garlic, and add enough cream to make a rather moist stuffing. Spread stuffing over courgettes and mushrooms.

Make a sauce with the flour, butter, cheese and enough milk to give a fairly thick but still pourable consistency. Season to taste and spoon over courgettes and mushrooms. Sprinkle grated cheese over all (a nice sharp Cheddar is good) and bake in a moderately hot oven (190 c, 375 f, gas 5) until golden brown and bubbling, about 20 minutes.

This is good as a starter or a vegetable dish with the main course. Or, if quantities are increased, it makes a lovely lunch or supper with some good bread. It can be made well in advance and just baked when everything else is nearly ready. SERVES 4.

Susan Coulson, Wooler, Northumberland

NETTLE SOUFFLÉ

about 225 g/8 oz nettle purée
300 ml/½ pint white sauce (25 g/
1 oz butter, 25 g/1 oz flour,
300 ml/½ pint milk)
5 eggs, separated

1 teaspoon finely chopped onion
½ teaspoon grated nutmeg
salt and pepper
whipped or soured cream for garnish

FIRST prepare nettle purée. Wear gloves to pick the young nettle tops. Discard any tough stalks, wash the leaves and cook gently in a little salted water until tender. Drain and purée.

Mix the sauce with the egg yolks, onion, nettle purée and nutmeg. Add seasoning to taste. Beat egg whites until stiff but not dry. Fold into mixture and pour into a greased soufflé dish. Bake in a moderately hot oven (200 c, 400 f, gas 6) for 30 minutes. Garnish with small dollops of whipped or soured cream, sprinkle with nutmeg and serve at once.

Nettles do make a good substitute for spinach, cooked in the same way, and this is splendid as a first course or as an impressive vegetable at a dinner party. SERVES 4–6.

Mrs W. D. Brown, Marlow, Buckinghamshire

VEGETABLE STEW

25 g/1 oz fat or 2 tablespoons oil
1 sliced onion
50–100 g/2–4 oz streaky bacon,
    chopped
1 tablespoon flour
300–450 ml/½–¾ pint stock

1 kg/2 lb mixed vegetables, sliced
bouquet garni
salt and pepper
3 tablespoons wine vinegar
chopped parsley

MELT the fat and fry the onion and bacon until golden. Add flour and cook gently. Pour in the stock, bring to the boil and then add vegetables, bouquet garni and seasoning. Cover and simmer until the vegetables are tender, remove bouquet garni. Add the vinegar, sprinkle parsley over and serve. SERVES 6.

Mrs W. A. Morton, Maplehurst, West Sussex

POOR MAN'S RATATOUILLE

1 medium onion
margarine or oil to fry
1 clove of garlic
2–3 tomatoes

3 medium courgettes
½ green or red pepper
salt and pepper
mixed herbs

CHOP onion and cook in the margarine or oil in a covered pan until soft. Peel and crush garlic and add to the onion. Add peeled, chopped tomatoes, sliced courgettes and sliced blanched pepper (blanch in boiling water for 3 minutes). Season with salt, pepper and herbs to taste.

Bring the mixture to the boil then continue cooking in a covered casserole in a moderate oven (180 c, 350 f, gas 4) for approximately 1 hour. SERVES 4.

Mrs Janet Earl, Newent, Gloucestershire

CHEESY VEGETABLE BAKE

1 medium aubergine
450 g/1 lb courgettes or marrow,
  sliced or cubed
225 g/8 oz onions, sliced
225–350 g/8–12 oz tomatoes,
  skinned and chopped
oil to fry

150 ml/¼ pint stock or water
salt, black pepper and pinch of
  dried mixed herbs
TOPPING
75 g/3 oz grated strong cheese
50 g/2 oz fresh breadcrumbs
butter to dot

SLICE aubergine unpeeled. Sprinkle with salt and leave for 15 minutes. Rinse and drain. Sauté the courgettes, aubergine, onions and tomatoes in a little oil for 5–8 minutes.

Put in ovenproof dish with lid. Add stock, salt, pepper and herbs. Cook for about 1 hour in a moderate oven (180 C, 350 F, gas 4). Remove the lid and sprinkle on cheese and breadcrumb mixture. Dot with butter and return to oven for about 30 minutes, until the topping is brown. SERVES 4–6.

Mrs R. Strang, St Neot, Cornwall

VEGETABLE MEDLEY

225 g/8 oz sliced celery stalks
350 g/12 oz sliced carrots
450 g/1 lb sliced leeks
225 g/8 oz button mushrooms
50 g/2 oz butter

50 g/2 oz flour
600 ml/1 pint milk
ground black pepper and salt
paprika pepper

COOK the celery and the carrots in 600 ml/1 pint boiling salted water for about 15 minutes. Add the leeks and cook for a further 10 minutes. Drain and keep back the stock.

Wash and trim the mushrooms. Keeping them whole, gently fry in the butter. Remove using a slotted spoon and add to the vegetables. Stir the flour into the juices left in the pan and cook for 1 minute. Remove from heat and gradually add 300 ml/½ pint of the vegetable stock followed by all the milk. Cook for a further few minutes and add the vegetables to the sauce. Heat through, season to taste and turn into a hot serving dish. Sprinkle with a pinch of paprika. SERVES 6.

Mrs Carole Ford, Warminster, Wiltshire

☆ HOT VEGETABLE LAYER ☆

175 g/6 oz streaky bacon, chopped
450 g/1 lb potatoes, peeled and
  thinly sliced
225 g/8 oz carrots, peeled and
  sliced
100 g/4 oz Cheddar cheese, finely
  grated

salt and freshly ground pepper
grated nutmeg
300 ml/½ pint double cream
2 tomatoes, sliced

FRY the bacon in its own fat until just beginning to brown. Drain well on absorbent paper.

Butter a 1.25-litre/2-pint ovenproof dish. Layer up the potato, bacon, carrots and grated cheese, finishing with a layer of cheese. Season as you go with salt, pepper and nutmeg, being careful not to over-season. Pour in the cream down the side of the dish.

Bake in a cool oven (150 C, 300 F, gas 2) for 2 hours, until set and golden in colour. Serve hot, garnished with tomatoes. SERVES 4.

Miss R. A. Page, Sibton, Suffolk

SUMMER VEGETABLE TERRINE

225 g/8 oz runner beans
350 g/12 oz carrots
450 g/1 lb spinach
175 g/6 oz mushrooms
5 eggs and 1 egg yolk

450 ml/¾ pint double cream
4 tablespoons grated Cheshire
  cheese
salt, pepper and nutmeg

PREPARE the vegetables. Top and tail the beans and drop them into a pan of boiling salted water. Cook for 1 minute after water returns to the boil then lift out and drain. Top and tail carrots and split into sticks. Drop into the water and cook for 5 minutes, lift out and drain. Wash spinach and pick out large leaves (do not discard smaller leaves, they can be used in salads, soups, etc.). Blanch for 1 minute and spread out to dry. Wipe and trim mushrooms.

Butter a 1.25-litre/2-pint terrine dish. Line with spinach leaves, completely and evenly.

Make the custard. Beat the eggs and egg yolk together, stir in the cream and mix. Place in the top of a double boiler, add the grated cheese and stir until the mixture thickens. Season with salt and pepper and a grating of nutmeg, and keep warm in the boiler.

Put first layer of mixed vegetables into the terrine and cover with custard. Place lid on terrine and set in a roasting tin with water coming halfway up the terrine. Bake in a moderate oven (180 C, 350 F, gas 4) for 30 minutes, until layer is just set. Add next layer of vegetables and custard and repeat baking. Continue until all vegetables and custard have been baked. Lift terrine from water and leave to cool before turning out. SERVES 8.

If using this dish as a starter at a dinner party use half quantity of all ingredients in a 600-ml/1-pint terrine dish, to serve four.

Mrs S. Carlyle, Ecclefechan, Dumfries-shire

HERB FRITTERS

Where we live in upland Cardiganshire (as was), spring comes rather late. There is a "hungry gap" period when there seem to be few vegetables in the garden or freezer, and those in the local shop look rather tired and un-springlike! Two minutes sauntering along an average hedge supplies delicious herb fritters (though avoid hedges along roadsides or sprayed fields). They aren't terribly slimming, I'm afraid, but they do provide a fresh tonic to the sluggish winter system.

BATTER
1 egg
100 g/4 oz plain flour
pinch salt
milk to mix

HERBS
finely chopped mixed handful of
 sorrel, chives, mint or any
 garden herbs

ADD the beaten egg to the flour and salt in a large bowl. Mix in enough milk to make a thick, but not stiff, batter. Chop a tight handful of herbs, and mix well in. I use half sorrel, in quantity, and half a mixture of chives and mint, together with any other garden herbs, or dandelion leaves etc.

Drop small spoonfuls of the batter mixture into hot (but not boiling) oil in a deep pan, and deep-fry until golden brown. These herb fritters can be served with virtually anything – instead of Yorkshire pudding, to accompany roast chicken, or with any cold meats or salads. SERVES 4.

Mrs M. Osborne, Bontnewydd, Dyfed

HOT PUDDINGS

PEARS WITH GINGER SAUCE

450 g/1 lb Conference pears
300 ml/½ pint water
75 g/3 oz fine breadcrumbs
50 g/2 oz margarine
25 g/1 oz butter

25 g/1 oz cornflour
25 g/1 oz castor sugar
½ teaspoon ground ginger
3 tablespoons preserved ginger

PEEL the pears thinly. Poach in the water for 10 minutes. Drain the water and reserve for the sauce. Roll the fruit in the breadcrumbs and place on a baking sheet. Dot with the margarine and bake in a moderately hot oven (200 c, 400 f, gas 6) until the crumbs are browned, about 10 minutes.

Meanwhile, make the sauce. Melt the butter in a saucepan. Stir in cornflour. Add the sugar and ground ginger to the reserved water from the fruit and stir well. Add to the saucepan and bring to the boil, stirring. While boiling add the chopped preserved ginger.

Serve pears in a hot dish accompanied by the sauce in a hot sauceboat. Serves 4 or 5, depending on number of pears.

Mrs M. Lewis, Cenarth, Dyfed

PINEAPPLE PUDDING

1 439-g/15½-oz can pineapple
  cubes or pieces
250 ml/8 fl oz water
juice of ½ lemon

100 g/4 oz sugar
2 tablespoons cornflour
2 eggs, separated

DRAIN 250 ml/8 fl oz pineapple syrup. Mix with the water, lemon juice, sugar and cornflour. Cook, stirring, in double saucepan until clear. Remove from heat. Stir in beaten egg yolks, then fold in whisked egg whites and pineapple cubes or pieces. Put in pretty buttered dish and cook in a cool oven (150 C, 300 F, gas 2) for 20 minutes.

When cooked cover or decorate with whipped cream and pineapple. Serve hot or cold. SERVES 4.

Mrs J. Harrison, Wainfleet, Lincolnshire

☆ ALMOND NUTTY APPLES ☆

1 small egg
4 medium cooking apples, peeled
  and cored
50 g/2 oz crushed Digestive
  biscuits

50 g/2 oz soft brown sugar
50 g/2 oz chopped nuts (almonds
  or mixed)
100 g/4 oz made almond paste

SEPARATE the egg and paint the outside of the apples with beaten egg white. Roll them in a mixture of the biscuits, sugar and nuts. Place in a baking dish.

Roll out the almond paste and make some leaf decorations – about two for each apple. Using the trimmings and rest of paste, work in the egg yolk. Fill the centre of the apples with this and decorate with the leaves. Cook in a moderate oven (180 C, 350 F, gas 4) for about 30 minutes. SERVES 4.

Patricia Neal, Inkberrow, Worcestershire

APPLE HEDGEHOG

9 cooking apples
175 g/6 oz granulated sugar
450 ml/¾ pint boiling water
50 g/2 oz tapioca
green food colouring

TOPPING
2 egg whites
150 g/5 oz moist brown sugar
25 g/1 oz shredded blanched
    almonds

PEEL the apples, core six of them and slice the rest. Bake or poach the whole apples in the sugar and water until just tender. Remove the apples to a dish and use the syrup to cook the sliced apples and tapioca until transparent (I use a double saucepan). Add colouring. Spread a layer of this mixture on a dish then place the whole cooked apples on top, fill up the spaces and make a dome in the centre with the rest of the mixture.

Whisk the egg whites until stiff and stir in the moist brown sugar. Spread lightly over the apples. Insert the almonds to represent the back of a hedgehog. May be served straightaway or browned first in the oven or under the grill. Good hot or cold. SERVES 6.

Patricia Neal, Inkberrow, Worcestershire

SPICED PINEAPPLE

1 fresh pineapple or 1 575-g/20-oz
    can pineapple chunks
castor sugar

6 cloves
½ teaspoon ground cinnamon
½ teaspoon ground ginger

IF fresh pineapple is used, prepare the previous day, removing skin and cutting flesh into chunky pieces. Place on a dish, sprinkle with sugar and leave overnight to allow juice to run.

Place all ingredients and the juice (fresh or canned) in an ovenproof dish, stir well. Cover and cook in a moderate oven (180 c, 350 f, gas 4) for 30 minutes. Serve hot with vanilla ice cream. SERVES 4.

Mrs P. A. Appleton, Holme-on-Spalding Moor, Yorkshire

PLUM AND PINEAPPLE FLAMBÉ

450 g/1 lb plums, halved and
stoned
1 medium pineapple, peeled and
cubed
4 tablespoons good marmalade

2 lemons
75 g/3 oz soft brown sugar
50 g/2 oz butter
½ teaspoon ground cinnamon
4 tablespoons rum

ARRANGE fruit in a shallow flameproof dish. In a small pan melt
the marmalade, add juice and grated rind of lemons, sugar, butter
and cinnamon. Pour over fruit and bake for about 20 minutes in a
moderately hot oven (190 C, 375 F, gas 5).

Just before serving heat the rum in a small pan; ignite and pour
over fruit. Serve with cream. SERVES 6.

N. V. Kinsey-Jones, Rowhook Hill, West Sussex

PINEAPPLE MERINGUE PUDDING

1 439-g/15½-oz can pineapple
pieces
1 medium banana, sliced
a little lemon juice
2 teaspoons custard powder

1 teaspoon sugar (optional)
1 large egg, separated
2 tablespoons castor sugar

MIX together drained pineapple pieces and sliced banana and
sprinkle with lemon juice. Place in a greased 18-cm/7-inch pie
dish.

Put custard powder and teaspoon sugar into a basin. Mix to a
smooth paste with pineapple juice and egg yolk and make up to
300 ml/½ pint with water. Mix well together, pour into a saucepan
and stir over medium heat until a creamy consistency. Leave to
cool a little then pour over the fruit.

Whisk egg white until fairly stiff, add castor sugar gradually and
whisk again until in peaks to form a meringue. Pipe or spread over
the top of dish, making sure the edges are sealed all round.
Sprinkle top with sugar and bake in a moderate oven (180 C, 350 F,
gas 4) for about 15 minutes, until golden brown and crisp on top.
SERVES 4.

This is a marvellous way to use up small amounts of leftover
stewed or tinned fruit (fresh raspberries or strawberries may also
be used). This favourite combination of pineapple and banana has
a sharp fresh tangy taste, and the sweet may be eaten hot or cold.
The pudding can also be made in a cooked pastry case.

Mrs P. M. Fox, Yattendon, Berkshire

PLUM CASTAWAYS

white bread
butter
ripe plums

granulated sugar
cinnamon

ALLOW one thick slice bread per person. Remove crusts, butter the slices and press onto each one as many halved stoned plums as will fit (say 4–6 halves).

Arrange slices flat in a large shallow, buttered, ovenproof dish. Dab with butter and sprinkle generously with sugar and a little cinnamon. Bake in a moderate oven (180c, 350f, gas 4) for 30 minutes, when plums should be cooked in syrup on golden crisp "rafts".

Mrs Kay Ohsten, Pulham St Mary, Norfolk

GOOSEBERRY AMBER

50 g/2 oz butter
450 g/1 lb gooseberries
190 g/7½ oz castor sugar

25–50 g/1–2 oz biscuit crumbs
(preferably Digestive)
2 eggs, separated

MELT butter in saucepan over low heat, add gooseberries and 100 g/4 oz sugar. Cook gently until fruit is a thick pulp. Stir in biscuit crumbs and beaten egg yolks and mix well. Place in buttered pie dish, cover and bake in a moderate oven (180c, 350f, gas 4) for about 15 minutes, until set. Remove from oven.

For meringue, whisk egg whites until stiff, beat in 50 g/2 oz sugar and fold in 25 g/1 oz sugar. Pile over pudding and sprinkle with remaining sugar. Bake in a cool oven (140c, 275 f, gas 1) until meringue is biscuit coloured and top is crisp, about 30–40 minutes. SERVES 4.

Mrs M. Winnington, Easterton, Wiltshire

RHUBARB AND ORANGE MERINGUE

675 g/1½ lb rhubarb	75 g/3 oz sugar
juice and grated rind of 1 large	2 egg yolks
orange	MERINGUE
300 ml/½ pint cold water	3 egg whites
1½ tablespoons cornflour	100 g/4 oz castor sugar

STEW rhubarb in a very little water, do not add sugar. Put juice and rind of orange with 2 tablespoons of the water and the cornflour in a basin, mix until smooth. Boil the remaining water, pour on to the cornflour, mix and pour back into saucepan. Stir until mixture thickens. Allow to cool slightly, add sugar, well beaten egg yolks and rhubarb. Turn into a flan dish.

For the meringue, whisk egg whites and half the sugar until thick, fold in remaining sugar. Cover rhubarb mixture with meringue and bake in a moderate oven (180 c, 350 f, gas 4) for 25–30 minutes, until golden brown and crisp.

If liked this could be put on to a pastry case to make it go further, but is quite filling as it is and is equally delicious either way. SERVES 4–6.

Mrs Helen Cole, Wormington Grange, Worcestershire

☆ ORANGE PUDDING ☆

4 oranges	2 eggs, separated
100 g/4 oz sugar	600 ml/1 pint milk
1 tablespoon cornflour	

PEEL the oranges, remove segments from skin. Put into a pie dish and sprinkle with a little of the sugar.

Make a custard with the cornflour, egg yolks, milk and 2 tablespoons of the sugar. Pour custard over the oranges.

Beat the egg whites until stiff and fold in the remaining sugar. Put on top of the custard in peaks. Bake in a moderate oven (180 c, 350 f, gas 4) until meringue is crisp and brown. SERVES 4–6.

Mrs Janet Ivins, Sutton Bonnington, Leicestershire

☆ AUNT ALICE'S SUMMER ☆ APPLE PIE

EGG CUSTARD
300 ml/½ pint milk
15 g/½ oz butter
25 g/1 oz castor sugar
4 tablespoons fresh white
  breadcrumbs
grated rind of 1 lemon

2 egg yolks
APPLE PURÉE
2 cooking apples
sugar to taste
MERINGUE
2 egg whites
100 g/4 oz castor sugar

HEAT the milk and add the butter and sugar. Stir until the sugar dissolves, then add the breadcrumbs and lemon rind. When the breadcrumb mixture has cooled slightly, mix in the egg yolks. Pour into a buttered pie dish and leave to stand for 30 minutes.

Bake in a moderate oven (180 c, 350 f, gas 4) for 25 minutes, or until the custard mixture is set. Remove and allow to cool slightly. Reduce the oven temperature to 160 c, 325 f, gas 3.

Peel, core and slice the apples and put into a pan. Add a little sugar and cook gently, without water, until very soft. Beat well and add sugar to taste. Carefully spread the apple purée over the custard.

Whisk the egg whites for the meringue until stiff. Whisk in 2 teaspoons sugar, whisk again until very stiff and shiny then fold in all but half a teaspoon of the remaining sugar. Pile the meringue on top of the custard and dust with the reserved sugar. Bake until the meringue is set and lightly straw-coloured, about 10 minutes. SERVES 4.

Elizabeth Pointing, Syresham, Northamptonshire

PLUM SUNSHINE

3 eggs
300 ml/½ pint single cream
75 g/3 oz fresh brown or white
  breadcrumbs
1 teaspoon ground cinnamon

1 kg/2 lb ripe plums, halved and
  stoned
175–225 g/6–8 oz syrup or honey,
  warmed

BUTTER pie dish (about 1.75 litre/3 pint size). Beat eggs and mix with cream to make a custard. Mix breadcrumbs with cinnamon and sprinkle half over base of dish. Cover with half the plums, neatly arranged cut side down, pour over half the syrup or honey and half the custard. Repeat all the layers once more.

Bake in a moderate oven (180 C, 350 F, gas 4) for about 1 hour, until golden and set. Serve hot, on its own, or with extra custard or cream. SERVES 6–8.

Mrs B. Adams, Charfield, Gloucestershire

RASPBERRY RIPPLE SPONGE

350 g/12 oz raspberries	75 g/3 oz castor sugar
75 g/3 oz granulated sugar	1 egg
300 ml/½ pint water	75 g/3 oz self-raising flour
75 g/3 oz butter	1 tablespoon cornflour

GENTLY poach the raspberries with sugar and water until juices run, strain through sieve and save clear juice to make sauce.

Cream butter and sugar, beat in egg then fold in flour to make a sponge mixture. Add strained raspberries. Pour into greased pie dish and cook in a moderate oven (180 C, 350 F, gas 4) until firm and golden – about 45–50 minutes.

Mix the cornflour with a little of the raspberry juice, bring rest to the boil and stir in the cornflour to make a sauce. Pour sauce over pudding portions and serve with fresh cream. Can be served hot or cold. SERVES 4.

Mrs R. J. Williams, Llangovan, Gwent

RASPBERRY CREAM PUDDING

450 g/1 lb fresh raspberries	2 eggs
75 g/3 oz castor sugar	1 tablespoon flour
300 ml/½ pint soured cream	sugar to sprinkle

PUT raspberries into a shallow ovenproof dish and sprinkle with 50 g/2 oz sugar. Stand the dish in a cool oven (150 C, 300 F, gas 2) until the raspberries are hot through.

Beat up the soured cream with the eggs, flour and remaining sugar. Pour the mixture over the raspberries and return to the oven until the topping is pale golden brown and firm, about 45 minutes. Sprinkle with a little more sugar before serving. This can be eaten hot or cold. SERVES 4–6.

Mrs E. Emo, Helston, Cornwall

RHUBARB DELIGHT

450 g/1 lb rhubarb	50 g/2 oz plain flour
2 medium eggs	½ teaspoon ground ginger
pinch of salt	25 g/1 oz butter, melted
100 g/4 oz castor sugar	300 ml/½ pint milk

WASH and cut rhubarb into 2.5-cm/1-inch pieces. Whisk eggs with salt, add 75 g/3 oz sugar and beat lightly. Beat in flour and ginger gradually, then blend in melted butter and milk a little at a time to make a smooth creamy batter. Scatter rhubarb and remaining sugar over a shallow buttered 20-cm/8-inch flan dish and cover with batter mixture.

Bake in a moderate oven (180 C, 350 F, gas 4) until golden brown, set but creamy. Serve with cream or ice cream. SERVES 4.

Mrs I. Thackeray, Rowley, Co. Durham

GRANNIE'S RHUBARB CAKE

75 g/3 oz soft margarine	1 teaspoon baking powder
40 g/1½ oz castor sugar	40 g/1½ oz plain flour
1 small egg	350 g/12 oz rhubarb, thinly sliced
3 tablespoons semolina or ground rice	little granulated sugar

BEAT margarine and sugar together, add egg and mix thoroughly. Mix in semolina or ground rice, baking powder and 3 tablespoons flour. Work in rest of flour with the hand; mixture should be stiff enough to roll out.

Halve mixture, roll out to fit a 19–20-cm/7½–8-inch round tin and place in the tin. Cover with rhubarb and sprinkle on sugar to taste. Roll out remainder of mixture to cover rhubarb and press edges together.

Cook in a moderate oven (180 C, 350 F, gas 4) for 20 minutes. Serve hot with custard or ice cream.

Other suitable fruits: apples, blackcurrants, gooseberries, dried apricots (soaked), and jam. This pudding freezes very well and can be put straight from the freezer into the oven to defrost and warm through. SERVES 4–6.

Mrs Alison M. Johnson, Yetholm, Roxburghshire

YORKSHIRE BRAMBLE PUDDING

1 medium egg
100 g/4 oz plain flour
pinch of salt
300 ml/½ pint milk
a little ice cold water

olive oil
225 g/8 oz blackberries
sugar to taste
600 ml/1 pint sweet white sauce
nutmeg

MAKE up batter by breaking egg into flour with salt and gradually beating together with milk, or combine all the ingredients in a liquidiser. Finally, when a smooth pouring consistency has been obtained, add water. Place a little oil in a four-ring Yorkshire pudding tin and heat in a hot oven (220 C, 425 F, gas 7). After a few minutes, pour batter into tin, dividing between the four compartments, and cook for 40–45 minutes.

Meanwhile, stew brambles if small and sweeten to taste, or leave fresh if large and sweet. When puddings are cooked, fill centres with fruit and serve with white sauce, sweetened with honey and topped with a little grated nutmeg. SERVES 4.

Mrs D. B. Broadhurst, Wetherby, West Yorkshire

BRAMBLE AND HAZELNUT SPONGE

450 g/1 lb brambles (or
blackberries south of the
border!)
50 g/2 oz sugar (or to taste)
TOPPING
100 g/4 oz butter or margarine
100 g/4 oz castor sugar

2 eggs, beaten
few drops almond essence
25 g/1 oz plain flour
25 g/1 oz ground almonds
50 g/2 oz ground hazelnuts
50 g/2 oz chopped hazelnuts

LIGHTLY grease an oblong ovenproof dish and add brambles and sugar in layers.

Cream butter and sugar until fluffy and beat in eggs and essence. Add flour, ground almonds and ground hazelnuts. Spread over brambles. Sprinkle with chopped hazelnuts and bake for 30–40 minutes in a moderate oven (180 C, 350 F, gas 4), until risen and golden. Serve hot or cold with cream or thin custard. SERVES 6.

This is an adaptation on a recipe from an elderly aunt and is a great family favourite.

Mrs Muriel Hume, Mains of Carmyllie, Arbroath

CRISP-TOPPED APPLE PUDDING

TOPPING
40 g/1½ oz butter or margarine
50 g/2 oz plain flour
65 g/2½ oz brown sugar, preferably
  demerara
1 teaspoon ground cinnamon
SPONGE MIXTURE
1 large cooking apple (about 275 g/
  10 oz), peeled, cored and
  quartered

175 g/6 oz soft brown sugar
175 g/6 oz butter or margarine,
  softened
3 eggs
175 g/6 oz self-raising flour
4–6 tablespoons apple juice or
  milk
100 g/4 oz sultanas or raisins

PREPARE topping. Rub butter into flour then stir in sugar and cinnamon.

Slice the apple thinly. Cream sugar and butter until fluffy, beat in eggs one at a time. Fold in the flour with apple juice or milk to give a soft dropping consistency. Add the sultanas or raisins. Spread two-thirds of this mixture into a well greased 1.25-litre/ 2-pint ovenproof dish, cover with apple slices then remaining one-third of sponge mix. Sprinkle topping mixture evenly over.

Bake in a moderate oven (160C, 325 F, gas 3) until firm to touch and top is crisp, about 1¼–1½ hours. Serve hot with custard or cream or it is especially delicious with plain yogurt. SERVES 6.

Leftovers can be served cold, cut as cake. Apples can be replaced by any autumn fruits – pears, plums, blackberries etc.

Mrs M. Loach, Sutton Coldfield, West Midlands

APPLE CRISP

A very superior apple crumble.

225 g/8 oz plain flour
¼ teaspoon salt
¾ teaspoon baking powder
225 g/8 oz granulated sugar
1 egg

3–4 large cooking apples, peeled
  and sliced
65 g/2½ oz butter or margarine,
  melted
sprinkle of ground cinnamon

SIFT flour, salt and baking powder together, mix with sugar. Beat egg and with a fork mix into flour and sugar mixture until it resembles crumbs.

Put apples in a 20×33-cm/8×13-inch dish, cover with crumb mixture. Pour melted butter over mixture, sprinkle with cinnamon. Bake about 30 minutes in a moderate oven (180C, 350F, gas 4). Serve with cream or ice cream.

I acquired this recipe from an American cousin about 18 years ago and have made it regularly since. Everyone who tries it asks for the recipe, and it is my husband's favourite dessert. SERVES 6.

Mrs Eileen Barmak, London NW11

MILLIN APPLE CHARLOTTE

175 g/6 oz butter, melted
225 g/8 oz fresh breadcrumbs
100 g/4 oz sugar
50 g/2 oz chopped mixed nuts or coconut

1 teaspoon ground mixed spice
grated rind and juice of 1 lemon
1 kg/2 lb cooking apples
100 g/4 oz sugar

GREASE a pie dish with a little of the melted butter. Add breadcrumbs, sugar, nuts, spice and lemon rind and juice to remaining butter. Peel, core and slice apples. Fill dish with alternate layers of crumbs and apple, sprinkle apple layers with sugar, finishing with crumbs. Cover with greased greaseproof paper and bake for about 1¼–1½ hours in a moderate oven (180 C, 350 F, gas 4). SERVES 6–8.

M. A. Brooks, Newent, Gloucestershire

BLACKBERRY AND APPLE DELIGHT

225 g/8 oz cooking apples
40 g/1½ oz sugar or syrup
225 g/8 oz crumble mixture (100 g/ 4 oz flour, 50 g/2 oz fat, 50 g/ 2 oz sugar)

100 g/4 oz blackberries

GREASE a pie dish well with butter. Peel and core apples and slice thinly. Place a substantial layer of slices in bottom of dish and a sprinkling of sugar or syrup over them, then a layer of crumble, finally a layer of blackberries. Repeat this process until the dish is filled; on the last layer of crumble put a final sprinkling of sugar. Place in a moderately hot oven (190 C, 375 F, gas 5) and bake until apples are cooked and pie is golden brown. Serve with custard or fresh cream. SERVES 3–4.

A. Richards, Lansstone, Gwent

Rhubarb Crisp

675 g/1½ lb rhubarb	100 g/4 oz wholemeal flour
100 g/4 oz sugar	75 g/3 oz brown sugar
1 orange	50 g/2 oz muesli or rolled oats
75 g/3 oz butter	

Cut rhubarb into 2.5-cm/1-inch pieces. Put in a pie dish with the sugar, grated orange rind and the orange segments cut small. Rub butter into flour, stir in brown sugar and muesli. Sprinkle over rhubarb. Bake until crisp, about 30 minutes in a moderately hot oven (200 c, 400 f, gas 6). Serves 4–5.

P. Russo, Reigate, Surrey

Winter Crumble

BASE	TOPPING
175 g/6 oz dried fruit, e.g.	100 g/4 oz butter
apricots, peaches, prunes	50 g/2 oz demerara sugar
1 tablespoon rum	75 g/3 oz self-raising flour
grated rind of 1 orange	100 g/4 oz rolled oats
sugar to taste	chopped walnuts to sprinkle

The fruit should be stewed in a little water and rum, with the orange rind, and sweetened to taste.

Make crumble. Cream together butter and sugar, work in flour and oats to form crumbly mixture. Spoon over fruit and bake in a moderately hot oven (190 c, 375 f, gas 5) for about 30 minutes, until golden brown. Sprinkle crumble with chopped walnuts and serve warm with whipped cream. Serves 4.

Miss Alex Welch, Cockerton, Co. Durham

Oranges and Lemons Pudding

FLANCRUST PASTRY	4 egg yolks
225 g/8 oz plain flour	2 egg whites
150 g/5 oz butter	100 g/4 oz castor sugar
75 g/3 oz icing sugar	grated rind and juice of 1 orange
2 egg yolks	grated rind and juice of ½ lemon
FILLING	
75 g/3 oz butter	

Sift flour into bowl and rub in butter. Stir in icing sugar and mix to a dough with egg yolks. Knead until smooth, on lightly floured board. Wrap in foil and chill for 30 minutes or up to 2 days. Then let pastry stand for 15 minutes at room temperature and roll out to line a 25-cm/10-inch flan or tart tin. Prick base and bake blind for 15–20 minutes in a moderately hot oven (190 C, 375 F, gas 5), removing greaseproof paper and beans, if used, for last 5 minutes.

Melt butter and cool. Whisk eggs and sugar until thick. Add rind and juice of orange and lemon. Gently stir in butter and pour into prepared flan case. Bake for about 15 minutes in a moderately hot oven (190 C, 375 F, gas 5), then reduce to moderate (160 C, 325 F, gas 3) for a further 15 minutes, or until filling sets. Serve hot or cold with cream if liked. SERVES 6–8.

Mrs Sheila Jerrard, Oldhamstocks, East Lothian

LEMON APPLE SLICE

FILLING
1 kg/2 lb cooking apples
juice of ½ lemon
sugar to taste
2 teaspoons cornflour
PASTRY BASE
½ beaten egg
50 g/2 oz castor sugar
100 g/4 oz block margarine

175 g/6 oz plain flour
50 g/2 oz self-raising flour
1 teaspoon salt
TOPPING
175 g/6 oz soft margarine
75 g/3 oz castor sugar
2 tablespoons beaten egg
175 g/6 oz plain flour
grated rind of ½ lemon

PEEL, core and slice apples, simmer gently with lemon juice, sugar and a little water. Cook until soft. Blend cornflour with a little cold water, stir in to thicken, and cool.

For the pastry, beat egg and castor sugar together. Rub margarine into sieved flour and salt. Add egg and sugar mixture, bind together into a ball. Stand for 5 minutes.

For the topping, cream together soft margarine and castor sugar. Beat in egg then flour and lemon rind. The mixture should be soft enough to pipe, if not add more beaten egg.

Roll out pastry to line oblong tin, about 36 × 18 × 3.5 cm/ 14 × 7 × 1½ inches. Spread apple filling on top. Place topping in piping bag fitted with a large star nozzle and pipe mixture over apple from corner to corner of tin, into a lattice pattern. Bake in a moderately hot oven (200 C, 400 F, gas 6) until golden brown. Cool slightly, cut into squares.

Delicious with cream or ice cream. Freezes beautifully. For a quick dessert just warm through, to thaw.

Mrs Eileen Bell, Torpenhow, Cumbria

ANGELA'S AUTUMN APPLE PIE

450 g/1 lb cooking apples, peeled
    and cored
1 tablespoon dark brown sugar
1 tablespoon honey
1 tablespoon homemade (or coarse
    cut) marmalade
100 g/4 oz mixed dried fruit

½ teaspoon ground ginger
½ teaspoon ground mixed spice
SHORTCRUST PASTRY
225 g/8 oz plain flour
pinch of salt
100 g/4 oz lard
ice cold water to mix

GRATE apples coarsely and put into a large basin, add all other ingredients and mix very thoroughly, leave to stand.

Make shortcrust pastry while apple mixture rests. Roll out pastry, line a 20-cm/8-inch round flat tin and fill with apple mixture. Put pastry crust on top to make a tart.

Cook in a moderately hot oven (200 C, 400 F, gas 6) for about 15 minutes then reduce to moderate (180 C, 350 F, gas 4) for a further 30 minutes, or until crisp and golden. Sprinkle with castor sugar and serve with cream or a thin custard. SERVES 4–6.

This is a fat free (no suet) mincemeat type of tart. For Christmas I add 1 tablespoon brandy to the apple mixture and serve with brandy butter.

Angela Parker, Branston, Lincolnshire

EGG, MINCEMEAT AND APPLE FLAN

2 tablespoons mincemeat
1 20-cm/8-inch cooked pastry flan
    case
few fresh breadcrumbs

1 large cooking apple
a little sugar
2 eggs

SPREAD mincemeat evenly over pastry case, add breadcrumbs with sliced apple and a little sugar to taste. Beat eggs and pour over. Bake for about 20 minutes until golden brown in a moderate oven (180 C, 350 F, gas 4). SERVES 4.

Mrs M. Pilcher, East Guldeford, East Sussex

APPLE AND MARZIPAN TART

ALMOND PASTRY
250 g/9 oz plain flour
75 g/3 oz ground almonds
¼ teaspoon salt
175 g/6 oz margarine
75 g/3 oz castor sugar
1 egg, beaten

FILLING
100 g/4 oz marzipan
100 g/4 oz margarine
50 g/2 oz castor sugar
2 eggs, separated
4 large apples, grated
beaten egg to glaze

SIFT flour, almonds and salt. Rub in margarine, stir in sugar. Bind to a firm dough with egg. Knead lightly, then place in fridge for 30 minutes.

Line a 25-cm/10-inch loose-based tin with pastry, leaving enough for lattice top. Grate marzipan over pastry. Cream fat and sugar. Beat in egg yolks and stir in grated apple. Stiffly whisk egg whites and fold into mixture. Spread apple mixture over marzipan. Cover with pastry strips to form lattice, brush with egg. Bake in a hot oven (220 c, 425 f, gas 7) for about 35–40 minutes. SERVES 6–8.

Mrs M. Whiteford, Cupar, Fife

COBURG PIE

6–8 cooking apples
about 175 g/6 oz shortcrust pastry
marmalade
50 g/2 oz cornflour

600 ml/1 pint milk
strip of lemon rind
3 eggs, separated
3 tablespoons sugar

PEEL, core and slice apples and stew until tender. Line and decorate the edges of a pie dish with shortcrust pastry. Put in a layer of stewed apple, cover with marmalade then the rest of the apple.

Mix the cornflour smoothly with a little of the milk and bring the remaining milk with the lemon rind slowly to the boil. Gradually add to the cornflour mixture, return all to the heat and stir until thickened and thoroughly cooked. Add the beaten egg yolks and pour over the apples.

Bake in a moderate oven (180 c, 350 f, gas 4) until the pastry is cooked and the custard set. Whip up the egg whites stiffly, fold in the sugar. Pile it on top of the pie and crisp in the oven.

Mrs P. Colclough, Betchton, Cheshire

BLACKBERRY AND APPLE STRUDEL

STRUDEL PASTRY
150 g/5 oz plain flour
½ beaten egg
2 teaspoons oil
2–3 tablespoons warm water

FILLING
25–50 g/1–2 oz butter, melted
40 g/1½ oz hazelnuts
350 g/12 oz cooking apples
100 g/4 oz blackberries
brown sugar

MAKE up the strudel pastry: sift the flour into a bowl and mix in the beaten egg, oil and water. Roll out and pull thinly over a floured tea cloth. Brush with melted butter. Sprinkle with the hazelnuts, browned and crushed. Scatter over thinly sliced apples and blackberries and sugar to taste. Roll up and place in shape on buttered baking sheet. Brush with butter and bake in a moderately hot oven (200 c, 400 f, gas 6) for 25 minutes, until browned. Dust with brown sugar and serve warm with cream. SERVES 6.

V. M. Frater, Goswick, Berwick-upon-Tweed

☆ SOUR CREAM PIE ☆

175 g/6 oz shortcrust pastry
25 g/1 oz flour
150 g/5 oz light brown sugar

250 ml/8 fl oz soured cream
5–6 cooking apples
large handful of blackberries

LINE pie plate with pastry. Beat flour, 100 g/4 oz sugar and cream until well mixed and smooth. Peel, core and slice apples and arrange nicely in pie plate. Sprinkle blackberries among apple slices. Pour cream mixture over fruit and sprinkle remaining sugar on top.

Bake in a hot oven (230 c, 450 f, gas 8) for 15 minutes, then reduce to moderate (180 c, 350 f, gas 4) for a further 30 minutes, until set and slightly browned. SERVES 6–8.

Mrs Susan Coulson, Wooler, Northumberland

BLACKBERRY ROLL

225 g/8 oz blackberries
100 g/4 oz cooking apples, peeled
    and finely chopped
75 g/3 oz raisins
175 g/6 oz sugar

1 teaspoon ground cinnamon
50 g/2 oz slivered almonds
225 g/8 oz shortcrust pastry
1 tablespoon apricot jam

SIMMER fruit with a tablespoon of water and the sugar and

cinnamon until quite thick, like marmalade. Let cool a little and add the almonds.

Roll out the pastry into a rectangle shape and spread with apricot jam. Spread a thick layer of fruit mixture on it. Roll up like a Swiss roll. Press edges together and glaze with milk or egg. Bake in a moderately hot oven (200 c, 400 f, gas 6) for 45 minutes. Serve with thick cream or custard. SERVES 4–5.

Mrs J. Cecil, Shorwell, Isle of Wight

ELDERBERRY PIE

450 g/1 lb elderberries
75 g/3 oz sugar

1 tablespoon cornflour
225 g/8 oz shortcrust pastry

PUT the elderberries, sugar and a little water in a saucepan and bring to the boil. Thicken with the cornflour blended with a little water, and allow to cool.

Line a 23-cm/9-inch ovenproof plate or casserole lid with pastry. Fill with the fruit and top with a pastry lid. Brush with water and sprinkle with sugar. Bake in a moderately hot oven (200 c, 400 f, gas 6) until golden and crisp. SERVES 4–6.

Mrs P. Parsons, Weston Longville, Norfolk

HOT APPLE SLICE

350 g/12 oz rough puff pastry
450 g/1 lb cooking apples,
    prepared
25 g/1 oz butter
sugar to taste

½ teaspoon ground mixed spice
50 g/2 oz raisins
beaten egg to brush
1 teaspoon castor sugar

ROLL out pastry to oblong 30 × 20 cm/12 × 8 inches. Cut in half lengthways, place one half on greased baking tray.

Poach apple in butter until soft. Purée and add sugar, spice and raisins. Spoon over bottom half of pastry, leaving a 2.5-cm/1-inch border all round. Fold top pastry in half lengthways and make cuts from fold to within 1 cm/½ inch of edges. Brush bottom edges of pastry with beaten egg and cover with top pastry. Seal carefully. Decorate edges, brush with egg and sprinkle over castor sugar. Bake in a moderately hot oven (200 c, 400 f, gas 6) for 35 minutes, until pastry is golden.

Serve hot with lashings of whipped cream. SERVES 6.

Mrs V. Drydon, Langley, Northumberland

PEAR TART WITH BRANDY CREAM

450 g/1 lb pears
1 tablespoon castor sugar
2 tablespoons brandy
rind and juice of ½ orange
150 ml/¼ pint double cream
PASTRY
225 g/8 oz plain flour
pinch of salt

100 g/4 oz block margarine, grated
3 egg yolks
1–2 drops almond essence
100 g/4 oz ground almonds
100 g/4 oz castor sugar
1 egg white and castor sugar to glaze

FIRST prepare the pastry one or two days in advance. Put the flour and salt into a large bowl. Add margarine, egg yolks, essence, ground almonds and sugar, and work until it looks like marzipan. Leave to rest for 1–2 days.

Peel, core and quarter pears. Put into a bowl and sprinkle with sugar. Pour over the brandy, orange juice and rind. Cover with cling film and stand for 30 minutes.

Take one-third of pastry for the lid. Roll out remainder to line a 20-cm/8-inch flan tin. Put in the drained pears, round side uppermost. Roll out the pastry lid and cut a 6-cm/2½-inch round out of it. Pop the lid on, damp the edges and seal. Bake in a moderately hot oven (190C, 375F, gas 5) for 30–40 minutes. Five minutes before cooking time is up, remove from oven, coat with lightly beaten egg white and sprinkle with castor sugar. Pop back in oven.

Whip up the cream with remaining liquid from pears. Spoon into hole in pastry. Serve hot or cold. SERVES 6–8.

Mrs E. M. Scott, Whitby, North Yorkshire

RASPBERRY ALMOND TART

FILLING
450 g/1 lb fresh raspberries
75 g/3 oz sugar
2 teaspoons cornflour
PASTRY
100 g/4 oz wheatmeal flour

50 g/2 oz ground almonds
100 g/4 oz margarine or butter
50 g/2 oz castor sugar
1 egg yolk
icing sugar to decorate

SIMMER raspberries gently with sugar, add cornflour mixed with a little cold water and boil to thicken, stirring carefully. Leave to cool while making the pastry.

Mix flour and ground almonds and rub in margarine until like breadcrumbs. Add sugar to mixture and bind with egg yolk and enough water to make a stiff dough. Leave to rest in fridge for 30 minutes.

Reserve a quarter of the pastry for the top and roll out the rest to fit a 20-cm/8-inch tin or flan dish. Fill with the raspberry mixture and use the reserved pastry to make a lattice pattern on top. Cook for 30 minutes in a moderately hot oven (200 c, 400 f, gas 6). Sieve icing sugar over the top when warm and serve warm or cold with cream. SERVES 4–6.

Mrs J. D. Bennett, Wymeswold, Leicestershire

GOOSEBERRY MERINGUE PIE

PASTRY
225 g/8 oz plain flour
pinch of salt
125 g/4½ oz butter
1 teaspoon icing sugar
1 egg yolk
½ teaspoon lemon juice
1–2 tablespoons cold water
FILLING
675 g/1½ lb young gooseberries

65 g/2½ oz butter
1 small head of elderflower
sugar to taste
2 egg yolks
MERINGUE
3 egg whites
165 g/5½ oz castor sugar
1½ tablespoons granulated sugar

SIFT the flour with the salt and rub in the butter. Add the icing sugar and bind with the egg yolk, lemon juice and sufficient cold water to make a firm dough. Chill in the refrigerator for 30 minutes then roll out to line a 20-cm/8-inch flan dish. Bake blind in a moderately hot oven (190 c, 375 f, gas 5) for 20–25 minutes, or until pale golden. Cool.

Top and tail gooseberries. Melt butter in a large pan, add gooseberries, stir with a wooden spoon, then add elderflower head. Cover and cook gently for about 7 minutes, or until fruit has softened. Remove elderflower head, take pan off the heat and crush fruit with wooden spoon. Add sugar to taste then stir in the egg yolks. When cool put mixture into prepared pastry shell.

Whisk egg whites until stiff, fold in half the castor sugar, whisk again until stiff then fold in rest of castor sugar and whisk until stiff. Pipe the meringue attractively over pie shell and gooseberry filling. Sprinkle with granulated sugar and bake for 30–35 minutes in a very cool oven (120 c, 250 f, gas ½) or until meringue is a delicate biscuit colour and crisp. Serve warm or cold. SERVES 6–8.

Mrs Eileen Massie, Swarestone, Staffordshire

BANANA MERINGUE PIE

PASTRY
100 g/4 oz margarine
75 g/3 oz icing sugar
1 egg yolk
225 g/8 oz self-raising flour
FILLING
1 tablespoon cornflour
6 tablespoons milk
1 tablespoon sugar
15 g/½ oz butter

2 egg yolks
½ teaspoon vanilla essence
jam of choice
2–3 bananas
3 egg whites
75 g/3 oz castor sugar for
  meringue
glacé cherries and angelica for
  decoration

MAKE pastry. Rub margarine into icing sugar, beat in egg yolk and cream together with flour, adding a little milk if necessary. Chill in fridge for 30 minutes.

Line an 18-cm/7-inch pie dish with pastry and bake blind in a moderately hot oven (200 c, 400 f, gas 6) for 10–15 minutes.

Make paste with cornflour and a little of the milk. Boil remaining milk, sugar and butter together. When boiling, pour on to cornflour, stirring all the time. Return to pan and cook until thickened. Cool slightly and stir in egg yolks. Add vanilla essence.

Spread jam on bottom of pastry case, slice bananas on top. Pour over the sauce. Whisk the egg whites stiffly and fold in the 75 g/3 oz castor sugar. Pile on top of tart and decorate with glacé cherries and angelica. Return to a hot oven (220 c, 425 f, gas 7) for 3–5 minutes, or until brown. Serve while still warm. SERVES 6.

Mrs Kathleen Smith, Slackbooth, Lancashire

MY GRANNIE'S CURD CHEESE CAKES

1.15 litres/2 pints milk
1 tablespoon rennet
100 g/4 oz butter
100 g/4 oz castor sugar
4 egg yolks
1 egg white

grated rind of 1 lemon
75 g/3 oz ratafias
2 tablespoons sherry
a few currants
nutmeg
225 g/8 oz pastry of choice

WARM milk and add rennet, leave until cold. Turn on to a hair sieve and press whey out, leaving the curds. Cream butter and sugar, add well beaten eggs, grated lemon rind, crushed ratafias, sherry, currants, a little grated nutmeg and the curds.

Line patty tins or a flan ring with pastry – I use a biscuit one – add filling and bake for 20–30 minutes in a moderately hot oven (200 c, 400 f, gas 6).

A good tip is to soak the currants in the sherry before adding to the mixture.

Mrs Dorothy Skinner, Bala, Gwynedd

☆ MINT AND CURRANT ☆ PASTY

100 g/4 oz prepared shortcrust
   pastry (100 g/4 oz flour etc.)
50 g/2 oz butter
50 g/2 oz sugar

75 g/3 oz currants
3 tablespoons chopped mint (apple
   mint is nicest)

EITHER roll pastry into a square, mix other ingredients together, place on one half then fold other half over and crimp edges; or make a plate pie, in which case fill pie rather thickly. Bake in a moderately hot oven (200 c, 400 f, gas 6) until golden brown – about 35–45 minutes. This is a traditional Yorkshire speciality. SERVES 4.

Mrs P. Lester, Broadwas-on-Teme, Worcestershire

ALMOND PUFF

If you're making almond paste for the Christmas cake, make a little extra for this delicious recipe, which can either be eaten hot as a sweet or cold for tea.

225 g/8 oz puff pastry

about 225 g/8 oz almond paste

ROLL out puff pastry into two oblong strips or into rounds, whichever is preferred. Roll almond paste to 1 cm/½ inch smaller and place between the two layers of puff pastry. Seal the edges with water, cut slits in the top layer to decorate and cook in a hot oven (220 c, 425 f, gas 7) for about 15–20 minutes, until golden. Delicious! SERVES 6–8.

Lavinia Dolbear, Holwell, Dorset

NORFOLK APPLE AND
BLACKBERRY PUDDING

100 g/4 oz margarine or butter
225 g/8 oz self-raising flour
50 g/2 oz castor sugar
4 tablespoons milk

FILLING
275 g/10 oz cooking apples
225 g/8 oz blackberries
175 g/6 oz dark soft brown sugar

WELL grease a 1.25-litre/2-pint pudding basin with butter and sift over a light coating of brown sugar.

Rub the margarine into the sifted flour until it resembles fine breadcrumbs. Stir in the sugar then the milk and bring together to form a stiff dough (similar to a scone mixture). Knead lightly in the bowl to form a ball. Turn on to a lightly floured surface and remove one-third of the dough for the lid. Roll out rest of dough to form a 20-cm/8-inch circle and use to line the pudding basin, moulding the dough to fit the basin if necessary.

For the filling, peel and thinly slice the apples and wash together with the blackberries. Layer the fruit and sugar into the pudding basin, starting with a layer of blackberries and ending with a top layer of apples, pressing down firmly. Roll out the remainder of the dough to form a lid. Cover the pudding with this, pinching the edges well together to seal. Cover with a layer of greaseproof paper and pleated aluminium foil. Place in a steamer or large pan two-thirds full of boiling water and steam for $2\frac{1}{2}$ hours.

Remove paper coverings, loosen with a knife around sides, and carefully turn out on to a flat serving dish. The butter and sugar outer coating will have melted to form a caramel glaze, while the brown sugar and fruits will form a rich syrup mixture inside. Serve with double cream and extra brown sugar if wished. SERVES 4.

Miss K. M. Roberson, Beetley, Norfolk

APPLE AND BLACKBERRY
SOUFFLÉ PUDDING WITH SHERRY
SAUCE

75 g/3 oz butter
75 g/3 oz flour
175 ml/6 fl oz milk
75 g/3 oz sugar

2 eggs, separated
100 g/4 oz blackberries
2 large cooking apples, peeled,
    cored and sliced

MELT the butter and stir in the flour. Pour over the milk a little at a time and stir until thick. Pull off the heat. Add the sugar, egg yolks, blackberries and apple. Lastly fold in the well beaten egg whites. Place in a covered greased pudding basin and steam for 1 hour, or until firm. Allow to stand for 5 minutes before turning out.

For sherry sauce, place 1 egg yolk and 1 whole egg, 2 tablespoons sugar and 2 tablespoons sherry in the top of a double boiler. Beat until thick over the hot water, then pour over the pudding. SERVES 4–5.

Mrs K. Y. Trounce, Portloe, Cornwall

MOCK CHRISTMAS PUDDING

2 tablespoons fine sago	50 g/2 oz shredded suet
250 ml/8 fl oz milk	½ teaspoon bicarbonate of soda
2 tablespoons soft brown sugar	½ teaspoon ground mixed spice
50 g/2 oz fresh breadcrumbs	handful currants, raisins or dates

SOAK sago for 10 minutes in the milk. Mix all ingredients together, place in a greased pudding basin, cover and steam 2–3 hours. Serve with rum sauce or custard. SERVES 4.

This recipe has been handed down and is a lovely light pudding.

Mrs Helen Douglass, Kirkwhelpington, Newcastle upon Tyne

STEAMED FRUIT ROLY-POLY

225 g/8 oz shortcrust pastry	25 g/1 oz castor sugar
75 g/3 oz currants or other dried fruit	50 g/2 oz butter

ROLL out pastry to rough oblong. Sprinkle currants over pastry, leaving space round edge. Sprinkle castor sugar on top and dot with knobs of butter. Roll up pastry and filling and seal edge; it should look like a Swiss roll. Gently bend shape round so it will fit into a steamer. Wrap loosely in greased greaseproof paper and a double thickness of cooking foil, then steam for about 1½ hours.

To serve, slice up as you would a Swiss roll. Can be served with butter and more sugar sprinkled over, or with custard. A simple, cheap and filling recipe for a winter's day. SERVES 4.

Mrs J. Shepperson, Poulton, Gloucestershire

SUSSEX POND PUDDING

225 g/8 oz self-raising flour, sieved
100 g/4 oz fresh breadcrumbs
100 g/4 oz shredded suet
pinch of salt
equal quantities of milk and
   water to mix

handful of currants
grated rind of 1 lemon
175 g/6 oz butter
175 g/6 oz brown sugar

MIX the flour, breadcrumbs, suet and salt with enough milk and water to form a soft, not sticky, dough. Divide the mixture into two-thirds and one-third. Roll each piece into a thick round, pressing a few currants in for decoration.

Line a 1.25-litre/2-pint greased pudding basin with the larger round. Mix lemon rind, butter, sugar and remaining currants together, and spoon into the crust. Gather the edges of the pudding together and cover with the second pastry round. Cover with greaseproof paper and a cloth, and steam for 2 hours, topping up saucepan with boiling water as necessary. SERVES 6.

Mrs J. C. Phillips, Caversham, Berkshire

DELICIOUS PUDDING

1 teacup milk
1 teaspoon bicarbonate of soda
1 teacup chopped suet

1 teacup plain flour
1 teacup breadcrumbs
1 teacup jam or golden syrup

WARM milk. Add bicarbonate of soda. Mix suet, flour, breadcrumbs and jam together. Add milk and mix well. Put into a greased 900-ml/1½-pint pudding basin and steam for 3 hours. SERVES 6.

Joan Crockett, Winterbourne, nr Bristol

CLOUTIE DUMPLING

450 g/1 lb plain flour
175 g/6 oz sugar
50 g/2 oz fresh breadcrumbs
225 g/8 oz shredded suet
1 teaspoon bicarbonate of soda
1 teaspoon ground ginger
1 teaspoon ground mixed spice
1 teaspoon ground cinnamon

1 teaspoon salt
225 g/8 oz sultanas or raisins
225 g/8 oz currants
1 tablespoon syrup
1 tablespoon treacle
1 egg
milk to mix

PUT all the dry ingredients into a bowl. Warm the syrup and treacle and mix to a soft consistency with the egg and milk. Put into a scalded and floured cloth; you wring the cloth out of boiling water and shake the flour over it. Tie the cloth above the contents, leaving space for the pudding to swell. Sit on a plate in a large pan with enough boiling water to come halfway up the pudding. Keep boiling, not too briskly, for 4 hours; top up with boiling water if necessary. Serve hot with custard.

This is very good sliced cold next day like cake, or fried for a dessert. It is very popular in Scotland, especially in cold weather. My mother used to make it for Sunday night tea long long ago. SERVES 6–8.

Mrs K. Macrae, Munlochy, Ross-shire

☆ LEMON PUDDING ☆

1 medium lemon
2 medium oranges
225 g/8 oz self-raising flour
pinch salt
100 g/4 oz margarine

100 g/4 oz castor sugar
½ teaspoon mixed spice
1 medium egg, lightly beaten
freshly made custard or whipped
cream

WASH the fruit and cut each into roughly eight pieces, place in blender and switch to fast speed. Blend to a pulp, adding a little water if liked. Strain and reserve the pulp; the juice can be diluted and sweetened to taste as a drink.

Sift the flour and salt and rub in margarine. Stir in the sugar, mixed spice, fruit pulp and beaten egg. Mix thoroughly. Turn into a greased and lined 18-cm/7-inch cake tin and bake for 1¼ hours at 180 C, 350 F, gas 4, or steam for 2 hours in a 1.25-litre/2-pint pudding basin covered with greaseproof paper.

Turn on to a warm plate and serve with custard or whipped cream. SERVES 6.

Mrs V. J. Creek, Woodmancote, Sussex

LEMON BATTER PUDDING AND LEMON SAUCE

PUDDING
100 g/4 oz plain flour
25 g/1 oz castor sugar
grated rind of 1 lemon
2 eggs, separated
300 ml/½ pint milk

1 small banana, sliced
SAUCE
juice of 1 lemon
1 tablespoon lemon curd
1½ teaspoons cornflour

Mix flour, sugar, lemon rind and egg yolks. Add milk to make a smooth batter and stir in banana. Whisk egg whites until stiff and fold into batter. Pour into buttered dish and cook for 30 minutes in a hot oven (220 c, 425 f, gas 7).

Meanwhile make sauce. Whisk together lemon juice and lemon curd, make up to 300 ml/½ pint with water. Mix a little with cornflour to make a paste and boil remainder. Add cornflour paste and stir until smooth and thickened.

Sprinkle pudding with castor sugar and serve immediately with sauce and whipped cream. SERVES 4.

Mrs M. E. Jones, Horton, Dorset

MERINGUE CITRUS CRUMBLE

225 g/8 oz sugar
350 g/12 oz flour
175 g/6 oz margarine
50 g/2 oz almond flakes
2 lemons
2 oranges

MERINGUE
3 egg whites
175 g/6 oz castor sugar
flaked almonds and orange slices
  to decorate

Mix sugar, flour, margarine as for crumble. Mix in almonds. Peel and thinly slice lemons and oranges, a little rind having been grated and added to the crumble first. Into a pie dish, layer one-third of crumble then sliced orange, then crumble, sliced lemon, then the final layer of crumble. Cook for 20 minutes in a moderately hot oven (190 c, 375 f, gas 5).

Meanwhile make meringue. Whisk egg whites. Whisk in 25 g/1 oz castor sugar, fold in remaining sugar. Place on top of crumble and cook for further 15 minutes. Decorate with a few flaked almonds and orange slices 15 minutes before end of cooking. SERVES 6–8.

Mrs Rosamond Smith, Wotton-under-Edge, Gloucestershire

☆ WALNUT PUDDING ☆

5 eggs
225 g/8 oz castor sugar
175 g/6 oz ground walnuts or
  hazelnuts

large pinch ground cinnamon

BEAT eggs with sugar till creamy and thick. Fold in ground walnuts and spice. Turn into a buttered pudding basin and cook in a moderate oven (180 C, 350 F, gas 4) until set, about 50 minutes.

For a less rich variation, use half the amount and spread on sweet crust pastry to cook as a tart. SERVES 6.

Mrs Holt, Crowsley, Oxfordshire

AUTUMN PANCAKES

PANCAKES
50 g/2 oz plain flour
pinch of salt
1 egg
150 ml/¼ pint milk
1 tablespoon cold water
lard or fat for cooking
FILLING
1 small Cox apple, peeled, cored
  and grated

100 g/4 oz blackberries
¼ teaspoon ground cinnamon
honey or brown sugar to sweeten
TOPPING
1 large egg white
50 g/2 oz castor sugar
25 g/1 oz toasted hazelnuts

FOR the pancakes, sieve the flour and salt. Add the egg and milk and beat until smooth. Mix in the water and leave in a cool place for approximately 20 minutes. Melt knob of fat in frying pan, add 2 tablespoons of batter. Cook until first side is golden, toss and cook other side. Repeat until all batter is used.

For filling, gently simmer apple, blackberries and cinnamon and sweeten to taste. Spoon the filling on to pancakes and roll up each one.

For topping, whisk egg white until stiff. Fold in sugar and whisk again. Spread over the pancakes and sprinkle with chopped, toasted hazelnuts. Cook in a hot oven (220 C, 425 F, gas 7) for about 3–5 minutes, or until beginning to brown. Serve with or without single cream. SERVES 4.

Mrs S. A. Rose, Bluntisham, Cambridgeshire

EGG AND SULTANA PUDDING

50 g/2 oz sultanas
600 ml/1 pint milk
4 eggs
75 g/3 oz sugar

pinch of salt
1 slice bread and butter
grated nutmeg

GREASE a deep round pudding dish. Sprinkle the sultanas on the bottom of the dish. Whisk together the milk, eggs, sugar and salt. Pour into the pudding dish. Break the slice of bread into small pieces and place buttered side down over the pudding. Sprinkle with grated nutmeg and bake for 25–30 minutes in a moderately hot oven (190 C, 375 F, gas 5), until brown on top and completely set. Serve hot or cold. SERVES 4.

Mrs E. M. Dale, Wetley Rocks, Staffordshire

PURPLE PUDDING

1 heaped tablespoon cornflour
600 ml/1 pint milk
2 heaped tablespoons blackberry
  and apple jam (preferably made
  so that blackberries are
  whole and chunks of apple
  remain)

sugar to taste

PUT all ingredients except for the sugar in a saucepan and stir frequently until mixture thickens. Simmer for 1 minute, taste and add sugar if you like, then serve hot. "Purple Pudding" should by this time be pale mauve with purple blackberry and apple spots.

If there is any leftover it can be served cold by which time it will have just set and actually taste quite different but equally delicious. Any other jam will do but blackberry and apple makes the best colour. SERVES 4.

Miss H. K. Faux, Tonbridge, Kent

COLD PUDDINGS

Swiss Toffee Apple

1 kg/2 lb cooking apples
150 g/5 oz granulated sugar
50 g/2 oz butter
1 rounded tablespoon golden
  syrup

100 g/4 oz cornflakes
150 ml/¼ pint double cream

PEEL, core and slice apples, put into a saucepan, add 100 g/4 oz sugar and 2 tablespoons water. Cook the apples gently until soft.

Strain off juice from apples, then liquidise fruit or press through a sieve to make a purée, adding some of the strained juice if necessary to make a thick sauce. Spread sauce into a serving dish and leave aside until cold.

Melt the butter and golden syrup together, add the remaining sugar and the cornflakes. Stir quickly together until the flakes are coated and spoon evenly over the apple sauce. Whip the cream until soft but stiff and spread over the top.

Chill before serving. SERVES 4.

Miss Caroline Oates, Belford, Northumberland

BLUSHING APPLES

THIS is an ideal pudding for autumn in the country and turns cooking apples into a party dish.

Peel and core six apples of even size. Put in lidded oven dish. Cover with a syrup made of sugar and water to which half a jar of redcurrant or plum jelly has been added. Baste apples frequently with red syrup and cook slowly in the oven until tender. Remove gently on to a dish. Pour remaining syrup round and leave until cold. Fill centres with whipped cream and a dusting of chopped hazelnuts. SERVES 6.

Mrs Elspeth Ritchie, Barbreck, Argyll

SPICY CREAM BAKED PEARS

Pears and cream, a classic and delightful combination, are a true reminder that autumn is on the way. This simple pudding can be served at the most sophisticated dinner party. A smooth creamy custard, flavoured with a hint of spice and the mellow taste of soft brown sugar, covers the pears, and the whole dish is offset by a delicious crunchy almond topping; irresistible and scrumptious!

4 ripe pears, peeled, poached and drained
300 ml/½ pint whipping cream
2 large egg yolks
2 tablespoons light soft brown sugar

1 teaspoon ground cinnamon
75 g/3 oz flaked almonds
demerara sugar to sprinkle

PLACE pears in a shallow ovenproof dish suitable for serving. Scald the cream. In a basin stir together the egg yolks, soft brown sugar and cinnamon, then blend in the hot cream. Pour over pears. Stand dish in a pan containing hot water and bake in a moderate oven (160 c, 325 F, gas 3) for about 30 minutes, until custard is just firm. Cool and chill in refrigerator.

About 1 hour before serving, sprinkle the top of the pears with almonds and demerara sugar to completely cover. Place under a hot grill until almonds are brown and the sugar has caramelised. SERVES 4.

Victoria Gray, Chilton, Buckinghamshire

STRAWBERRIES IN CIDER

1 kg/2 lb strawberries
600 ml/1 pint sweet cider

3 heads well-opened elderflowers
sugar to taste

CUT the strawberries in half or quarter if very large. Marinate overnight in the cider with the elderflowers in a muslin bag.

Drain and set strawberries aside. Boil the cider and elderflowers briskly until reduced by half. Sweeten if necessary, allow to cool, strain and pour over strawberries.

Chill well and serve in individual glasses with thickly whipped cream. SERVES 6–8.

David Alexander, Wye, Kent

BLACKCURRANT ROYALE

450 g/1 lb blackcurrants
6 tablespoons water
50 g/2 oz sugar
a little cornflour
75 g/3 oz margarine

75 g/3 oz demerara sugar
175 g/6 oz rolled oats
175 ml/6 fl oz double cream
75 g/3 oz plain chocolate

COOK the blackcurrants, water and sugar in a saucepan until tender. Thicken with a little cornflour, made into a paste with cold water. Leave to cool.

Melt the margarine and demerara sugar in a saucepan. Add the rolled oats and mix well. Spread half this mixture over the base of the serving dish, tip in the blackcurrants and spread the remaining oat mixture on top. Whip the cream until thick and spread it over the oat mixture. Grate the chocolate and sprinkle evenly over the cream. Chill until ready to serve. SERVES 6.

Mrs N. Kay, High Post, Wiltshire

BRAMBLE DESSERT

450 g/1 lb cooking apples
175 g/6 oz blackberries
50 g/2 oz sugar
100 g/4 oz fresh breadcrumbs

50 g/2 oz soft light brown sugar
50 g/2 oz butter
whipped cream to decorate

PEEL and core apples, slice and put in a pan with the blackberries and sugar. A very little water may be added. Stew gently until soft. Cool.

Mix breadcrumbs with brown sugar. Melt butter in a pan, add breadcrumb mixture and stir well. Cool.

In a glass serving dish layer the fruit then breadcrumbs alternately, finishing with a layer of crumbs. Chill for 2 hours and decorate with cream to serve. SERVES 6.

Anon.

APPLE MERINGUE

5 cooking apples
water
sugar to taste
3 egg whites

175 g/6 oz castor sugar
1 teaspoon sieved cornflour
¼ teaspoon vanilla essence
½ teaspoon malt vinegar

PEEL, quarter, core and slice apples. Cook with a little water and sugar to taste.

Whisk egg whites until stiff, add sugar, whisk until very stiff, fold in cornflour, vanilla and vinegar.

Put cooled apple into a shallow ovenproof dish, spoon meringue mixture on top to cover the apple, flat or rough.

Cook in a cool oven (150 c, 300 f, gas 2) for 1 hour. Turn off oven, leaving meringue inside to dry out for a further 30 minutes.

Cool and serve at room temperature with whipped cream. SERVES 4–6.

Mrs J. Earl, Newent, Gloucestershire

PEACH PUDDING

40 g/1½ oz cornflour
50 g/2 oz sugar, plus 1 tablespoon
2 eggs, separated

1 425-g/15-oz can peach halves
450 ml/¾ pint milk
50 g/2 oz butter

MIX cornflour, 1 tablespoon sugar, the egg yolks and juice from the peaches in a bowl until smooth. Put milk and butter in a pan and bring gently to the boil. Stir in the cornflour mixture and cook until it thickens.

Arrange peaches over the base of an ovenproof dish and pour mixture over. Beat egg whites until they stand in peaks. Add sugar to make a meringue. Put in a hot oven (230 c, 450 F, gas 8) for a few minutes to brown and then place in the fridge for 3–4 hours. SERVES 4.

This is a handy pudding in winter as it uses tinned fruit, when fresh fruit is not so readily available. Any other fruit can be used such as pineapple or pears.

Mrs R. Jones, Llanfachraeth, Holyhead

RHUBARB SPRING PUDDING

1 kg/2 lb young rhubarb
juice of ½ lemon
150 g/5 oz soft brown sugar
few drops red food colouring
   (optional)

butter
about 8 slices white bread, crusts
   removed

CUT leaves and bottom part of rhubarb off. Wash and drain well and slice into 5-cm/2-inch pieces.

Place rhubarb in saucepan with lemon juice, sugar, food colouring and 3 tablespoons water. Simmer gently, turning the rhubarb occasionally, until tender. Strain the rhubarb and cool, reserving the liquid.

Butter a 1.25-litre/2-pint mould well and fit the slices of bread over the sides and bottom of the mould, to completely cover. Press the rhubarb firmly into the bread-lined mould. Pour enough of the reserved liquid on to the rhubarb to soak the bread down the sides of the mould. Cut the remaining slices of bread to fit the top of the mould and press into place. Weight down with a saucer and heavy weights and chill until quite firm.

Unmould the pudding carefully on to a platter and serve with cream. SERVES 6.

Claire Wootton, Battlers Green, Hertfordshire

RASPBERRY MARSHMALLOW CREAM

350 g/12 oz fresh or frozen
　raspberries
25 marshmallows
175 ml/6 fl oz single cream

3 tablespoons apricot brandy
150 ml/¼ pint double cream
a few whole raspberries

PUT defrosted raspberries in shallow glass dish. Melt marshmallows in single cream over low heat. When melted allow to cool thoroughly. Add apricot brandy and fold in stiffly whisked double cream, pile on to raspberries and decorate with whole raspberries. SERVES 4–6.

Mrs Eaton Goldsmith, Wattisfield, Norfolk

☆ RASPBERRY AND ORANGE ☆ CREAMY DESSERT

2 large oranges
675 g/1½ lb raspberries
2 rounded tablespoons castor
　sugar

300 ml/½ pint double cream
150 ml/¼ pint natural yogurt
2 rounded tablespoons icing sugar

TAKE a narrow sliver of orange peel and shred finely for decoration. Reserve 10 raspberries.

Peel and slice one orange, then mix with 450 g/1 lb raspberries and the castor sugar. Put into a glass serving bowl.

Crush remaining raspberries and sieve to extract the juice, leaving the seeds in the sieve (to be discarded). Extract the juice from the second orange. Whip together the raspberry juice, orange juice, cream, yogurt and icing sugar until thick. Pile this creamy mixture on top of the raspberries and orange slices.

Decorate by placing the reserved raspberries alternately with a few shreds of orange peel around the edge of the dish. Set aside in a cool place or refrigerator. Make at least 2 hours before required to allow the flavours to blend. SERVES 6.

Mrs Barbara Briggs, Winmarleigh, Lancashire

CRUNCHY RASPBERRY CREAM

100 g/4 oz plain flour
100 g/4 oz butter
50 g/2 oz demerara sugar
50 g/2 oz chopped hazelnuts
4 tablespoons hot water
15 g/½ oz powdered gelatine

450 g/1 lb raspberries
juice of 1 lemon
175 g/6 oz castor sugar
300 ml/½ pint double cream
extra cream to decorate

FIRST make the crunchy mixture by rubbing together the flour and butter, then stir in the demerara sugar and nuts. Scatter over a shallow baking tin and bake for 10–15 minutes in a moderately hot oven (200 C, 400 F, gas 6). Leave to cool, then crumble it into a mixing bowl.

Put the water into a small bowl, sprinkle over the gelatine and leave to soften. Mash a quarter of the raspberries in a saucepan, add the lemon juice and castor sugar and bring to the boil. Take off the heat, add the softened gelatine and stir until completely dissolved. Pour a little of this mixture through a strainer into the base of an 18-cm/7-inch cake tin, rubbed with oil, to a depth of 1 cm/½ inch, and leave to cool but not quite set. Whip the cream until just holding its shape. Fold the cream and whole raspberries into the remaining half-set raspberry mixture then immediately fill the tin with alternate layers of raspberry cream and crumble, starting with raspberry cream and ending with crumble. Leave in refrigerator for 24 hours if possible to set.

Turn the Crunchy Raspberry Cream out on to a plate; first dipping the tin into hand-hot water, then place plate on top of tin and turn upside-down. Decorate with cream, whipped until it just holds its shape; using a large star pipe, pipe round base and top with a whirl in the centre.

This pudding is really good made with other summer fruits, strawberries, blackberries etc, and is successful using frozen fruits too. SERVES 6.

Mrs C. J. McCulloch, Hopton, Staffordshire

RASPBERRIES IN PORT JELLY

450 g/1 lb frozen raspberries
½ raspberry jelly

6 tablespoons port
150 ml/¼ pint double cream

LET raspberries thaw at room temperature. Make raspberry jelly with 150 ml/¼ pint boiling water. When cool add port. Pour over raspberries.

When set, serve with double cream. SERVES 4.

Edna Cullimore, Berkeley, Gloucestershire

QUICK AND EASY PINK PUD

TAKE 600 ml/1 pint strained mixed pink fruit juice – say strawberry, raspberry, any currants or rhubarb, damson, blackberry. Add sugar to taste.

Dissolve 15 g/½ oz powdered gelatine in 150 ml/¼ pint of above juices, mix and leave to cool with remainder of juice. Leave to setting point.

Whisk 300 ml/½ pint cream and mix with setting juice. Pour into glass dish and allow to set in fridge. Decorate with a little leftover fruit. SERVES 4.

Mrs P. S. Nicholson, Whithorn, Wigtownshire

SRAWBERRY YOGURT JELLY

1 strawberry jelly
150 ml/¼ pint boiling water

600 ml/1 pint natural yogurt

DISSOLVE the jelly in the water, cool and mix in the yogurt. Pour into a dish or individual containers, place in refrigerator and leave to set.

This refreshing dessert can be made with any of the favourite flavoured jellies, and tinned fruit can be added, the juice being used to dissolve the jelly and the fruit being mixed in with the yogurt. This is an extremely economical recipe if homemade yogurt is used. SERVES 6.

Mrs Celia Haynes, Headley, Hampshire

EASY SUMMER SWEET

350–450 g/12–16 oz fruit
300 ml/½ pint whipping cream

450 ml/¾ pint natural yogurt
8 tablespoons demerara sugar

PREPARE fresh fruit, such as strawberries, peaches or raspberries, or gently poach and sweeten to taste apricots, apples and blackberries, or any fruit of choice; canned peaches, apricots and crushed pineapple are also good. Drain fruit and place in deep serving dish.

Whip the cream then mix in the yogurt and pour on top of fruit. Sprinkle thickly with the sugar and leave overnight in fridge.

I also like to flavour this with grated lemon rind or a little grated nutmeg. SERVES 6.

Mrs Clara Black, Kentmere, Cumbria

PINEAPPLE FLUFF

15 g/½ oz powdered gelatine
2 tablespoons lemon juice
3 eggs, separated
225 g/8 oz castor sugar

1 large can evaporated milk
1 376-g/13¼-oz can crushed
   pineapple

DISSOLVE gelatine in heated lemon juice. Beat egg yolks and sugar until thick and light, add cooled dissolved gelatine. Fold in whipped evaporated milk, stiffly beaten egg whites and lastly pineapple and juice. Allow to set in fridge. SERVES 6.

If evaporated milk is boiled in the tin for 1½ hours then cooled overnight, it whips up stiffer.

Anon.

PINEAPPLE PUDDING

50 g/2 oz margarine
150 ml/¼ pint milk
2 tablespoons flour
2 tablespoons sugar

pinch of salt
2 eggs
1 439-g/15-oz can pineapple pieces

MELT margarine in milk in saucepan over heat. Do not boil. Mix flour, sugar and salt with a little extra milk and add to milk in saucepan. Bring this mixture to the boil and stir until it becomes a thick paste. Allow to cool. Add eggs and drained pineapple juice and beat well with electric mixer. Pour on to pineapple pieces in a dish and allow to stand in refrigerator. SERVES 4.

Mrs Madge Burton, Raunds, Northamptonshire

Spring Blancmange

675 g/1½ lb rhubarb
900 ml/1½ pints water
275 g/10 oz sugar
175 g/6 oz ground rice

50 g/2 oz flaked almonds
few drops of almond essence or
lemon juice

Put rhubarb and water into a saucepan and cook until tender, then strain through sieve or put into liquidiser. Return purée to pan, add sugar and when dissolved add ground rice (made into a paste with cold water).

Add nuts and boil until rice is cooked. Add essence or lemon juice to taste, pour into a wetted mould, turn out when quite cold and set. Serves 6.

Mrs Pamela Burge, Brafield-on-the-Green, Northamptonshire

Jellied Rhubarb Delight

450 g/1 lb rhubarb
sugar to taste
1 red jelly – raspberry is best

150 ml/¼ pint double cream
whole raspberries and angelica
strips to decorate

Wash and trim rhubarb. Cut into 2.5-cm/1-inch lengths and stew gently with sugar to taste and 4 tablespoons water until it resembles a pulp when stirred. Leave to cool.

Dissolve jelly in 300 ml/½ pint boiling water. Add rhubarb and enough juice to make up to 600 ml/1 pint. Pour into four individual jelly moulds and leave in refrigerator to set.

When set turn on to small plates and pipe whipped cream around sides and on top of each jelly, using a large star nozzle. Decorate each star with a fresh raspberry and thin strips of angelica on each side of raspberry to resemble leaves.

This sweet is very economical and refreshing on hot summer days. Serves 4.

Mrs Anne Bailey, Long Clawson, Leicestershire

Fluffed Rhubarb Cream

450 g/1 lb rhubarb
175 g/6 oz sugar
15 g/½ oz powdered gelatine

2 egg whites
150 ml/¼ pint whipping cream

Gently stew the rhubarb with the sugar and a little water until soft. Dissolve the gelatine in 2 tablespoons hot water and stir into the hot fruit. When cold, but not setting, stir in the stiffly beaten egg whites and then the whipped cream. Pour into a dish and chill until set. SERVES 4–6.

Mrs Ann Shrive, Brigstock, Northamptonshire

TANGY RHUBARB MOUSSE

450 g/1 lb rhubarb
50–75 g/2–3 oz sugar
1 raspberry jelly

½ large can evaporated milk, chilled

WASH rhubarb and cut into 2.5-cm/1-inch pieces, stew gently with sugar to taste until tender. Dissolve the jelly directly into the stewed fruit. The resulting mixture is then made up to approximately 450 ml/¾ pint with water and allowed to cool until just about setting (this is important). Reserve a little of the jelly mixture to decorate.

In a large bowl whisk the evaporated milk until really frothy and thick. Gradually and slowly beat in the fruit/jelly mixture until you have a lovely pink dessert. Pour the dessert into a bowl, then swirl the reserved jelly on top to decorate. Leave until quite set.

You can serve this with whipped cream but it is equally delicious on its own – sharp, tangy and mouth-watering. Children love it as well as adults. You can set it in individual glasses or in plastic or paper cups for picnics, lovely too for kids' lunches. SERVES 4–5.

Mrs L. Rawlings, Littleton Drew, Wiltshire

APPLE POSSET

4 large Cox's Orange Pippin
  apples
1 medium jar homemade
  raspberry jam

600 ml/1 pint custard
300 ml/½ pint whipping cream
toasted flaked almonds

PEEL apples and grate into serving dish. Mix together thoroughly apples and jam. Pour custard over. Leave to cool. Decorate with whipped cream and almonds. SERVES 4–6.

Mrs Marjorie Gatley, Rushwick, Worcestershire

☆ BLACKBERRY CREAM ☆

450 g/1 lb blackberries
150 ml/¼ pint double cream
100 g/4 oz castor sugar

2 tablespoons Calvados (apple brandy)

RESERVING a few blackberries for decoration, liquidise the rest then strain to remove pips. Whip cream, gradually adding blackberry purée and sugar. Add Calvados a little at a time to taste. Serve in glass goblets, each topped with whole reserved blackberries. SERVES 4.

J. Pilgrim, Queens Camel, Somerset

BLACKBERRY CLOUDS

1 kg/2 lb freshly picked
    blackberries
100 g/4 oz granulated sugar

600 ml/1 pint water
1 packet lime jelly
150 ml/¼ pint double cream

PUT blackberries, sugar and water into a covered casserole, stir well and leave in the bottom of a cool oven (150 C, 300 F, gas 2) until the berries are mushy. Remove the casserole from the oven and cool; strain the fruit mixture through a jelly bag overnight, then discard pips.

Snip the lime jelly cubes into small pieces and dissolve them in 3 tablespoons boiling water; add this to the blackberry juice and stir very thoroughly.

Divide between six individual bowls (glass ones look best) and leave until the mixture begins to set. Add cream to each, pouring slowly, and a cloud-like shape will set just under the surface. Keep until needed on the "cold shelf" or other cool place – not in the refrigerator, as the jelly should only be very lightly set. SERVES 6.

Elizabeth Turner, Ogbourne St Andrew, Wiltshire

BRAMBLE MOUSSE

450 g/1 lb blackberries
100 g/4 oz castor sugar
juice of ½ lemon
15 g/½ oz powdered gelatine
3 tablespoons water

1 small can evaporated milk,
  chilled
3 egg whites
cream and blackberries for
  decoration

PUT blackberries in saucepan with sugar and lemon juice. Gently simmer for a few minutes until sugar has dissolved and juices run from blackberries. Soften gelatine in the water then stir into blackberries until dissolved. Sieve and leave until they start to thicken.

Put evaporated milk in a bowl and whisk briskly with an electric whisk until thick. Put egg whites in a clean bowl and whisk until stiff. Whisk blackberry purée into evaporated milk until evenly blended then fold in egg whites carefully.

Turn into a 1.75-litre/3-pint dish and leave to set. Decorate with piped whipped cream and a few blackberries. SERVES 6.

Rita Robinson, Yaddlethorpe, South Humberside

BLACKCURRANT FLUMMERY

300 ml/½ pint water
25 g/1 oz margarine
25 g/1 oz plain flour
100 g/4 oz castor sugar

1 egg, separated
450 g/1 lb fresh blackcurrants,
  puréed and sieved
whipped cream to decorate

HEAT water and margarine together until hot, not boiling. Remove from heat. Add the flour and sugar mixed together and beat until smooth. Whisk egg yolk into mixture; return to heat and stir for 5 minutes, do not boil. Remove and stir in blackcurrant purée. Whisk egg white until stiff, fold into mixture. Mix very well. Put into glass serving dishes and chill.

Decorate with piped whipped cream and a bunch of currants dipped in egg white then castor sugar. Serve with thin shortbread biscuits. SERVES 4.

Paula Middleton, Bishops Castle, Shropshire

☆ BLACKCURRANT VELVET ☆

2 small eggs
75 g/3 oz castor sugar
½ teaspoon powdered gelatine
1 tablespoon warm water

225 g/8 oz blackcurrants, cooked
and puréed
pinch salt
whipped cream for decoration

SEPARATE eggs. Mix yolks and sugar well together until creamy. Dissolve gelatine in the water and stir into the blackcurrant purée. Add yolks and sugar. Whisk egg whites until stiff with a pinch of salt and fold into mixture. Chill before serving and decorate with whipped cream. SERVES 4.

Mrs A. Morgan, Builth Wells, Powys

GOOSEBERRY HONEYCOMB

1 410-g/14½-oz can gooseberries or
350 g/12 oz fresh gooseberries,
cooked and sweetened

1 packet lime jelly
2 large eggs, separated

STRAIN the juice from fruit and add water to make up to 475 ml/ 16 fl oz. Heat the liquid and dissolve jelly in it. Allow to cool for 3 minutes approximately.

Beat the egg yolks into slightly cooled liquid and add the fruit. Whisk the egg whites until fairly stiff and fold into the mixture. Pour into individual dishes or a serving dish and allow to set. SERVES 4.

Mrs J. M. Rapson, Burpham, Sussex

FLUFFY STUFF

1 lemon jelly
450 ml/¾ pint boiling water
1 large can evaporated milk,
chilled

fruit in season or canned fruit

BREAK up cubes of jelly and add the boiling water, stir until jelly dissolves. Put jelly in large mixing bowl in fridge.

When the jelly is just setting remove from the fridge and very gradually add the evaporated milk, whisking vigorously all the time until the mixture is frothy.

Add the fruit, either drained tinned fruit or fresh, varying the jelly flavour to go with the fruit. Pour jelly mixture into a serving bowl and put in fridge to set.

A delicious sweet that is easy to make and is enjoyed by all members of the family. SERVES 6.

Mrs Rachel Kitchin, Burton-on-Trent, Staffordshire

HEATWAVE LEMON

1 lemon jelly
300 ml/½ pint boiling water
1 tablespoon sugar
1 egg, beaten

juice of ½ lemon
300 ml/½ pint milk
whipped cream to decorate
(optional)

DISSOLVE jelly in water, add sugar, stir and leave to cool.

Add egg, lemon juice and milk, whisk until fluffy. Put into individual dishes, leave to set, then decorate with cream if liked. SERVES 4.

Mrs Susan Jacob, Craig-Cefn-Parc, West Glamorgan

LEMON HAZE

1 packet lemon jelly
3 lemons

3 eggs, separated
90 g/3½ oz castor sugar

MELT jelly in 300 ml/½ pint boiling water. Cool. Grate lemon rinds and squeeze juice. Beat egg yolks and sugar together until pale and thick. Add this to cooled jelly with lemon juice and rind.

Beat egg whites until stiff. Whisk half of this into jelly and the other half fold in. Leave to set.

Decorate with piped whipped cream or clotted cream and strips of lemon rind, if liked. SERVES 4–5.

Ann Morgan, Builth Wells, Powys

DUTCH FLUMMERY

THINLY peel 2 lemons. Put the rind in a saucepan with 450 ml/
$\frac{3}{4}$ pint water, 175 g/6 oz castor sugar and 20 g/$\frac{3}{4}$ oz powdered
gelatine. Heat, without boiling, until dissolved. Stand the cold
mixture over a low heat for at least half an hour. Remove peel, add
squeezed lemon juice and 150 ml/$\frac{1}{4}$ pint sherry. Heat slowly, but do
not boil.

Beat 2 egg yolks until light and fluffy, pour slightly cooled
mixture over them. Pour back into pan, stir gently until thick. Cool
and when almost cold, pour into glass bowl. Refrigerate overnight
and before serving decorate with 150 ml/$\frac{1}{4}$ pint whipped cream and
leaves of angelica. SERVES 6.

Mrs E. S. Nicolson, Lochinver, Sutherland

LEMON PUDDING

2 lemons	CRUNCHY TOPPING
4 tablespoons cornflour	25 g/1 oz butter
2 eggs	75 g/3 oz Digestive biscuits
50 g/2 oz butter	$\frac{1}{4}$ teaspoon ground cinnamon
175–225 g/6–8 oz granulated sugar	1 tablespoon demerara sugar

GRATE the rind from the lemons and squeeze out the juice (add at
least another tablespoon of pure lemon juice if you like it to really
taste of lemon). Make the juice up to 600 ml/1 pint with water. Put
this into a pan and bring to the boil. Meanwhile put the cornflour
into a bowl, add the eggs and beat well, then whisk in the hot
lemon liquid. Return to pan and stir all the time over a low heat
until it thickens and comes to the boil. Remove from the heat and
beat in the butter, then the sugar to taste.

Leave the mixture to cool then beat up with a whisk and put into
a serving bowl.

Melt the butter for the topping in a small saucepan, crush the
biscuits into it and stir in the cinnamon and sugar. Sprinkle this
over the surface of the lemon mixture.

This is also nice made with oranges but then leave the cinnamon
out of topping mixture. SERVES 4.

Mrs D. Percy, Buglawton, Cheshire

LEMON FOOL

juice of 3 lemons
3 eggs, well beaten

600 ml/1 pint single cream
65 g/2½ oz castor sugar

PLACE the lemon juice and eggs in a bowl and mix well together. Stir in the cream and sugar. Place the bowl over a pan of hot water and cook the mixture, stirring until thickened. Pour into serving dish and chill. Serve cold. SERVES 6.

Mrs B. Brinkler, Hill Ridware, Staffordshire

LEMON YOGURT SOUFFLÉ

3 eggs, separated
75 g/3 oz castor sugar
grated rind and juice of 2 lemons
2 tablespoons water

1 tablespoon powdered gelatine
150 ml/¼ pint plain yogurt
150 ml/¼ pint double cream

PREPARE a 13-cm/5-inch soufflé dish with a band of double greaseproof or foil, forming a collar 5 cm/2 inches above the rim.

Whisk egg yolks, sugar, lemon rind and juice in a deep bowl over hot water until thick. Into a small bowl add water and sprinkle on gelatine. Place bowl over a pan of hot water and stir until dissolved. When lukewarm whisk into egg mixture and leave in a cool place until half set; add yogurt and whipped cream. Lastly, fold in stiffly whisked egg whites. Turn into prepared soufflé dish and leave to set.

Before serving remove collar and decorate with crystallised lemon slices, mimosa balls and strips of angelica. SERVES 6.

NB I pour into yogurt containers to freeze before sending with children for school pudding!

Mrs J. Barker, Billingsley, Shropshire

ORANGE MOUSSE

juice of 1 lemon
15 g/½ oz powdered gelatine
3 eggs
150 ml/¼ pint double cream

100 g/4 oz castor sugar
1 177-g/6¼-oz can frozen
   concentrated orange juice

MAKE lemon juice up to 5 tablespoons with water and use to dissolve gelatine in a small bowl over hot water.

Separate yolks from egg whites and put in separate bowls. Whisk egg whites until stiff. Whip cream until thick. Whisk egg yolks and castor sugar until thick and pale in colour; whisk in gelatine mixture and orange juice (still slightly frozen), add cream and lastly fold in egg whites.

Pour into glass bowl; sets and is ready to eat in minutes. This mousse is very rich so serve plain or with slices of fresh orange. Freezes very well. SERVES 6.

Mrs S. A. Clayton, Carlton Husthwaite, Yorkshire

GRAPEFRUIT CREAM

15 g/½ oz powdered gelatine
4 tablespoons cold water
1 567-g/1 lb 4-oz can grapefruit
   segments

175 ml/6 fl oz double cream

SOFTEN gelatine in cold water in a cup then stand in hot water until quite clear. Liquidise or finely chop the grapefruit. Add the grapefruit juice and dissolved gelatine and stir well. Put into refrigerator until just beginning to set.

Whip cream until fairly stiff. Stir gently into grapefruit mixture. Pour into serving dish or individual dishes and top with a cocktail cherry before serving. SERVES 6.

Mrs D. M. Procter, Tillingham, Essex

SCOTTISH DELIGHT

15 g/½ oz powdered gelatine
300 ml/½ pint hot water
4 eggs, separated
175 g/6 oz castor sugar

vanilla essence
raspberry jam
whipped cream

DISSOLVE the gelatine in the hot water and leave to cool slightly. Beat egg yolks and sugar until thick. Add warm gelatine mixture and continue whisking until mixture is frothy. Add vanilla essence to taste and carefully fold in the stiffly whisked egg whites. Pour the mixture into a glass dish and chill until set. Spread a thin layer of jam over and pile whipped cream on top. SERVES 4–6.

Mrs Agnes Neill, Dunning, Perth

SNOW PUDDING

300 ml/½ pint water
100 g/4 oz sugar
3 tablespoons cornflour mixed
   with 3 tablespoons cold water

2 firmly whisked egg whites
fruit, nuts and angelica

PUT water and sugar in pan and bring to the boil. Add cornflour mixture, bring to the boil and cook for 1 minute, stirring, until mixture thickens. Remove pan from heat and add to this hot mixture the whisked egg whites; thoroughly mix, using a wooden spoon. Place mixture into a rinsed 600-ml/1-pint mould and allow to set for a couple of hours.

Turn out the pudding on to a wetted 5-cm/2-inch deep dish, surround it with loganberries or raspberries (the fruit may be either fresh or cooked) and decorate top with chopped almonds and angelica. Serve with custard made from the egg yolks.

Simple to make, attractive to look at, easy on the calories and inexpensive. SERVES 6.

Mrs Cicely Jones, Guilsfield, Powys

SOUTHERN CREAM SPLENDOUR

15 g/½ oz powdered gelatine
1 397-g/14-oz tin sweetened
   condensed milk
2 large eggs
6 tablespoons single cream

2 tablespoons coffee essence or
   strong black sweetened coffee
250 ml/8 fl oz whisky
toasted flaked almonds

DISSOLVE gelatine in heated condensed milk. Put all ingredients into liquidiser and whizz for 2 minutes. Turn into glass dish, allow to cool and set. Sprinkle with toasted flaked almonds. SERVES 6.

Mr R. I. McCoskrie, Hemel Hempstead, Hertfordshire

SHADES OF DELIGHT

15 g/½ oz powdered gelatine
grated rind and juice of 1 orange
100 g/4 oz milk chocolate
100 g/4 oz plain chocolate
4 eggs, separated
2 tablespoons brandy

100 g/4 oz castor sugar
1 small can evaporated milk,
  chilled
whipped cream and chocolate
  curls to decorate

PLACE gelatine, orange rind and juice in a small basin. Place in pan of hot water, stir until gelatine dissolved.

Melt chocolates in separate basins over hot water. Add 2 egg yolks and 1 tablespoon brandy to each basin, remove from heat and stir until smooth. Add half the gelatine mixture to each chocolate mix, stir well and leave to cool.

Whisk egg whites until stiff, add sugar gradually. Whisk evaporated milk until thick. Fold half egg white and half evaporated milk into each bowl of chocolate mixture.

When almost setting layer two stripes of each flavour in a bowl or separate glasses; allow each layer to set (a few minutes) before adding the next.

To serve, pipe a whirl of cream on the top and decorate with chocolate curls or leaves.

Will freeze for 2 months; thaw for 3 hours in fridge. SERVES 4.

Mrs E. Banks, Egmanton, Nottinghamshire

SHEILA'S STRAWBERRY SPECIAL

175 g/6 oz Digestive biscuits
75 g/3 oz butter or margarine
½ strawberry jelly
150 ml/¼ pint boiling water

1 small tin evaporated milk,
  chilled
fresh strawberries
whipped cream

LINE a 20-cm/8-inch loose-bottomed cake tin with foil – sides as well as base. Crush the biscuits to resemble crumbs. Melt butter over a low heat, add crumbs, press mixture into bottom of lined tin and put in fridge to set.

Melt jelly in the boiling water, leave to cool. Whip the evaporated milk until very thick, whisk in jelly. Slice strawberries (reserve some for decoration) and stir into jelly mixture. Pour over the biscuit base, then put into fridge until set.

When set remove from tin very carefully, put on to serving dish and decorate with strawberries and whipped cream. SERVES 6.

Mrs Sheila Ashby, Sturry, Kent

PRINCESS CHARLOTTE

225 g/8 oz Digestive biscuits	vanilla essence
100 g/4 oz butter	450 ml/¾ pint whipping cream
1 packet sponge fingers (about 18)	4 teaspoons powdered gelatine
2 egg yolks	1 425-g/15-oz can apricot halves
50 g/2 oz castor sugar	apricot jam to glaze
2 tablespoons honey	

CRUSH biscuits, melt butter and stir into crumbs. Press firmly over the base of an 18 or 20-cm/7 or 8-inch loose-based tin. Leave in refrigerator for 2 hours to harden.

Place sponge fingers around edge of tin, sugar side out.

Whisk egg yolks with castor sugar until light. Add honey and vanilla essence to taste. Whip cream, add carefully to egg mixture. Soften gelatine in a little of drained apricot juice then dissolve over a gentle heat. Cool and add to mixture. Turn into tin and smooth top.

Leave to set, then turn out. Arrange apricots on the top and glaze with jam. Decorate if liked with extra piped whipped cream. SERVES 6.

Mrs Pyett, Chipping Sodbury, Bristol

CHARLOTTE DELIGHT

50 g/2 oz plain chocolate	150 ml/¼ pint double cream,
2 eggs, separated	whipped
1 heaped tablespoon sugar	100 g/4 oz sponge fingers
600 ml/1 pint milk	a little fruit juice
25 g/1 oz powdered gelatine	a few glacé cherries
vanilla essence	

FIRST melt the chocolate in a basin over hot water. Make a custard in a double saucepan, using the egg yolks, sugar and milk, then stir in the melted chocolate and leave to cool.

Dissolve the gelatine in a little warm water and when quite melted add to the custard. When nearly set add vanilla essence to taste and fold in the stiffly beaten egg whites and some of the whipped cream. Moisten the sponge fingers with a little fruit juice and use them to line the sides of a soufflé dish or cake tin.

Carefully pour in the mixture and put in refrigerator to set. Turn out before serving and decorate with remaining cream and cherries. SERVES 6.

Mrs P. Lewis, Hobarris, Shropshire

RASPBERRY CHIFFON

few slices day-old sponge cake or
  trifle sponges
little sherry
225 g/8 oz raspberries
1 raspberry jelly

150 ml/¼ pint raspberry
  juice/water
2 large eggs, separated
75 g/3 oz castor sugar
whipped cream to decorate

BREAK sponge cake into a trifle dish and soak with a little sherry. Lightly stew raspberries and strain off any juice.

Dissolve jelly in a saucepan with raspberry juice/water. Place raspberries over sponge cake. If sponge is not completely soaked with sherry moisten with a little jelly. Leave remaining jelly to cool.

Whisk egg whites until white and stiff. Whisk egg yolks and sugar until thick and pale in colour. Whisk yolks and sugar and cooled jelly lightly into whites, pour over raspberries and chill.

Decorate with whipped cream before serving. SERVES 6.

Mrs B. Sutton, Bignall End, Staffordshire

CITRUS SUMMER SWEET

175 g/6 oz butter, softened
175 g/6 oz castor sugar
3 large eggs
2 large lemons
2 small oranges

12 trifle sponge cakes
150 ml/¼ pint double cream
1 298-g/10½-oz can mandarin
  oranges

LINE a 1-kg/2-lb loaf tin with foil.

Cream butter and sugar until fluffy. Beat in eggs one by one. Grate rind of lemons and oranges, squeeze out and strain juice. Beat all into creamed mixture.

Split sponge cakes in half and arrange in base of tin. Pour in part of creamed mixture. Layer more cakes and creamed mixture until mixture is used and end with layer of cake. Press firmly down, cover with a lid to fit and put heavy weight on top. Chill in refrigerator for 3 hours until set.

Turn out on to plate, cover with whipped cream and decorate with mandarin orange pieces. SERVES 6.

Mrs Shirley Weatherup, Lockerbie, Dumfries

CRINDLEDYKES SEVILLE SURPRISE

225 g/8 oz cream cheese
4 tablespoons castor sugar
1 large orange
300 ml/½ pint double cream

1 tablespoon orange liqueur
18 sponge fingers (1 packet)
about 2 tablespoons orange
   marmalade

GREASE and line a 450-g/1-lb loaf tin.

Cream together cheese and sugar. Grate orange rind, add to cream with orange liqueur and whip until thick. Beat into cheese and sugar. Put 6 sponge fingers in bottom of tin, spread with marmalade, then orange segments cut up and de-pithed, then cream cheese mixture. Repeat three times, finishing with cream.

Refrigerate overnight. Remove from tin. Decorate with fresh orange segments and a little grated chocolate. SERVES 4–6.

Mrs Judy Davidson, Bardon Mill, Northumberland

BRAMBLE DELIGHT

350 g/12 oz blackberries
sugar to taste
3 tablespoons medium sherry
100 g/4 oz pink and white
   marshmallows

150 ml/¼ pint double cream
1 packet sponge finger biscuits
   (about 18)
extra cream for decoration

SAVE 12 blackberries for decoration and simmer the remainder very gently with approximately 25 g/1 oz sugar; do not add water to blackberries or allow colour to boil out. Cool, drain off juice.

Into a pan put the sherry, 3 tablespoons of the blackberry juice and the roughly chopped marshmallows (easy to cut with wet scissors). Heat gently, stirring occasionally, until marshmallows have melted. Allow to cool.

Whip cream until stiff, fold into cooled marshmallow mixture. Line base of an 18-cm/7-inch square cake tin with sponge fingers, first dipping each one into remaining blackberry juice. Cover with half the blackberries, then half the marshmallow mixture. Repeat layers, finishing with layer of sponge fingers. Cover with greaseproof paper, press down slightly and refrigerate overnight.

Turn out upside down, decorate with blackberries and cream whirls. A super rich sweet, but not too expensive as the fruit is free! SERVES 6.

Mrs V. Lowe, Urchfont, Wiltshire

SWEET POACHED EGGS

4 trifle sponge cakes
a little apricot jam
1 213-g/7½-oz can apricot halves

150 ml/¼ pint whipping or double
cream
25–50 g/1–2 oz icing sugar

CUT the trifle sponges in half and sandwich together with apricot jam. Arrange the sponge cakes in a fruit dish and soak them with the apricot juice; reserve the apricots.

Mix the whipped cream and icing sugar to taste until smooth. Spread gently over the sponges and arrange the apricots on top to look like eggs. It is then ready to serve. SERVES 4.

Mrs Sandra Warne, St Kew, Cornwall

RICH RASPBERRY TRIFLE

3 tablespoons raspberry jam
12–16 trifle sponge cakes, or
     equivalent homemade sponge
1 small glass sherry
2 226-g/8-oz cans raspberries or
     450 g/1 lb fresh fruit
3 egg yolks
50 g/2 oz custard powder

2 tablespoons sugar
600 ml/1 pint milk
1 raspberry jelly
300 ml/½ pint double or whipping
     cream
glacé cherries, angelica, ratafias
     or chopped nuts to decorate

LINE the trifle bowl with raspberry jam. Place the sponge in the bowl and soak with sherry. Strain the fruit and reserve the juice. Scatter the fruit on top of the sponge.

Make the custard as follows: beat the egg yolks and mix together with the custard powder, sugar and a little milk taken from the 600 ml/1 pint. Heat the remaining milk until boiling and add the custard mixture, stirring constantly. Boil for 1 minute and remove from the heat. Allow to cool, stirring to prevent skin forming, then pour over the raspberries.

Use a little boiling water to dissolve the raspberry jelly and make up to 600 ml/1 pint with water and the strained fruit juice. Add the jelly to the trifle, piercing through the custard with a knife, so that the jelly runs through to the sponge. Leave to cool and set.

Whip the cream, spread over the trifle and decorate as desired – with cherries and angelica, ratafia biscuits or chopped nuts. Serve chilled. SERVES 8–10.

Mrs Margaret Morrison, Castle Fraser, Aberdeenshire

☆ ROLLED RASPBERRY ☆
DELIGHT

SPONGE
3 eggs, separated
75 g/3 oz castor sugar
grated rind and juice of ½ lemon
1 tablespoon ground hazelnuts
50 g/2 oz self-raising flour
FILLING
175 ml/6 fl oz double cream

few drops of vanilla essence
icing sugar
225 g/8 oz fresh raspberries
25 g/1 oz roughly chopped
  hazelnuts

PREPARE a Swiss roll tin by brushing a little melted lard or oil on the bottom and sides. Place in it a piece of greaseproof paper cut to fit the base of the tin exactly and brush again with melted fat. Dust with flour and sugar. (If no Swiss roll tin is available a baking sheet fitted with a tray of doubled greaseproof paper will do.)

Place the egg yolks and castor sugar in a bowl and whisk until thick and pale, then whisk in the lemon juice. Fold in the lemon rind, ground hazelnuts and flour. Whisk the egg whites in a separate clean bowl until stiff and fold into the mixture. Turn into the prepared tin and bake in a moderately hot oven (190 C, 375 F, gas 5) for 15 minutes, until well risen and springy to the touch.

Meanwhile, prepare a sheet of greaseproof paper by liberally dusting with castor sugar and laying it on a dampened clean teacloth. Turn the cooked sponge on to the paper immediately it is taken out of the oven and, using a sharp knife, neaten the edges. Lightly mark one end of the sponge with the knife 2.5 cm/1 inch from the edge and proceed to roll the sponge up with the paper and tea-towel inside. Leave on a wire rack to cool completely.

Whisk together the cream, vanilla essence and sieved icing sugar to taste. Add the raspberries.

To fill the sponge: unroll the sponge carefully allowing it to keep its natural shape. Spread with the cream and raspberries and lightly roll up. Place on an oblong serving dish with the end tucked under. Sift over icing sugar and scatter the chopped hazelnuts on top. Use any raspberries left over to lie along the two sides of the dessert. Serve with fresh double cream as an accompaniment. SERVES 6.

Miss A. Jeanes, Sibsey, Lincolnshire

LEMON SPONGE MOUSSE

SPONGE FLAN
2 eggs
50 g/2 oz castor sugar
50 g/2 oz plain flour
FILLING
2 medium eggs

grated rind and juice of 1 small
   lemon
1 tablespoon castor sugar
scant 15 g/½ oz powdered gelatine
2 tablespoons water

WHISK eggs and sugar for sponge until thick and creamy. Sieve
flour over mixture and fold in. Pour into a greased and sugared 20-
cm/8-inch sponge flan tin. Bake in a hot oven (220 C, 425 F, gas 7)
for 10 minutes, turn out when cool.

Meanwhile prepare filling. Separate eggs. Add lemon rind and
sugar to yolks and beat until light and creamy. Add strained lemon
juice. Stiffly beat egg whites. Dissolve gelatine in the water, cool
and add to egg mixture thoroughly. Fold in whites, pour into flan
case and leave to set.

Before serving decorate with crystallised primroses with thin
strips of angelica for the stems. SERVES 4.

Crystallised primroses

gum arabic crystals
rose water

fresh primroses
castor sugar

PLACE gum arabic crystals (about equal to the size of a walnut) in a
screw-topped jar with 2 teaspoons rose water. Screw on top and
leave overnight to dissolve gum. Using dry primroses, carefully
paint with soft paintbrush every part of primrose evenly, not
missing any as it will go brown. Dredge lightly with castor sugar
and shake off surplus. Put flowers on to strips of sugared greaseproof paper on a wire cake cooling rack and place in an airing
cupboard until the flowers are quite crisp. Store in airtight tins.

Mrs A. Marris, Tregony, Cornwall

FRUIT SPONGE

½ packet jelly
225 g/8 oz plums or other seasonal
   fruit, cooked in 300 ml/½ pint
   water

1 20-cm/8-inch sponge cake
300 ml/½ pint custard
300 ml/½ pint double cream
green grapes to decorate

MAKE jelly up to 300 ml/½ pint with plum fruit juice and extra water if necessary. Cut a large round out of the centre of the sponge cake, leaving base as for a flan.

When the jelly is beginning to set arrange the warm plums in centre of cake and pour the jelly over, letting it sink into sponge base. When jelly has set pour over the cool custard.

Pipe whipped cream round edge of cake and spread remainder over the custard. Arrange the cut out round of sponge as for butterfly cakes, and decorate with grapes or other suitable fruit. SERVES 6.

Mrs M. Dent, Mickleton, Co. Durham

PEAR AND PLUM HARVEST FLAN

PASTRY
175 g/6 oz flour
pinch of salt
50 g/2 oz ground almonds
75 g/3 oz butter
1 egg yolk
1 tablespoon cold water

FILLING
225 g/8 oz stoned plums, halved
3 pears, peeled and halved
3 tablespoons clear honey
2 teaspoons arrowroot
150 ml/¼ pint double cream,
    whipped

PUT flour, salt and ground almonds in mixing bowl. Rub in the butter and bind together with the egg and water. Chill for 10 minutes. Roll out and use to line a 20-cm/8-inch flan dish or ring. Fill with foil and baking beans and bake blind in a moderately hot oven (190 C, 375 F, gas 5) for 20 minutes. Remove foil and beans and bake a further 5 minutes. Cool.

Meanwhile, put plums and pears in saucepan with 150 ml/¼ pint water. Simmer for 10 minutes. Cool in liquid then lift out. Add honey to the juice. Bring to the boil. Add a little cold water to the arrowroot, blend and stir into the syrup to thicken. Spread cream over base of flan, arrange the fruit on top and spoon over the cooled syrup. Serve at once. SERVES 6.

Mrs Helen Thomson, Strachan, Kincardineshire

SUMMER FRUIT FLAN

PASTRY
175 g/6 oz plain flour
pinch of salt
50 g/2 oz hard margarine
25 g/1 oz lard
aspoon castor sugar
2 tablespoons cold water

FILLING
350 g/12 oz mixed soft fruit
(strawberries, loganberries,
raspberries, blackcurrants,
blackberries)
sugar to taste
FOR THE GLAZE
150 ml/¼ pint juice
2 teaspoons cornflour
2 teaspoons castor sugar

MAKE pastry, use to line an 18-cm/7-inch flan dish and bake blind in a moderately hot oven (200 c, 400 f, gas 6) for 20–25 minutes. Allow to cool.

Put the fruit into a saucepan and cook very gently until the juice starts to run. Carefully lift out the fruit with a perforated spoon into a large sieve and allow to drain. It is important to let the fruit drain so that the pastry stays crisp. Put the drained fruit on to a large plate, sprinkle with sugar to taste and then arrange in the flan case.

Measure the juice drained from the fruit and make up to 150 ml/ ¼ pint with fresh orange juice if necessary. Put the cornflour into a small saucepan with the castor sugar. Stir in the juice and cook over a low heat to start with, then turn up the heat and stir all the time until it bubbles. Remove from the heat, allow to cool a little then spoon over the fruit. Serve with pouring cream. SERVES 4–6.

Dorothy Redgate, Moorgreen, Nottingham

INDIVIDUAL CHOCOLATE STRAWBERRY GÂTEAUX

PASTRY
175 g/6 oz plain flour
2 tablespoons cocoa powder
100 g/4 oz butter
40 g/1½ oz castor sugar
1 large egg yolk
¼ teaspoon vanilla essence

FILLING
450 g/1 lb firm strawberries, thinly
sliced
1 tablespoon castor sugar
1 teaspoon lemon juice
TOPPING
100 g/4 oz plain dark or cooking
chocolate
4 very firm large strawberries

SIFT flour and cocoa into a mixing bowl. Add butter and cut into small pieces. Rub fat into flour until like coarse breadcrumbs. Add sugar, egg yolk and vanilla and mix to a firm dough, adding a little water if necessary. Put to rest in fridge for 30 minutes.

Roll out dough until thin and cut into twelve 7.5-cm/3-inch rounds. Put these on a greased baking sheet and bake in a moderately hot oven (190c, 375 f, gas 5) for about 10–12 minutes, until just firm. Leave to cool.

Take four of the cooked pastry circles and put on a rack. Melt chocolate for the topping in a bowl over hot water. Dip the four large strawberries into melted chocolate until half covered and put aside. Pour rest of melted chocolate on to tops of the four pastry circles and spread evenly. Put a chocolate strawberry on top of each chocolate circle.

Assemble filling by mixing strawberries, sugar and lemon juice gently together.

Cover four of the plain pastry circles with half the filling. Place remaining plain pastry circles on top. Spread rest of filling on top of these, finally topped by the chocolate-covered pastry circles. Ready to serve. SERVES 4.

Mrs J. C. Gemmill, Neuney Green, Essex

MILE HIGH PIE

BASE
225 g/8 oz crushed Digestive
  biscuits
150 g/5 oz melted butter
pinch of ground cinnamon
FILLING
450 g/1 lb frozen strawberries

100 g/4 oz castor sugar
1 tablespoon lemon juice
⅛ teaspoon salt
2 egg whites
250 ml/8 fl oz whipping cream
25 g/1 oz icing sugar
1 teaspoon vanilla essence

MIX the crushed biscuits, butter and cinnamon thoroughly and press into base of a deep-sided 23 × 33-cm/9 × 13-inch tin.

Combine frozen berries, castor sugar, lemon juice, salt and egg whites in a large bowl. Leave until berries can be crushed with a wooden spoon but are not fully thawed. Beat in electric mixer for 15 minutes. Whip cream with icing sugar and vanilla and fold into strawberry mixture. Pile on to biscuit crust and freeze until firm. When ready to serve, slice into squares and decorate with fresh fruit. SERVES 6–8.

Mrs E. Matthews, Bangor, Co. Down

APPLE AND BRANDY CREAM FLAN

BASE
50 g/2 oz butter
100 g/4 oz Digestive biscuit
  crumbs
FILLING
2 large Bramley cooking apples
  (about 575 g/1¼ lb in weight)
25 g/1 oz butter

50 g/2 oz demerara sugar
1 225-g/8-oz packet Philadelphia
  cream cheese or full fat soft
  cheese
TOPPING
150 ml/¼ pint double cream
1 tablespoon brandy
1 tablespoon icing sugar

LINE the base of an 18-cm/7-inch deep loose-bottomed flan or cake tin with greased greaseproof paper, also lightly grease the rest of the tin. Melt the butter for the base, add to the biscuit crumbs and mix. Press down evenly all over base of prepared tin and put in refrigerator while preparing the filling.

Peel, core and slice apples, cook gently with butter and demerara sugar until soft. Remove from heat, beat apples to a pulp, allow to cool. Finally beat cream cheese into apple mixture until smooth. Spread this filling evenly over biscuit base. Put into refrigerator to chill for 4–6 hours.

Remove flan from tin and place on a serving dish. Make topping by whisking double cream, brandy and icing sugar together until thick. Spread over top of flan, swirl surface with a knife, or place cream mixture in a piping bag fitted with a star pipe, pipe cream stars all over surface of flan. A few toasted flaked almonds could also be used for decoration on top of the cream. SERVES 4–6.

Mrs R. W. Braithwaite, Romsley, Shropshire

☆ CHILLED RHUBARB PIE ☆

BASE
12 Digestive biscuits
1½ tablespoons castor sugar
75 g/3 oz butter
FILLING
225 g/8 oz rhubarb
100 g/4 oz castor sugar

pinch salt
juice of 1 orange
15 g/½ oz powdered gelatine
red food colouring (optional)
600 ml/1 pint thick-set natural
  yogurt
50 g/2 oz slivered almonds, toasted

FOR pie base, line a deep 23-cm/9-inch pie dish with foil or greaseproof paper. Crush the Digestive biscuits and mix in the sugar. Melt butter in a saucepan, mix in the biscuits and, while still warm, line the sides and base of the pie dish with the mixture. Leave until cold.

Wash and trim rhubarb and cut into 2.5-cm/1-inch lengths. Place in a heavy pan with the sugar, salt and 1 tablespoon of the orange juice. Cook slowly until soft, stirring occasionally. Cool and chill until needed.

Put rest of orange juice into a saucepan and sprinkle in the gelatine until thick. Stir over a low heat until dissolved.

Drain rhubarb in a colander, put into a bowl, stir in gelatine and a little red colouring if used. Stir in the yogurt until smooth, pour into the pie base and chill. Set for 2–3 hours in the refrigerator and then sprinkle with the almonds. Remove from the pie dish to serve. SERVES 4–6.

Mrs P. Beveridge, Danestreet, Kent

BLACKCURRANT DELIGHT ON BISCUIT BASE

BASE
225 g/8 oz crushed biscuits
100 g/4 oz melted butter or
  margarine
TOPPING
175 g/6 oz sugar

150 ml/¼ pint water
15 g/½ oz powdered gelatine
450 g/1 lb fresh or frozen
  blackcurrants
300 ml/½ pint double cream

MIX well together biscuit crumbs and melted fat, press into base of a 20-cm/8-inch flan dish. Chill in refrigerator to set.

Put sugar and all but 2 tablespoons water in pan, dissolve over gentle heat then bring to boil for 3 minutes. Use remaining water to dissolve gelatine. Sieve blackcurrants to a purée. Lightly whip cream. Retain a very little sugar syrup and few blackcurrants for decoration.

Gently stir blackcurrant purée into sugar syrup then add dissolved gelatine. When cool fold in whipped cream. Pour on to biscuit base and leave to set.

Decorate with piped whipped cream and a few blackcurrants dipped in sugar syrup. SERVES 6.

Mrs L. Laughton, North Cockerington, Lincolnshire

FRESH BERRY TORTE

A delightful combination of flavours and colours produces an intriguing dessert sure to catch the eye. Fresh strawberries and raspberries are the main ingredients of this luscious pudding, light and creamy with the refreshing taste of summer fruits – very tempting and mouth-watering!

BISCUIT CRUST
40 g/1½ oz butter
2 teaspoons soft brown sugar
about 75 g/3 oz Digestive biscuits, crushed
FILLING
⅓ tablet (4 cubes) orange jelly
⅓ tablet (4 cubes) lime jelly
350 g/12 oz fresh raspberries and strawberries

1 heaped teaspoon powdered gelatine
5 tablespoons orange juice
150 ml/¼ pint double cream
1 tablespoon castor sugar
few drops vanilla essence
whipped cream for decoration

DISSOLVE each of the jellies in 6 tablespoons boiling water and leave to set in separate dishes.

Melt butter for the biscuit crust, add sugar and crumbs. Line a 15-cm/6-inch loose-based cake tin with greaseproof paper and then press two-thirds of the crumbs into the base of the tin.

Chop jelly into fairly small cubes. Reserve a few raspberries and strawberries for decoration. Slice remaining strawberries, but leave raspberries whole. Soften gelatine in 2 tablespoons orange juice. Heat remainder and then dissolve softened gelatine in this mixture. Allow to cool. Whip cream, add sugar and vanilla essence. Fold dissolved gelatine into cream, then jelly cubes and fruit. Turn into tin lined with crumbs and top with remaining crumbs. Chill until firm.

Invert on to a serving dish and remove greaseproof paper. Decorate with remaining berries and whirls of cream. Slice a portion from the dessert so that the inside effect can be seen. SERVES 4.

Miss Rosalind Gray, Billingshurst, West Sussex

JAMAICAN CRUNCH PIE

100 g/4 oz ginger nuts
50 g/2 oz melted butter
150 ml/¼ pint double cream
1 198-g/7-oz tin sweetened
condensed milk

6 tablespoons lemon juice (2–3
lemons)
grated rind of 1 lemon
glazed lemon slices to decorate

CRUSH ginger nuts with a rolling pin, place in a bowl and blend with melted butter. Line an 18-cm/7-inch pie plate or flan ring placed on a flat plate with the biscuit mixture.

Lightly whip the cream, stir in condensed milk, lemon juice and rind. When beginning to thicken, pour into biscuit shell and chill in the refrigerator overnight. Decorate with glazed lemon slices. SERVES 4–6.

Glazed Lemon Slices

Poach 8 thick slices of lemon (free of pips) in enough water to cover, until tender. Drain slices, add 75 g/3 oz sugar to liquid left in pan. When sugar has dissolved, boil to reduce to a glaze. Pour over the slices and cool.

Mrs Audrey Brown, Little Billington, Bedfordshire

KIWI AND PEACH FLAN

¼ peach jelly
2 eggs
50 g/2 oz sugar

50 g/2 oz self-raising flour
6 kiwi fruit
whipped cream to decorate

MAKE up the jelly using 150 ml/¼ pint boiling water, leave to cool and set.

Grease well and line the centre piece of a sponge flan tin. Whisk up the eggs and sugar until thick and fluffy. Fold in the flour carefully so as not to knock out the air you have trapped in the mixture. Pour into the flan tin and cook in a moderately hot oven (190 c, 375 f, gas 5) for 15–20 minutes, until the sponge springs back when lightly pressed. Remove from tin straightaway and peel off lining paper, leave to cool.

Remove the thin skin from the kiwi fruit and thinly slice. Arrange slightly overlapping in rings to fill the flan. When the jelly has nearly set spoon over the fruit and decorate with whipped cream before serving. SERVES 6.

Mrs C. E. Jackson, Slaithwaite, Yorkshire

Chocolate Ginger Delight

225 g/8 oz crushed biscuits
100 g/4 oz butter, melted
15 g/½ oz powdered gelatine
4 tablespoons cold water
100 g/4 oz cooking chocolate
3 eggs plus 1 egg yolk
75 g/3 oz castor sugar

2 tablespoons ginger syrup
shake of ground ginger
150 ml/¼ pint double cream, lightly
   whipped
4 pieces stem ginger, chopped
   fairly small

Lightly grease a 20-cm/8-inch flan tin. Combine crushed biscuits with melted butter and press firmly on to base and sides of tin. Leave to set.

Soak gelatine in cold water. Melt chocolate in dry pan over very low heat. Place eggs, egg yolk and sugar in a bowl and whisk over hot water until thick and creamy. Dissolve the softened gelatine in the ginger syrup over a low heat and strain into the egg mixture. Beat in the melted chocolate and ground ginger.

When cool and on the point of setting, fold in three-quarters of the cream, lightly whipped. Fold in the chopped stem ginger.

Turn into prepared flan case and when set decorate with the rest of cream, more stiffly whipped. This will freeze well. Can be served straight from flan case. Serves 6.

Mrs Gwen Gay, Upper Swainswick, Avon

Drambuie Dream Baskets

BRANDY BASKETS
40 g/1½ oz golden syrup
25 g/1 oz butter
25 g/1 oz soft brown sugar
15 g/½ oz plain flour
½ teaspoon ground ginger
½ teaspoon lemon juice

FILLING
100 g/4 oz fresh raspberries
50 g/2 oz castor sugar
3 tablespoons Drambuie liqueur
2 teaspoons orange juice
300 ml/½ pint double cream
raspberries to decorate

Make baskets. Melt syrup, butter and sugar together in a pan until fat has melted. Remove from heat then stir in flour, ginger and lemon juice. Mix well. Place teaspoons of mixture on to a well-greased baking tray, leaving plenty of room for expansion. Cook in a moderate oven (160 c, 325 f, gas 3) for 8–10 minutes, until golden brown. Cool for half a minute then, using a palette knife, carefully lift biscuits off tray and while still warm, mould round oranges to form basket shapes. Leave until cold then gently lift off.

Purée raspberries and sieve to remove seeds. Add sugar, Drambuie and orange juice to cream and whip together until cream forms stiff peaks. Place in a piping bag with a 1-cm/½-inch plain nozzle. Insert palette knife down opposite sides of piping bag and pour raspberry purée down each space. Pipe into baskets to make pink and white swirl effect. Decorate tops of swirls with a raspberry and small raspberry leaves. SERVES 4.

Miss Sheila Gray, Fochabers, Morayshire

SODA CRACKER PIE

BEAT 3 egg whites until stiff, gradually add 175 g/6 oz castor sugar and beat well, add 1 teaspoon vanilla essence.

Crush 8 cream crackers into fine crumbs, then add ½ teaspoon baking powder, 50 g/2 oz chopped walnuts and 50 g/2 oz chocolate chips. Combine with the egg white mixture and spread evenly over a well buttered 23-cm/9-inch pie plate. Bake for 30 minutes in a moderate oven (180 c, 350 F, gas 4), do not allow to get too brown. Cool.

Whip 150–300 ml/¼–½ pint cream. Add 1 tablespoon castor sugar and spread all over the pie. Decorate with chocolate flake, coloured sugar and chocolate curls. SERVES 6.

Mrs Isabella Burns, Path Head, Midlothian

PEANUT BUTTER PIE

175 g/6 oz shortcrust pastry	450 ml/¾ pint custard
2–3 tablespoons crunchy peanut butter	3 eggs, separated
	175 g/6 oz castor sugar

ROLL out shortcrust pastry to line a 20-cm/8-inch flan tin and spread the peanut butter on to the base.

Make the custard in advance, cool slightly and add the egg yolks. Place custard on to peanut butter layer and leave until set.

While custard is setting make meringue. Whisk egg whites until stiff, beat in half the sugar then fold in the remainder. Place on top of the cooled custard, and fork into peaks.

Place in a moderate oven (180 c, 350 F, gas 4) until pastry and meringue are cooked, about 30–40 minutes. SERVES 6.

Miss Jane Edwards, St Mary Hill, Glamorgan

SUMMER CHEESECAKE

BASE
25 g/1 oz butter
25 g/1 oz sugar
50 g/2 oz chocolate Digestive
    biscuits, finely crushed
FILLING
225 g/8 oz soft cheese or sieved
    cottage cheese
2 tablespoons melted redcurrant
    jelly
100 g/4 oz castor sugar
2 eggs, separated
150 ml/¼ pint single cream

15 g/½ oz powdered gelatine
3 tablespoons water
50 g/2 oz raspberries, finely
    chopped
50 g/2 oz strawberries, finely
    chopped
1 large ripe peach, skinned and
    finely chopped
2 tablespoons lemon juice
TOPPING
150 ml/¼ pint double cream
1 tablespoon Cointreau liqueur
raspberries and strawberries

MELT the butter and sugar in a pan over gentle heat and mix in the biscuit crumbs. Press evenly on a greased loose-bottomed 18-cm/7-inch cake tin or flan ring.

Soften the cheese, beat in the redcurrant jelly, 50 g/2 oz sugar, the egg yolks and cream. Put the gelatine and water in a bowl over a pan of hot water and stir until gelatine dissolves. Beat the gelatine into the cheese mixture and leave until nearly set.

Whisk the egg whites until stiff, whisk in the remaining sugar. Mix lightly into the cheese mixture with the chopped fruit and lemon juice. Turn on to the biscuit base and chill until set.

Whip the cream with the Cointreau until thick and decorate the cheesecake with fruit and cream. SERVES 6.

Anne Thornton, Forton, Lancashire

TANGY LEMON CHEESECAKE

1 18–20-cm/7–8-inch sponge flan
    case
275 g/10 oz cream cheese
2 medium eggs, separated
grated rind and juice of 1 lemon
50 g/2 oz castor sugar
2 tablespoons milk
few drops of vanilla essence
600 ml/1 pint double or whipping
    cream

15 g/½ oz powdered gelatine
TOPPING
6 Digestive biscuits
15 g/½ oz sugar
½ teaspoon ground cinnamon
lemon slices and angelica to
    decorate

PLACE sponge flan case in bottom of a suitable-sized mould (a cake tin with removable base is ideal).

Blend cheese, egg yolks, lemon rind and juice, sugar, milk and vanilla essence in a large bowl. Whisk double cream in another bowl until thick. Dissolve gelatine in 6 tablespoons hot water and leave to cool. Whisk egg whites until stiff enough to stand in peaks.

When gelatine has cooled add to cheese mixture and blend thoroughly. Stir in whipped cream gently and then fold in egg whites. Pour over sponge base in the mould.

Crush biscuits and mix with sugar and cinnamon. Sprinkle over cheesecake and place in refrigerator to set.

Although this cheesecake may be served after 2–3 hours it is best if made 24 hours before needed.

Before serving, slide base out of mould and decorate top with lemon slices and angelica. SERVES 6–8.

Mrs L. Davies, Meriden, West Midlands

BLACK CHERRY CHEESECAKE

BASE	300 ml/½ pint whipping cream
50 g/2 oz butter	350 g/12 oz cottage cheese
100 g/4 oz plain biscuits	1 lemon
TOPPING	50–75 g/2–3 oz sugar
7 g/¼ oz powdered gelatine	1 396-g/14-oz can cherry pie filling

MELT the butter, crush the biscuits until they are fine crumbs and combine together. Press into the base of a 20–23-cm/8–9-inch loose-bottomed tin. Chill.

Dissolve the gelatine in 1–2 tablespoons water. Whip the cream until peaks are formed. Sieve half the cottage cheese into the bowl with the cream, add the remainder unsieved; this gives the cheesecake a lovely textured consistency. Grate the lemon rind finely and add to the bowl, then add lemon juice and sugar to taste. Mix this together gently and stir in the gelatine, best passed through a sieve. Mix well.

Turn on to the biscuit base and spread level. Chill in the fridge for 24 hours if possible, although it can be used once it is set.

Open the pie filling and spread over the cheesecake evenly. When ready to serve push the cheesecake through the tin and slide it on to a serving dish. SERVES 6.

Mrs Gillian Jones, Castleton, nr Cardiff

FLUFFY PINEAPPLE CHEESECAKE

BASE
100 g/4 oz butter or margarine
50 g/2 oz castor sugar
225 g/8 oz Digestive biscuits,
  finely crushed
FILLING
225 g/8 oz full fat soft cream
  cheese
2 egg yolks
2 tablespoons castor sugar
2 tablespoons desiccated coconut
2 tablespoons ground rice
1 425-g/15-oz tin pineapple pieces
  or rings
25 g/1 oz powdered gelatine
4 tablespoons boiling water
2 egg whites
2 tablespoons castor sugar
  (optional)
150 ml/¼ pint double or whipping
  cream

MELT the butter for the base in a saucepan, add sugar and biscuit crumbs. Press into a loose-bottomed round cake tin. Chill in fridge.

Beat cream cheese until soft and fluffy. Add the egg yolks and beat. Add castor sugar, beat in. Stir the coconut and ground rice into the cheese mixture. Reserve a little pineapple to decorate and blend the remainder in a liquidiser with 4 tablespoons of the juice, until puréed. Add to the cream cheese mixture, fold in but do not beat. Dissolve gelatine in 4 tablespoons boiling water, add to the mixture and beat.

Whisk egg whites until stiff and forming peaks, fold in extra sugar if liked. Whip cream until forming peaks. Fold the cream and egg whites into the cream cheese mixture lightly but thoroughly. Pour on to the biscuit base and chill.

Decorate the cheesecake top with whipped cream and pineapple pieces. SERVES 6–8.

Mrs Anne Wightman, Kirkby Lonsdale, Lancashire

MANDARIN AND CHOCOLATE CHEESECAKE

225 g/8 oz cottage cheese
225 g/8 oz cream cheese
15 g/½ oz powdered gelatine
1 298-g/10½-oz can mandarin
  oranges

a little icing sugar
1 chocolate Swiss roll
1 chocolate flake

SIEVE the cottage cheese and mix with the cream cheese. Dissolve the gelatine in half the juice from the oranges, in a bowl over a pan of hot water, stirring continuously. Pour gelatine mixture into cheese mixture, mix well and stir in one-third of the oranges chopped up. Stir in a little icing sugar if you like.

Slice Swiss roll thickly and line bottom of 18-cm/7-inch round cake tin with it. Sprinkle on remainder of juice and arrange over another one-third of oranges. Spread cheese mixture on top and level. Decorate with remainder of oranges and chill in fridge.

Decorate with crumbled flake just before serving, push cheesecake out when ready. SERVES 4–6.

L. J. Waller, Great Witley, Worcestershire

WAISTLINE HONEY AND NUT CHEESECAKE

175 g/6 oz Digestive biscuits
75 g/3 oz low-calorie margarine
scant 150 ml/¼ pint skimmed milk
1 44-g/1½-oz sachet dessert topping
  mix

225 g/8 oz cottage cheese
1 packet nuts and raisins
honey

CRUSH Digestives, add to melted margarine. Use to line a very lightly greased pie plate. Cool.

Whisk milk and dessert topping, preferably in electric mixer, until very stiff. Add cottage cheese, draining off any liquid, and whisk again. Pile on biscuit base, level. Sprinkle on nuts and raisins and pour over warmed honey (easier pouring). SERVES 4–6.

Mrs Anne Collins, Port Isaac, Cornwall

☆ LEMON CURD MERINGUE ☆

LEMON CURD
(to be made in advance)
225 g/8 oz unsalted butter
450 g/1 lb granulated sugar
6 standard eggs and
   2 standard egg yolks, beaten
   together

6 medium lemons
MERINGUE
6 fresh large egg whites
350 g/12 oz castor sugar
CREAM
600 ml/1 pint whipping cream

To make lemon curd, melt butter in a double saucepan, or a large basin over a pan of simmering water. Add sugar, eggs and finely grated rind and juice of the lemons. Stir the mixture frequently until it thickens – allow about 20–30 minutes. Pour into clean dry warm jars. Cover as for jam, cool and keep in the refrigerator until required.

For the meringue, whisk egg whites until they form soft peaks. Add sugar gradually, whisking all the time. Divide meringue into three with a metal spoon and place on prepared baking sheets, making rounds of 30 cm/12 inches, 20 cm/8 inches and 10 cm/ 4 inches. Cook in a cool oven (140 c, 275 f, gas 1) for about 1 hour. If browning, unlatch oven door. When firm, turn heat off but leave meringues in the oven until completely dried out. Remove from baking sheet and store in tins until required.

To make up, whisk the cream until fairly stiff. Starting with the 30-cm/12-inch meringue, build a pyramid by layering meringue, lemon curd and whipped cream until you have the three layers. Decorate with grated plain chocolate, cherries or little flowers made from coloured icing. SERVES 12.

Mrs Gwenda Bendall, Marksbury, Bath

CITRUS WHAM

MAKE sweet 2 days before required and store in refrigerator, covered with cling film.

Make a meringue with 4 egg whites, 225 g/8 oz castor sugar and $\frac{3}{4}$ teaspoon cream of tartar. Spread over the lightly oiled base of a 25-cm/10-inch ovenproof flan dish or dinner plate. Bake until pale golden in a cool oven (150 c, 300 f, gas 2), about 1–1½ hours. Remove from oven and cool.

Blend in a liquidiser or food processor: 4 egg yolks, 100 g/4 oz castor sugar, grated rind of 1 orange and the juice of 2 oranges and

1 lemon. Cook in a double boiler until thick and then cool slightly. Whip 300 ml/½ pint double cream until fairly thick and fold into orange mixture. Pour on to the meringue base and decorate just before serving with fresh orange segments and toasted flaked almonds. SERVES 8.

Mrs E. Hutchinson, Ponteland, Northumberland

SUMMERTIME FLAN

MERINGUE
2 egg whites
pinch of salt
100 g/4 oz castor sugar
FILLING
75 g/3 oz raspberries

2 tablespoons redcurrant jelly
100 g/4 oz low fat soft cheese
150 ml/¼ pint double cream
225 g/8 oz strawberries

COVER two baking trays with non-stick baking parchment, marking an 18-cm/7-inch circle on each.

Beat egg whites and salt until stiff, add half the sugar again beating until stiff, fold in remaining sugar. Using a forcing bag fitted with a 1.5-cm/¾-inch wide tube, place just under half the meringue mix in it and pipe a ring on one tray, keeping just within the marked out circle, then neatly pipe blobs on top of this meringue ring. Spread smoothly all remaining meringue mixture within the other marked out circle.

Bake in a very cool oven (110 C, 225 F, gas ¼) for 2 hours; if not quite dried out leave in oven with heat off for a further hour. Do not assemble flan until meringue has gone cold.

Press raspberries through a sieve, discard seeds, place the raspberry purée and redcurrant jelly in a liquidiser, mix at high speed until blended. Beat soft cheese with a fork, gradually adding raspberry and redcurrant mixture until all is thoroughly blended.

Place solid circle of meringue on a serving plate. Spread the cheese mixture to within 1 cm/½ inch of outer edge, gently place meringue ring over the meringue base.

Whip the cream and spread over cheese mixture in centre of ring. Hull strawberries then arrange them neatly on the whipped cream. SERVES 4.

Mrs Barbara Briggs, Winmarleigh, Lancashire

Strawberry and Redcurrant Pavlova

PAVLOVA meringue made in usual way with 3 egg whites, 175 g/ 6 oz castor sugar, 1 teaspoon cornflour and 1 teaspoon wine or fruit vinegar (both added with last teaspoon of sugar); spread into a round on Bakewell paper and cooked for 1 hour in a cool oven (150 c, 300 f, gas 2), then left to cool in oven.

300 ml/½ pint double Jersey cream, whipped and mixed with purée of strawberries (about 300 ml/½ pint) and a few redcurrants, and either sugar or honey to taste.

At serving time, place pavlova on large plate or round tray, add strawberry cream mixture piled high. Decorate with frosted redcurrant clusters, fresh strawberries and rose geranium leaves. SERVES 6.

Mrs H. P. Platt, Tostock, Suffolk

Hazelnut Meringue Cake with Brandy Chocolate Filling

CAKE
4 large egg whites
pinch of salt
225 g/8 oz castor sugar
50 g/2 oz ground hazelnuts
1 teaspoon vinegar
1 teaspoon vanilla essence
FILLING
4 large egg yolks
½ teaspoon cornflour

25 g/1 oz castor sugar
1½ tablespoons brandy
150 ml/¼ pint milk
75 g/3 oz plain chocolate, coarsely grated
TO DECORATE
whipped cream
hazelnuts
sliced kiwi fruit

GREASE two 20-cm/8-inch sandwich tins with a disc of Bakewell paper in base.

Whisk the egg whites with the salt until stiff and then add the sugar a little at a time and whisk until peaky. Lightly stir in nuts, vinegar and essence with a metal spoon. Divide mixture between tins and bake for 30–40 minutes in a moderate oven (180 c, 350 f, gas 4), until firm and golden. Cool cakes slightly, ease edges with a sharp knife, remove from tin and cool on wire racks.

Put yolks in double boiler top with cornflour, sugar and brandy, mix and stir in the milk. Cook over simmering water until mixture becomes thick, stirring constantly with a wooden spoon. Stir in chocolate until melted and smooth. Transfer to bowl to cool.

Spread cooled chocolate mixture over two meringue cakes and sandwich together. Decorate with whipped cream rosettes and place a hazelnut on each whirl. Chill in fridge before serving and arrange slices of kiwi fruit between cream rosettes just before placing on table. SERVES 6–8.

Mrs A. E. Bebbington, Craven Arms, Shropshire

QUICK AND EASY ICE CREAM

4 eggs
100 g/4 oz castor sugar

vanilla essence
300 ml/½ pint double cream

SEPARATE eggs. Whisk whites until stiff, whisk and mix in sugar, 1 teaspoon at a time.

Beat egg yolks, fold into mixture, add vanilla to taste. Whip cream until thick, fold into mixture.

Put into shallow container and freeze. SERVES 6.

Mrs N. Burton, Brailsford, Derby

DAIRY CREAM PUDDING

600 ml/1 pint single cream
2 egg yolks
100 g/4 oz castor sugar
2 teaspoons vanilla essence

1 slice pineapple
40 g/1½ oz candied apricots
25 g/1 oz maraschino cherries
25 g/1 oz chopped walnuts

ADD a quarter of the cream to the egg yolks and heat for a few minutes over boiling water, stirring all the time. Add sugar and vanilla, then remove from heat, cool and partly freeze. Mince fruit and nuts and stir them into the frozen mixture, then stir in the rest of the cream. Freeze to a mush, then turn into a mould and finish freezing. SERVES 4–6.

Miss C. Rolfe, Hitcham, Suffolk

BOMBE PRINCESSE

meringues made with 3 egg
   whites and 175 g/6 oz castor
   sugar
3 pieces stem ginger
450 ml/¾ pint double or whipping
   cream

2 tablespoons castor sugar
3 tablespoons Cointreau liqueur
grated rind of 1 lemon
whipped cream and lemon slices
   to decorate

LIGHTLY crush the meringues. Finely chop the ginger. Whip the cream until just holding its shape. Fold meringues and ginger into cream with remaining ingredients. Spoon into a loose-bottomed 18-cm/7-inch tin. Level surface and cover with foil. Freeze for at least 4 hours until firm.

Run a hot knife around edge of tin and turn out on to chilled serving plate. Decorate top with whirls of cream and lemon slices and return to freezer. Remove from freezer 10 minutes before serving and leave at room temperature to soften slightly. SERVES 8.

Mrs Diana Homewood, New Romney, Kent

☆ LEMON ICE CAKE ☆ DESSERT

3 eggs, separated
100 g/4 oz castor sugar
5 tablespoons lemon juice

2 teaspoons grated lemon rind
pinch of salt
300 ml/½ pint double cream

BEAT egg yolks until thick and then beat in sugar. Add lemon juice, rind and salt. Fold in lightly whipped cream and then stiffly beaten egg whites.

Put into a lightly oiled 21–23-cm/8½–9-inch loose-bottomed tin, and place in freezer.

When required, defrost for about 20–30 minutes and gently push out. Cover with soft fruit and whipped cream before serving. Very refreshing. SERVES 6.

Mrs S. M. Jerrard, Oldhamstocks, East Lothian

MIDSUMMER GLORIES

A delicious fruity dessert – fresh peaches steeped in liqueur with a hint of almond are served with a creamy fruit ice masked with raspberry sauce. Served in cocktail or tall-stemmed glasses this produces a very attractive, mouth-watering sweet.

FRUIT ICE
150 ml/¼ pint double cream
150 ml/¼ pint sweetened fruit
  purée, made from fresh
  raspberries and canned peaches
2 tablespoons sieved icing sugar
1 tablespoon each fresh
  raspberries and diced canned
  peaches
TO FINISH
4 large ripe peaches, skinned and
  sliced

a little lemon juice
castor sugar to taste
2 tablespoons Kirsch or liqueur of
  your choice
4 macaroons, roughly crushed
50 g/2 oz sieved icing sugar
150 ml/¼ pint sieved raspberry
  purée (225 g/8 oz raspberries)
150 ml/¼ pint double cream,
  whipped

TURN refrigerator to coldest setting 1 hour before making ice. Half whip cream and add sieved purée, continue whisking until stiff. Stir in sugar and pour into ice cube tray. Place in freezing compartment. When ice has frozen around the edges, turn into chilled bowl and beat with an electric whisk until smooth. Return to rinsed out tray and freeze again for approximately 30 minutes. Beat once more as before. Add pieces of chopped fruit and freeze again until just firm, about 1½–2 hours.

Place prepared peaches in a bowl. Turn in lemon juice and sprinkle with sugar. Spoon over Kirsch, add crushed macaroons and leave for 1 hour.

To make raspberry sauce, add icing sugar to raspberry purée and fold into whipped cream.

To complete dessert, divide peach mixture among six cocktail glasses. Top with a slice of fruit ice and mask with the raspberry cream. Decorate with a few whole berries if desired. Serve straightaway.

The ice may be made and stored in the deep freeze, but do allow time for it to soften before serving. SERVES 6.

Miss Rosalind Gray, Billingshurst, West Sussex

SIMPLE FRUITY ICE CREAM

100–175 g/4–6 oz soft ripe fruit
(strawberries, raspberries,
blackcurrants, blackberries or
bananas)

100 g/4 oz granulated sugar
1 large can evaporated milk,
chilled

PULP fruit with sugar in a liquidiser, sieve if necessary to remove seeds. Whisk evaporated milk with electric whisk until fluffy, gently add fruit purée.

Place in a covered container and freeze in freezer or fridge at low setting.

Serve with crisp oatmeal or shortbread fingers. SERVES 4–6.

Mrs Jennifer Bastard, Launceston, Cornwall

ELDERFLOWER SORBET

225 g/8 oz granulated sugar
600 ml/1 pint water

2 lemons
2 good elderflower heads

PLACE sugar and water in a fair-sized pan. Heat gently, stirring well, until sugar is dissolved. Add thinly pared lemon rinds and boil briskly for 5 minutes. Remove from heat, add elderflower heads and squeezed lemon juice. Leave to cool then strain and freeze, stirring all the edges to middle as they harden. When all is set fairly hard beat well until the mixture is soft and light (or use a food processor if available). Re-freeze. Remove to refrigerator 40 minutes before required.

Any sorbet left can be refrozen, beating again if necessary. This dish freezes superbly and so can be an all year round treat – but of course you can only make the ice when the elderflower blooms. SERVES 4–6.

Mrs Audrey Williams, St Austell, Cornwall

☆ GOOSEBERRY SORBET ☆

450 g/1 lb gooseberries
600 ml/1 pint medium sweet cider
4 tablespoons castor sugar

2 egg whites
almonds and fruit for decoration

SIMMER the fruit in half the cider with half the sugar until tender. Liquidise in a food processor or blender and sieve to eliminate any pips. Chill.

Lightly whisk the egg whites with rest of sugar.

Pour the gooseberry purée, remaining cider and whisked egg whites into the gelato chef and switch on to freeze/churn for 25 minutes. If no machine is available, combine ingredients, put in freezer for 3–4 hours then process and freeze again until set. SERVES 6.

Mrs Bridget Best, Saltash, Cornwall

RASPBERRY CREAM DELIGHT

300 ml/½ pint double cream	100 g/4 oz castor sugar
3 eggs, separated	75–100 g/3–4 oz raspberries

WHIP cream in a bowl. In another large bowl whisk egg whites until stiff and gradually add sugar, whisking then stirring. Mix in lightly beaten egg yolks and fruit, add whipped cream and mix thoroughly. Put in freezer-proof container and freeze. Take out 45 minutes before serving and decorate with fresh raspberries and crushed cornflakes.

This is very good also when you replace berry fruit with rind and juice of 2 lemons. Very refreshing. SERVES 4–6.

Mrs Pam Lock, Landcross, North Devon

RASPBERRY CREAM PIE

BASE LAYER	175 g/6 oz icing sugar
12 Rich Tea biscuits	TOP LAYER
50 g/2 oz butter	300 ml/½ pint whipping cream
MIDDLE LAYER	225 g/8 oz fresh raspberries
1 large egg	biscuit crumbs to sprinkle
50 g/2 oz butter	

CRUMB biscuits, melt butter, add biscuits, stir and press mixture on to an 18-cm/7-inch ovenproof plate. Cook in a moderate oven (180 C, 350 F, gas 4) for 15 minutes. Cool.

Beat all ingredients for middle layer together until light and creamy. Spread on to biscuit base.

Whip cream for top until fairly stiff, fold in most of raspberries. Pile this on to middle layer. Decorate with reserved raspberries and dust with biscuit crumbs. Refrigerate until needed. This pudding freezes well. SERVES 4.

Mrs G. M. Parker, Gretton, Gloucestershire

STRAWBERRY ICE CREAM

225 g/8 oz strawberries
65 g/2½ oz castor sugar

1 tablespoon lemon juice
150 ml/¼ pint double cream

FRESH fruit is the best of course, but frozen may be used.

Hull fruit, rinse and allow to drain. Liquidise fruit or mash with potato masher. Stir in sugar and lemon juice. Whip cream until stiff and fold in purée. Pour into freezer tray and cover with film. Leave in freezing compartment of fridge, or freezer, for about 1½ hours, until partly set. Remove, lightly whip again then return to freezer for about another hour. Delicious. SERVES 4.

Mrs Eileen Foss, Chale Green, Isle of Wight

STRAWBERRY SORBET

225 g/8 oz castor sugar
300 ml/½ pint water
juice of 1 lemon

450 g/1 lb strawberries
red food colouring (optional)

PUT sugar and water in a saucepan, heat gently without stirring until dissolved. Boil for 1 minute then stir in strained lemon juice. Leave to cool.

Wipe and hull strawberries and liquidise with a little of the lemon syrup. Stir fruit into syrup, adding a few drops of red food colouring if liked. Pour into plastic container and put in freezer. When half-frozen beat with a hand or electric whisk until smooth and light. Re-freeze for 1–2 hours until just firm, then beat again. Refreeze until firm. SERVES 6.

Mrs M. Kerr, Kirkholm, Stranraer

TEA BREADS,
CAKES AND BISCUITS

OVALTINE LOAF

450 g/1 lb self-raising flour
100 g/4 oz sugar
40 g/1½ oz dry Ovaltine
175 g/6 oz dried fruit (sultanas are
 best)

1 tablespoon golden syrup
½ teaspoon bicarbonate of soda
pinch of salt
about 300 ml/½ pint milk

MIX all ingredients well together in a basin with enough milk to make rather moist. Bake for 1½–2 hours in a greased 1-kg/2-lb loaf tin in a cool oven (150 C, 300 F, gas 2).

This recipe has been handed down the family. It is quick and easy to make and proves very popular with all our visitors, young and old alike. It is very good in packed lunches, not breaking up and providing nourishment without being heavy.

Packed in foil the loaf will keep well for several weeks. It is best left 2–3 days before eating as buttered slices.

Mrs S. J. Deli, Singleborough, Milton Keynes

TEA CAKES

100 g/4 oz self-raising flour	1 egg
100 g/4 oz butter	vanilla essence
pinch of salt	milk
100 g/4 oz castor sugar	50 g/2 oz currants

SIFT the flour and rub in the butter, add salt and sugar and mix well. Beat the egg until frothy and add to dry ingredients. Beat well and add a few drops of vanilla essence. Beat again and add a little milk, until the mixture just drops from wooden spoon. Lastly mix in currants.

Line a flat tin 28 × 18 cm/11 × 7 inches with greased greaseproof paper, spread mixture over it. Bake in a moderately hot oven (200 c, 400 f, gas 6) for 15 minutes. Turn off oven and leave inside a further 5 minutes. When cold cut into squares.

Mrs P. D. Dyke, Upton Lovell, Wiltshire

CARROT CAKE

This is my version of a recipe given to me by New Zealand farming friends. It's unusual, healthy and adaptable. It can be served hot or cold: hot as a pudding with custard or cream, cold as a gâteau with whipped cream or a cream cheese frosting (25 g/1 oz butter, 50 g/2 oz cream cheese, 200 g/7 oz icing sugar, grated lemon rind). It uses ingredients to be found in anyone's store cupboard, it's inexpensive, quick and easy to make, kids love making it – and eating it. And lastly it is, of course, absolutely delicious.

2 eggs	100 g/4 oz wholemeal or plain
225 g/8 oz demerara sugar	white flour
175 ml/6 fl oz corn oil	175 g/6 oz grated carrot
1 teaspoon vanilla essence	75 g/3 oz sultanas (or any other
1 teaspoon bicarbonate of soda	dried fruit)
½ teaspoon salt	50 g/2 oz chopped nuts (optional)
1 teaspoon ground cinnamon	

WHISK the first seven ingredients together until really thick and foamy. Fold in the flour first, then the carrot and dried fruit and nuts, if used. Mix thoroughly.

Turn into a 1.25-litre/2-pint capacity tin (I use a ring tin) and bake in a moderate oven (180 c, 350 f, gas 4) for 60–65 minutes.

Miss Alison Compton, Forfar, Angus

BOILED FRUIT CAKE

450 g/1 lb sultanas or mixed dried fruit	225 g/8 oz butter or margarine, melted
350 g/12 oz castor sugar	450 g/1 lb self-raising flour
2 eggs	

BOIL fruit in water to cover for 10 minutes. Meanwhile, beat sugar and eggs, add butter. Drain the fruit and add it to the egg mixture. Stir well then add flour.

Turn into a 20-cm/8-inch greased cake tin and bake in a moderate oven (180 C, 350 F, gas 4) for 1½ hours.

This is an old Welsh recipe from West Wales.

Miss Rhian James, Llanon, Dyfed

CHERRY GINGER CAKE

150 g/5 oz crystallised ginger	3 medium eggs
75 g/3 oz glacé cherries	few drops of vanilla essence
225 g/8 oz self-raising flour	1 tablespoon milk
175 g/6 oz castor sugar	ICING
175 g/6 oz butter and margarine (half of each)	50 g/2 oz icing sugar
	1–2 drops of vanilla essence

GREASE and line a 23-cm/9-inch loaf tin. Reserve 6 pieces of ginger and 3 cherries for decoration. Cut remaining ginger into small pieces, halve cherries and flour them. Cream sugar and butter/margarine mixture. Beat eggs lightly and add alternately with sifted flour. Add vanilla essence and milk. Turn into tin and bake for 50 minutes in a moderate oven (180 C, 350 F, gas 4) then reduce to 160 C, 325 F, gas 3 for a further 25–30 minutes, until cooked. Cool.

To ice, beat a small amount of boiling water into icing sugar and vanilla. Ice top of cake. Cut ginger and cherries in half and use to decorate.

Mrs Alina Herbert, Stowe-by-Chartley, Staffordshire

MOTHER'S LAMBING CAKE

225 g/8 oz castor sugar
225 g/8 oz margarine
3 medium eggs
2 teaspoons ground mixed spice
1 teaspoon ground cinnamon

½ teaspoon ground ginger
450 g/1 lb self-raising flour
100 g/4 oz mixed dried fruit
about 200 ml/7 fl oz water
sugar to sprinkle

CREAM together sugar and margarine, beat in eggs. Mix spices well with the sifted flour and mixed fruit. Fold into the creamed mixture a little at a time. Add water as required to make a dropping consistency.

Put mixture, evenly divided, into two greased 1-kg/2-lb loaf tins and sprinkle with sugar. Bake in the centre of a cool oven (150c, 300 f, gas 2) for 30 minutes then reduce to 140c, 275 f, gas 1 for a further 1 hour.

When cooked turn out on to wire rack and cool. Makes 2 cakes.

Mrs S. R. Alderson, Craven Arms, Shropshire

APPLE CAKE

3 cooking apples
75 g/3 oz lard
225 g/8 oz self-raising flour
40 g/1½ oz sugar

1 teaspoon baking powder
1 egg, beaten
little milk

PEEL and core apples and put through mincer. Rub lard into flour, sugar and baking powder, add apples and mix with egg. If necessary add a little milk but it must be a very stiff dough as apples moisten when cooking. Bake in a greased flat cake tin about 30 minutes in a hot oven (220c, 425 f, gas 7).

Split whilst hot, spread with butter and dredge with sugar. Can also be served as a pudding with custard or cold.

Mixed spice and/or sultanas may be added for variety.

Mrs E. J. Large, Down-Ampney, Gloucestershire

AUTUMN APPLE CAKE

2–3 cooking apples
150 g/5 oz margarine
150 g/5 oz brown sugar
2 eggs
½ teaspoon ground cinnamon
½ teaspoon ground mixed spice

½ teaspoon bicarbonate of soda
225 g/8 oz plain flour
50 g/2 oz glacé cherries
50 g/2 oz chopped nuts
grated lemon rind

PREPARE and cook the apples with a little water and mash or sieve. You should have 100–175 g/4–6 oz pulp. Cool.

Cream margarine and sugar, add eggs. Sieve the spices, soda and flour and add to creamed mixture. Add cherries and nuts, lastly stir in apple pulp and grated lemon rind to taste.

Put into a greased and lined 18-cm/7-inch cake tin and sprinkle with castor sugar (it gives a crunchy topping). Cook in a moderate oven (180 C, 350 F, gas 4) for 45–55 minutes.

This keeps very moist.

Mrs R. Pugh, Monkhopton, Shropshire

SPICY APPLE CAKE

275 g/10 oz plain flour
¼ teaspoon baking powder
½ teaspoon bicarbonate of soda
pinch of salt
175 g/6 oz granulated sugar
100 g/4 oz soft margarine
1 egg
3 tablespoons milk
225 g/8 oz peeled and chopped
   cooking apples

TOPPING
40 g/1½ oz melted butter
100 g/4 oz soft brown sugar
1 tablespoon flour
2 teaspoons ground cinnamon
50 g/2 oz chopped nuts or
   desiccated coconut

SIFT dry ingredients, add sugar. Combine margarine, egg and milk, stir into dry ingredients, fold in chopped apples. Pour into a greased 23-cm/9-inch square tin.

Combine the topping ingredients and spread over cake mixture. Bake in a moderate oven (180 C, 350 F, gas 4) for about 30 minutes, or until cooked. Can be served warm or cold.

Mrs W. M. McIntyre, How Mill, Cumbria

HAZELNUT RING

100 g/4 oz margarine	chopped hazelnuts to sprinkle
275 g/10 oz self-raising flour	FILLING
100 g/4 oz castor sugar	200 g/7 oz minced hazelnuts
1 egg	75 g/3 oz sugar
2 tablespoons milk	1 egg plus 1 egg white
egg yolk to glaze	

RUB margarine into flour and sugar. Knead into dough with beaten egg and milk. If sticky, put in fridge for an hour. Roll out into a rectangle 1 cm/½ inch thick.

Mix nuts and sugar with beaten egg plus egg white, add a little water if too stiff. Spread over rectangle. Roll up lengthways, join ends, cut slits across top, glaze with egg yolk and sprinkle top with chopped nuts. Bake in a moderate oven (180 c, 350 f, gas 4) until the pastry is cooked and golden brown – about 45–50 minutes.

Ms M. Lintel, Otterham, Cornwall

SPRING LEMON CAKE

SPONGE	grated rind of 1 lemon
6 eggs, separated	25 g/1 oz flour
175 g/6 oz castor sugar	juice of 1 lemon made up to
2 tablespoons water	150 ml/¼ pint with water
grated rind of 1 lemon	300 ml/½ pint double or whipping
pinch of salt	cream
75 g/3 oz self-raising flour	100 g/4 oz chopped and toasted
25 g/1 oz cornflour	almonds
LEMON TOPPING	whipped cream and chocolate
1 egg	curls to decorate
150 g/5 oz castor sugar	

BEAT egg yolks, sugar, water, lemon rind and salt until light and fluffy. Sift together flour and cornflour and gradually blend into egg yolk mixture. Whisk egg whites until stiff but not dry and fold gently into yolk mixture. Place equal quantities of batter into three greased 18-cm/7-inch sandwich tins.

Bake in a moderate oven (180 c, 350 f, gas 4) for 35–40 minutes, or until golden brown. When cool remove from tins on to wire rack.

Make the topping. Beat egg, sugar and lemon rind together until foamy, add sifted flour and lemon juice and cook in top of double saucepan, stirring all the time until smooth and thick. Cool and fold in whipped cream, reserving some for decoration.

Spread two layers of sponge with lemon topping and sandwich all together. Cover sides of cake with topping and pat chopped almonds firmly round, then cover top and decorate with whipped cream whirls and chocolate curls.

Isobel Joyce, Baschurch, Shropshire

EASTER GÂTEAU

SPONGE	100 g/4 oz unblanched almonds,
5 eggs, separated	chopped
2 teaspoons tepid water	175 g/6 oz butter
215 g/7½ oz castor sugar	175 g/6 oz icing sugar
165 g/5½ oz plain flour	3 egg yolks
1 teaspoon baking powder	ASSEMBLY OF CAKE
FILLING	150 ml/¼ pint sherry
150 ml/¼ pint milk	150 ml/¼ pint milk

GREASE and line two 19-cm/7½-inch sandwich tins.

Beat egg yolks and water until pale and creamy. Beat whites until very stiff, add sugar gradually then beat in yolk mixture. Sift flour and baking powder twice and fold into egg mixture. Divide between tins and bake in a moderately hot oven (190 c, 375 f, gas 5) for 20–25 minutes, until springy. Leave in tins on a damp cloth for a few minutes. Remove from tins and cool.

Boil milk for filling, add almonds and leave to cool. Cream butter and icing sugar until light, add egg yolks one at a time. Then beat in cooled nut mixture.

Lightly grease tins in which cakes were cooked. Cut four strips of greaseproof paper and place in tins to make a cross on base and to come up above sides, to ensure easy removal of cakes.

Split each cake in two. Mix the sherry and milk together. Pour a quarter of this mixture on to a plate and dip in one cake round to soak. Place in prepared tin. Repeat with base of second cake. Cover each with one-third of filling mixture. Soak remaining sponge halves in sherry and milk and place on top of filling. Leave overnight in fridge. Turn out one cake on to serving plate and spread with remaining one-third of nut mixture. Place second cake on top.

Mrs J. Shanks, Ballynahinch, County Down

APRICOT CREAM CASHEW

175 g/6 oz dried apricots
450 ml/¾ pint water
175 g/6 oz soft margarine
175 g/6 oz dark muscovado sugar
3 large eggs
175 g/6 oz plain 100% wholewheat flour

2 teaspoons ground cinnamon
1 teaspoon ground mixed spice
1 tablespoon baking powder
150 ml/¼ pint double cream
2 tablespoons cashew nut pieces

SOAK the apricots in the water overnight. Simmer gently for about 30 minutes, drain and retain the liquid.

Cream the margarine and sugar. Add the beaten eggs gradually and beat well (a wooden spoon used throughout is ideal). Mix the flour, spices and baking powder well and add gradually to the creamed mixture. Beat well. Bake for about 1 hour in a moderate oven (180 C, 350 F, gas 4), in a greased and base-lined 18-cm/7-inch cake tin. Turn out and leave to cool.

Cut cake horizontally into three. Well moisten each layer with the retained apricot liquid, spread with apricots and whipped cream and sandwich together. Moisten the top with any remaining liquid, decorate with apricots and piped whipped cream. Sprinkle with cashew nut pieces and serve on a pedestal cake stand for maximum effect.

Mrs S. A. Rose, Bluntisham, Cambridgeshire

GRANDMOTHER'S SHORTBREAD

100 g/4 oz margarine
50 g/2 oz castor sugar

175 g/6 oz plain flour
½ teaspoon baking powder

CREAM fat and sugar, then add flour and baking powder. Press into a lightly greased 18-cm/7-inch sandwich tin.

Bake in a moderate oven (160 C, 325 F, gas 3) until just turning colour, about 40–50 minutes. Leave to cool for 5 minutes.

Mark into eighths. Remove from tin and finish cooling on a wire rack.

K. Brough, Caton, Lancashire

☆ SHORTBREAD DATE ☆ SLICES

FILLING
225 g/8 oz stoned dates
1 tablespoon honey
1 teaspoon ground cinnamon
150 ml/¼ pint cold water
2–3 teaspoons lemon juice

SHORTBREAD
175 g/6 oz margarine
85 g/3 oz castor sugar
175 g/6 oz self-raising flour
175 g/6 oz semolina

PUT all the filling ingredients into a pan and simmer until soft.

Melt the fat and sugar for the shortbread in another pan. Add flour and semolina and mix well. Put rather less than half the shortbread mix into a Swiss roll tin and spread with a palette knife. Put all the date mixture over this and spread rest of shortbread on top. Cook in a moderately hot oven (190 c, 375 F, gas 5) for about 25 minutes.

Cut into slices or squares and serve as a hot pudding with custard or cold at teatime.

Mrs T. Mobbs, Oulton, Suffolk

OAT BISCUITS

100 g/4 oz margarine or butter
100 g/4 oz sugar (brown or white)
1 tablespoon golden syrup
100 g/4 oz self-raising or
wholemeal flour

250 g/9 oz rolled oats
1 teaspoon bicarbonate of soda
dissolved in 4 tablespoons
boiling water

CREAM margarine and sugar until fluffy. Add golden syrup and beat in flour, oats and soda until a stiff dough. Roll into a long sausage shape and cut 40 pieces. In the palm of your hand, roll each piece into a ball, then squash flat and put on a baking tray. Cook in a moderate oven (180 c, 350 F, gas 4) for 15 minutes, or until brown.

These help at coffee time during winter to fill the men and there are still some left for the next day! Makes 40.

Mrs J. M. B. Stanley, Harvington, Worcestershire

☆ ROYAL HORNS ☆

BISCUITS
25 g/1 oz blanched almonds
2 egg whites
100 g/4 oz castor sugar
50 g/2 oz plain flour
½ teaspoon vanilla essence

50 g/2 oz melted butter
FILLING
300 ml/½ pint double or whipping
cream
225 g/8 oz strawberries
castor sugar to sprinkle

LIGHTLY grease at least three baking sheets and a rolling pin.

Cut the almonds into fine slivers or shreds. Place the egg whites in a bowl and beat in the sugar with a fork; the egg white should be frothy but by no means snowy. Sift in the flour and add the vanilla and almonds. Mix with the fork. Cool the butter (it should be melted but not hot), add to the mixture and stir well. Place the mixture in teaspoonfuls at least 13 cm/5 inches apart on the baking sheets and flatten well.

Bake in a moderate oven (180 c, 350 F, gas 4) until a good brown at the edges and pale biscuit-coloured in the middle, about 6 minutes. Remove from the oven and cool for a few seconds. Lift the biscuits off carefully with a palette knife. Lay them individually, while still warm and pliable, over the rolling pin to form into a slightly curved shape. As soon as they are stone cold put into an airtight tin or plastic bag to keep crisp.

Whip the cream. Halve if small or slice large strawberries, saving the best whole for decoration. Sprinkle with a little castor sugar. The biscuits must not be filled until just before serving or they will not remain crisp. This is not difficult as both the strawberries and cream can be prepared and ready in the refrigerator. Combine strawberries and cream, do not include too much juice, fill cones and top with one lovely berry.

Mrs George, Peterston Super Ely, Cardiff

PRESERVES

Mrs Lily Byford's Recipe for Mincemeat

This is my mother's recipe for mincemeat, and it was her mother's; it is different from all other mincemeat recipes because it is cooked and does not contain suet. It is deliciously moist – can be eaten from the pot!

450 g/1 lb peeled and chopped cooking apples
450 g/1 lb soft brown sugar
450 g/1 lb currants
450 g/1 lb raisins (large if possible)
450 g/1 lb sultanas

225 g/8 oz whole mixed peel, thinly sliced
grated rind and juice of 1 lemon
grated rind and juice of 2 oranges
1 teaspoon ground mixed spice
225 g/8 oz butter

Mix all thoroughly together in a preserving pan or large saucepan. Bring to the boil, stirring, and simmer for 15 minutes. Allow to cool before potting.

I make this every other autumn and it keeps that long. Makes about 3.25 kg/7 lb.

Mrs E. E. Hern, Billingborough, Lincolnshire

RICH MINCEMEAT

450 g/1 lb peeled and finely
  chopped cooking apples
  (prepared weight)
450 g/1 lb dates, finely chopped
450 g/1 lb shredded beef suet
675 g/1½ lb sultanas
100 g/4 oz ground almonds

grated rind and juice
  of 1 large or 2 small oranges
2 teaspoons ground mixed spice
450 g/1 lb soft brown sugar
150 ml/¼ pint cooking sherry
1 wineglass whisky, brandy or
  rum

PUT the first six ingredients in a large bowl and mix well. Sprinkle on the spice and sugar, then stir in all the alcohol.

Stir well and leave overnight in bowl, stir again next day and put into clean dry jars. Keeps for as long as 3 months (maybe longer but we eat ours quickly). Makes about 2.75 kg/6 lb.

Mrs L. Kenworthy, Mansfield-Woodhouse, Nottinghamshire

PEAR CONSERVE

1.75 kg/4 lb pears, peeled and
  quartered

900 g/2 lb granulated sugar
grated rind and juice of 2 lemons

COVER pear pieces with sugar and leave to stand overnight. Put into a pan with lemon rind and juice. Bring to the boil, cover the pan and simmer very gently for 2 hours, until pink and syrup thick. Make sure that the liquid does not dry up during cooking. Place into warm thoroughly scalded jars and seal. Serve as a topping for ice cream. Makes about 1.75 kg/4 lb.

Mrs J. Robinson, Beeley, Derbyshire

MICHAELMAS PEARS

4 kg/9 lb Conference pears
2 kg/4½ lb sugar

600 ml/1 pint malt vinegar
few cloves

PEEL pears and quarter them. Dissolve sugar in vinegar in a large saucepan. Add pears and boil until tender. Add a few cloves at last. Allow to cool then bottle. Leave for one month before eating – delicious with cold meats or cheese. Makes about 4 kg/9 lb.

Mrs L. Boor, Crowland, nr Peterborough

☆ HEDGEROW CHEESE ☆

an autumn afternoon's picking of crab apples, elderberries, sloes and
blackberries

To every 450 g/1 lb of crab apples, add 450 g/1 lb of mixed fruit as
above. Wash and roughly chop the crab apples and place in a
preserving pan. Wash and remove elderberries from stalks. Wash
and pick over sloes and blackberries. Add to pan with water,
600 ml/1 pint to every 1.5 kg/3 lb fruit. Simmer until all fruit is
soft. Sieve softened fruit and measure pulp. To every 600 ml/1 pint
of pulp, add 450 g/1 lb sugar. Boil to setting point. Skim, pot and
cover in the usual way.

Use as jelly or jam, but it has a thicker, old-fashioned consistency. It would be possible to use any combination of the berries
and sloes, but half the total amount of fruit must be crab apples.
Makes about 1.5 kg/3 lb (using 1 kg/2 lb fruit).

Mrs M. Nuttal, Great Washbourne, Gloucestershire

PICKLED PLUMS

1.5 kg/3 lb plums	3 blades mace
600 ml/1 pint vinegar	1 stick of cinnamon
675 g/1½ lb sugar	½ teaspoon ground allspice
1 tablespoon cloves	

PIERCE each plum and place in a large bowl. Boil the vinegar with
the sugar and spices tied in a muslin bag for 15 minutes, then pour
over plums. Stand for 24 hours and then boil together again for a
few minutes.

Bottle and tie down. Ready at once. Serve with cold meats or
cheese. Makes about 1.5 kg/3 lb.

Mrs R. Gilling, Rooksbridge, Somerset

APPLE CHUTNEY

1 kg/2 lb cooking apples, peeled
and cored
350 g/12 oz seedless raisins or
sultanas
1 medium onion, peeled and sliced
600 ml/1 pint malt vinegar

350 g/12 oz brown sugar
2 teaspoons ground ginger
1 teaspoon dry mustard
2 teaspoons salt
2 red chillies

CHOP or mince apples, raisins and onion. Put into saucepan with
vinegar, sugar, ginger, mustard, salt and chillies. Bring to the boil
then simmer gently until the mixture is a thick pulp, about 1 hour.
Turn into dry, warm jars and cover when cold. (Don't forget to
remove chillies.) Makes about 1.5–1.75 kg/3–4 lb.

Mrs Margaret Carter, Wingate, Co Durham

NELLIE'S HARVEST CHUTNEY

450 g/1 lb onions, peeled and
sliced finely into rings
450 g/1 lb Bramley cooking
apples, peeled, sliced and
quartered
450 g/1 lb ripe tomatoes, cut into
thin slices and then halved
225 g/8 oz courgettes or marrow,
peeled and diced (seeds
removed)

225 g/8 oz sultanas
450 g/1 lb soft brown sugar
20 g/¾ oz salt
pinch of ground ginger
pinch of ground mixed spice
750 ml/1¼ pints vinegar

PLACE all the ingredients in an enamel pan and boil for 2½ hours;
stir often during cooking with a wooden spoon. Remove from heat
and allow to cool slightly. Stir again, and with a cup ladle it into
clean warm jars. Cover with cling film and keep for a fortnight.
Delicious with cold meats. Makes about 2–2.25 kg/4–5 lb.

Mrs Nellie Brocklehurst, North Rode, Cheshire

MIXED VEGETABLE CHUTNEY

300 ml/½ pint vinegar
225 g/8 oz brown sugar
225 g/8 oz onions
225 g/8 oz celery
225 g/8 oz red tomatoes

225 g/8 oz cooking apples
225 g/8 oz cooking dates
½ teaspoon salt
½ teaspoon pepper
½–1 teaspoon ground ginger

PUT vinegar into a saucepan with the sugar and heat gently until dissolved. Put vegetables and dates through a mincer then add to pan with seasoning and spice. Cook until liquid has gone. Pot and then cover when cold. A most appetising chutney. Makes about 1.5 kg/3 lb.

Mrs C. A. Freeman, Newbold Verdon, Leicestershire

GREEN BEAN CHUTNEY

This is a good recipe for using up a surplus of runner beans. Very good with cold meats and cheese.

1.5 kg/3 lb sliced runner beans	1½ teaspoons dry mustard
1.5 kg/3 lb sliced onions	1½ teaspoons turmeric powder
900 ml/1½ pints vinegar	2 teaspoons cornflour
675 g/1½ lb demerara sugar	

BOIL beans in water and a little salt until tender. Boil onions in a separate pan until tender. Strain both, combine together in one saucepan, add vinegar (except 2 tablespoons) and sugar. Boil for 15 minutes.

In a basin mix mustard, turmeric and cornflour to a paste with the reserved vinegar. Add to the beans and onions and boil for another 15 minutes. Put into hot jam jars and cover. Makes about 2.25 kg/5 lb.

Mrs Eileen Hambly, Pengover, Cornwall

SHOOTING PARTY CHUTNEY

2.25 kg/5 lb green tomatoes	225 g/8 oz sliced apples
salt	½ teaspoon cayenne pepper
1.15 litres/2 pints malt vinegar	225 g/8 oz dates or sultanas
675 g/1½ lb demerara sugar	½ teaspoon ground ginger
225 g/8 oz sliced onions	

CHOP or mince the tomatoes and sprinkle with salt. Leave overnight, strain and add all remaining ingredients.

Bring to the boil slowly and simmer for 2 hours. Leave to cool. Put down when cold.

A mild, sweet chutney. Good with salads and curry. Makes about 3.5 kg/8 lb.

Mrs L. Dallyn, Petworth, Sussex

APPLE AND TOMATO CHUTNEY

1.5 kg/3 lb apples, peeled and
   cored
1 kg/2 lb tomatoes
450 g/1 lb seedless raisins, cut up
450 g/1 lb brown sugar
25 g/1 oz ground ginger

1 large onion, cut up
50 g/2 oz mustard seed
1 tablespoon salt
1.15 litres/2 pints vinegar
cayenne pepper to taste

SIMMER all the ingredients together steadily until thick, about 2 hours. Cool down and put into pots. Makes about 3.25 kg/7 lb.

Mrs M. Vickers, Legsby, Lincolnshire

AUTUMN FRUIT CHUTNEY

1 kg/2 lb stoned plums
1 kg/2 lb Bramley cooking apples
1 kg/2 lb tomatoes
1 kg/2 lb onions
1–2 cloves garlic
25 g/1 oz salt
½ teaspoon cayenne pepper

½ teaspoon ground mixed spice
½ teaspoon powdered mace
50-g/2-oz piece fresh root ginger,
   peeled
450 g/1 lb sultanas
600 ml/1 pint vinegar
450 g/1 lb demerara sugar

CLEAN and mince all fresh fruit and vegetables. Put in pan, add spices and sultanas. Boil in vinegar until thick and tender. Add sugar and continue cooking for up to 2 hours in all, until thick and you can smell the aroma of good old chutney to eat with a good old ploughman's lunch which is very popular in the old-fashioned farmhouse. Makes about 3.5 kg/8 lb.

Mrs M. Jude, Stacksford, Norfolk

WINTER SALAD

225 g/8 oz green tomatoes
1 whole head celery
3 large onions
1 white cabbage
600 ml/1 pint vinegar

450 g/1 lb sugar
1 tablespoon salt
1 tablespoon cornflour
1½ teaspoons dry mustard
1½ teaspoons turmeric powder

PEEL and quarter the tomatoes. Prepare and chop the celery, onions and cabbage. Simmer in the vinegar until soft then add all remaining ingredients. Cook until it thickens, stirring from time to time. Cool and pot in airtight jars, then store in a cool place. Lovely with cold meats. Makes about 4 kg/9 lb.

Mrs J. F. McClurg, Willington, Co. Durham

QUICK AND EASY DISHES

SHRIMPS AND AVOCADO

TAKE a ripe avocado, cut in half lengthways and remove stone. Fill with a mixture of shrimps, mayonnaise and half a hard-boiled egg, mashed. Season to taste and serve on lettuce.

Superior for a lazy hazy day. SERVES 2.

Mrs M. Clark, Grange-over-Sands, Cumbria

CHEESE SHRIMP

8 drained pineapple rings
225 g/8 oz full fat soft cream cheese
225 g/8 oz small shrimps
salt, pepper and paprika to taste

1 teaspoon lemon juice
3 tablespoons double cream
1 lettuce
stuffed olives and parsley to garnish

DRAIN pineapple rings. Beat cheese until smooth, add shrimps. Season with salt, pepper, paprika and add lemon juice and cream.

Put four small lettuce leaves on each plate, place a pineapple ring on top. Fill rings with shrimp cheese mixture and garnish with halved stuffed olives and parsley. Serves 8 as a starter.

Anon.

EGG PRAWN CURRY

25 g/1 oz butter
50 g/2 oz onions, chopped
1 teaspoon curry powder (or to taste)
1 298-g/10½-oz can condensed cream of mushroom soup
2 tablespoons cream

175 g/6 oz prawns (fresh, frozen or canned)
2 tablespoons cooked stir fry vegetables
275 g/10 oz long-grain rice, cooked
4 hard-boiled eggs, halved
2 tablespoons chopped parsley

MELT butter in saucepan and fry onion until soft but not coloured. Stir in curry powder and cook for 1 minute. Add the soup and bring to the boil. Stir in the cream, prawns and vegetables.

Put the hot cooked rice on a large plate or dish, pour the curry in the middle, arrange over the eggs and sprinkle with parsley. This is a very nice meal and quite cheap. SERVES 4.

M. V. Chesworth, Vicars Cross, Cheshire

QUICK AND EASY FISH DISH

450 g/1 lb filleted fish (cod, haddock or any fish without bones)
1 425-g/15-oz can peeled tomatoes

100–225 g/4–8 oz mushrooms
50 g/2 oz grated cheese
50 g/2 oz fresh breadcrumbs

PLACE the fish in a shallow baking dish. Pour over whole tin of tomatoes including juice, making sure that juice has passed over all parts of fish.

Wash or wipe mushrooms and place in dish. Sprinkle cheese and breadcrumbs over all and cook in a moderate oven (180 C, 350 F, gas 4) for about 30 minutes, or until fish is cooked and cheese has melted and browned. Make sure it is not overcooked.

Serve with a sprig of parsley and potatoes and colourful vegetables. SERVES 4.

Mrs L. M. Halton-Farrow, Framingham Earl, Norfolk

BAKED CHEESE AND SALMON MOULD

1 212-g/7½-oz can salmon, red or
    pink
75 g/3 oz cheese, grated

3 large eggs
450 ml/¾ pint milk
salt and pepper

GREASE a deep pie dish well. Drain salmon and flake, discarding any skin and bone. Place in the pie dish and sprinkle over half the cheese. Beat eggs and milk well together, add salt and pepper to taste and pour over contents in the dish.

Place the dish in a baking tin with 2.5 cm/1 inch of water in it and cook in a moderate oven (180 c, 350 F, gas 4) for about 30 minutes, or until set. Take from oven, sprinkle on rest of cheese and brown slightly under hot grill.

When cold garnish with cress and sliced radish and serve with a crispy lettuce salad. SERVES 4.

Mrs B. D. Jackson, Austwick, Lancashire

TUNA MACARONI

175 g/6 oz macaroni
600 ml/1 pint milk
2 tablespoons cornflour
salt and pepper
¼ teaspoon mustard powder

175 g/6 oz Cheddar cheese
4 tablespoons chopped parsley
1 198-g/7-oz can tuna fish
1 small packet potato crisps

BRING 1.15 litres/2 pints salted water to boil in a large pan, add macaroni and boil without lid for time stated on packet.

Meanwhile make a sauce by blending 2 tablespoons of the milk with the cornflour, salt, pepper and mustard powder. Bring rest of milk to boil, remove from heat and stir in the cornflour mixture. Put pan back on to heat and stir until sauce boils. Simmer for 2 minutes. Add 75 g/3 oz grated cheese to sauce and stir until melted. Mix in parsley and flaked tuna fish.

Drain the macaroni. Combine the sauce with the macaroni and pour into a baking dish. Sprinkle the rest of the grated cheese on top and place under a hot grill until golden brown and bubbling. Garnish with potato crisps and serve immediately.

This recipe is nice served with a green vegetable, for lunch or supper on a cold day. SERVES 4.

Mrs M. A. Griffiths, Bayton, Worcestershire

DABS WITH SAGE DERBY AND A STRAWBERRY SALAD

1 or 2 dabs per person, depending
on size and appetite
about 25 g/1 oz Sage Derby cheese
per fish

a dash of cream
black pepper

GRILL the dabs. Meanwhile grate cheese and mix it with cream and pepper. When the dabs are nearly done, pile the cheese mixture on to them and continue to grill until bubbling.

Serve with buttered new potatoes, green beans and this strawberry salad: rip a crisp lettuce into neat pieces, mix with watercress and strawberries and a few black olives, then toss in a favourite vinaigrette dressing.

Nancy Green, Goldhanger, Essex

ITALIAN BACON

225 g/8 oz spaghetti
450 g/1 lb bacon pieces or rashers
2 tablespoons oil

2 large onions, chopped
1 64-g/2¼-oz tin tomato purée
100 g/4 oz grated cheese

COOK spaghetti in plenty of boiling salted water. Fry bacon in oil until cooked, remove from pan. Fry chopped onion, drain off oil, add tomato purée and 300 ml/½ pint water.

When sauce has thickened combine with drained spaghetti and cooked bacon. Heat through then serve on warmed dish with grated cheese on top. SERVES 4.

Barbara Burchmore, Great Horwood, Milton Keynes

CORNED BEEF HOT POT

1 kg/2 lb potatoes
1 340-g/12-oz can corned beef
1 454-g/16-oz can garden peas
1 447-g/15¾-oz can baked beans in
tomato sauce

2 beef stock cubes (Oxo or Bovril)
600 ml/1 pint boiling water
salt and pepper
butter to dot

PEEL and put the potatoes on to boil. Dice the corned beef into approximately 1-cm/½-inch cubes, place in a large oval ovenproof dish and add the peas and baked beans. Dissolve the beef cubes in the boiling water and pour over. Add salt and pepper to taste. Drain the potatoes when cooked, slice and place on top of the beef and vegetables. Dot with butter and cook in a moderately hot oven (190 c, 375 f, gas 5) until nicely browned on the top – about 45 minutes.

I devised this recipe for Corned Beef Hot Pot and have been making it for well over 30 years. It is quick and easy to make, hot and nourishing, packed with protein and a useful standby as the ingredients can be found in every pantry. It can be made from start to finish in just over an hour and, so useful on a farm, kept warm without spoiling. SERVES 6.

Mrs Dorothy Faraday, Tatham Fells, Lancashire

MINCE ROLL

450 g/1 lb minced beef
2 tablespoons rolled oats
1 medium onion, finely chopped
1 tablespoon apple chutney

1 tablespoon tomato ketchup
1 egg, beaten
salt and pepper

MIX all ingredients together and spread on greased tin foil. Fasten edges of foil to make a roll and cook in a moderate oven (180 c, 350 f, gas 4) for about 1 hour. Can be eaten hot or cold. SERVES 4.

Mrs E. J. Sidley, Brill, Buckinghamshire

AUTUMN SAUSAGE

8 large pork sausages
4 rashers bacon
450 g/1 lb cooking apples, peeled
   and sliced

about 150 ml/¼ pint dry cider
salt and pepper

WRAP each sausage in half a bacon rasher and place in a shallow casserole.

Cover with slices of apple, pour in cider and season to taste.

Cook in a moderately hot oven (190 c, 375 f, gas 5) for ¾–1 hour, depending on thickness of sausage. Serve with mashed potatoes and green vegetables. SERVES 4.

Mrs E. Overington, Whixall, Shropshire

SPEEDY SAUSAGE PIE

LINE the base of a pie dish with sausagemeat, cook in a moderately hot oven (190 C, 375 F, gas 5) for about 30 minutes, then drain off the fat. Slice tomatoes on top, followed by cheese sauce. Bake through in the oven until piping hot.

Mrs P. Uthwatt-Bouverie, Ashfield, Suffolk

CHEESE AND CHOPS

4 lamb or pork chops	salt and pepper
2 medium onions	1 teaspoon sugar
1 396-g/14-oz can tomatoes (or	50 g/2 oz grated cheese
sliced fresh tomatoes)	50 g/2 oz fresh breadcrumbs

REMOVE most of fat from chops and bone if liked. Brown chops in hot fat to seal each side. Peel and slice onions thinly.

Place chops in a shallow casserole in a single layer. Put sliced onions over chops, pour on tomatoes, sprinkle with salt, pepper, sugar and finally the cheese and breadcrumbs mixed. Cover with foil and cook for 1 hour in a moderate oven (180 C, 350 F, gas 4), then a further 30 minutes uncovered, until a crispy top is formed. Serve with a green salad and potatoes. SERVES 4.

E. J. Sidley, Brill, Buckinghamshire

LAMB IN DEVIL SAUCE

50 g/2 oz butter	½ teaspoon salt
2 tablespoons chopped onion	¼ teaspoon cayenne pepper
1 tablespoon vinegar	piece cold roast lamb
2 tablespoons redcurrant jelly	1 tablespoon tomato purée
½ teaspoon French mustard	

HEAT butter in frying pan. Fry onion until transparent. Add vinegar, then redcurrant jelly and stir over a low heat until the jelly melts. Add mustard, salt and pepper.

Cut cold roast lamb into slices. Lay these in the sauce and keep at simmering point for 5 minutes. Transfer meat to a hot dish. Add the tomato purée to the sauce, reheat and pour over meat. Serves up to 4 people (depending on amount of lamb).

Mrs K. I. Martin, Great Missenden, Buckinghamshire

TIPSY CHICKEN

2 tablespoons oil
1 large onion, chopped
4 chicken portions
1 64-g/2¼-oz can tomato purée
6 tablespoons medium sherry

175 ml/6 fl oz cold water
2 teaspoons curry powder
1 teaspoon dried sweet basil
salt and pepper to taste

HEAT the oil in a large saucepan. Add the chopped onion and fry gently until transparent. Stir in the chicken portions and remaining ingredients. Bring to the boil and simmer for approximately 1 hour, or until the chicken is cooked.

If desired, the portions of chicken can be removed 10 minutes before serving and grilled to a golden brown.

Serve with spring cabbage and potatoes or with a crisp salad. SERVES 4.

Mrs Shelley Greensmith, Skeffington, Leicestershire

CHICKEN DIVINE

1 cooked chicken, shredded
2 298-g/10½-oz cans condensed
  cream of chicken soup
250 ml/8 fl oz mayonnaise
2 teaspoons lemon juice

½ teaspoon curry powder
TOPPING
50 g/2 oz grated cheese
25 g/1 oz fresh breadcrumbs

WHEN cooking the chicken add 600 ml/1 pint water and use this stock produce to thin the sauce, although not too much as it goes thinner when hot.

Mix all the sauce ingredients together, adding stock to make required consistency, and pour over shredded chicken in an ovenproof dish.

Adjust curry powder to suit but it should not taste of curry.

Top with the cheese and breadcrumbs mixed together and bake for 30 minutes in a moderate oven (180 C, 350 F, gas 4). Serve with peas and potatoes or rice. SERVES 6.

Mrs C. M. Johnson, Malpas, Cheshire

SUMMER CHICKEN

4 chicken thighs or breasts (about 175 g/6 oz each)	50 g/2 oz butter
	salt and black pepper
grated rind and juice of 1 lemon	225 g/8 oz strawberries, sliced
200 ml/7 fl oz dry cider	150 ml/¼ pint double cream
sprig of fresh tarragon	parsley sprigs to garnish

SKIN the chicken pieces and secure in a neat shape with a wooden cocktail stick. Place in an ovenproof dish, pour over the lemon juice and cider, add the lemon rind and sprig of tarragon. Dot chicken with the butter and season lightly with salt and pepper. Cover the dish with foil and cook for 25–30 minutes in a moderately hot oven (200 c, 400 f, gas 6).

When cooked, remove chicken from dish and drain, place on a serving dish lined with the sliced strawberries and keep warm.

Remove the sprig of tarragon and boil the remaining liquor rapidly until reduced to half the quantity. Gradually stir in the cream and then adjust seasoning. Pour sauce over the chicken, garnish with sprigs of parsley and serve immediately. Delicious in summer served with a crisp green salad and minted new potatoes. SERVES 4.

Mrs H. J. Cooke, Upper Sunden, Bedfordshire

FRICASSÉE OF CHICKEN OR TURKEY

25 g/1 oz margarine	1 227-g/8-oz can button mushrooms
25 g/1 oz flour	
300 ml/½ pint milk	450 g/1 lb cooked chicken or turkey meat
salt and pepper	

MAKE a sauce with the margarine, flour and milk, and cook for a few minutes. Season to taste, add mushrooms and water from the tin, and mix well with the sauce. Lastly stir in the diced chicken meat, cover and allow to heat thoroughly. Serve with rice or potatoes, green peas, beans or broad beans.

My own recipe which is very acceptable after salads all summer. SERVES 4–6.

Mrs N. Gray, Hethel, Norfolk

MELTED CHEESE AND ONIONS

*I am not a cookery enthusiast and appreciate quick simple
dishes, all the more so if the dish is inexpensive and enjoyed
by the whole family.*

450 g/1 lb onions
margarine or oil to fry
1 425-g/15-oz can tomatoes or
equivalent fresh tomatoes

pinch herbs (optional)
100 g/4 oz sliced Cheddar cheese

PEEL and chop onions, cook gently in margarine or oil until tender,
usually about 10 minutes. Add tomatoes, mix thoroughly, sprinkle
in herbs if required and pour into casserole. Top with sliced cheese
and place in a hot oven (220 c, 425 f, gas 7) for 5 minutes.

Serve on its own or on halved "stotty cake" as it is known locally.
We often eat this dish as high tea or for supper. SERVES 4.

Mrs A. M. Stott, Croxdale, Co. Durham

NUT ROAST

100 g/4 oz mixed nuts, milled or
ground
3 tablespoons sunflower seeds
3 tablespoons soya flour
seasoning and herbs (use fresh if
available)

1 large onion, grated
2 large eggs, beaten
1 tablespoon sunflower oil
100 g/4 oz mushrooms, chopped
sesame seeds and butter/
margarine for topping

MIX nuts, seeds, flour, seasoning and herbs to taste. Add onion,
mix in eggs and oil and fold in mushrooms. Turn mixture into a
greased 23-cm/9-inch pie or quiche dish, sprinkle with sesame
seeds and dot with butter or margarine. Bake in a moderately hot
oven (190 c, 375 f, gas 5) for about 30 minutes, until golden.
SERVES 3–4.

Miss G. C. Carrington, Bradford on Avon, Wiltshire

WINTER FRUIT SALAD

ADD some orange juice to tinned or bottled rhubarb, sweeten to taste and bring to the boil. Remove from heat and while still hot add some raisins and sliced banana; it is the hot banana that enriches the flavour. When cold, chop into it any other available fruit – apples, oranges, grapes, etc.

This is filling but refreshing after a heavy main course. I invented it one day when a family of six arrived unexpectedly and I had to stretch a small amount of cold rhubarb to feed eight.

Mrs Mary Beardshaw, Treswell, Nottinghamshire

SPEEDY, EASY AND LUXURIOUS

4 large cooking apples (end of season which have turned a bit sweet)
1 heaped tablespoon honey
6 tablespoons hot water
1 298-g/10½-oz can mandarin oranges

100 g/4 oz raisins or sultanas
1 227-g/8-oz can pineapple pieces
100 g/4 oz dried figs
50 g/2 oz dates
3 bananas
about 175 g/6 oz seedless grapes

PREPARE apples into little chunks and place in a large bowl. Melt honey in water and pour over apples. Pour juice from mandarins over raisins or sultanas and leave to soak. Save all excess juice from both tins of fruit. Add drained pineapple pieces and mandarin oranges to the apple. Cut up figs and dates into small pieces and add to rest. Slice bananas and fold into fruit gently. Wash and drain grapes and add to the bowl of fruit. Add plumped dried fruit and stir gently.

Taste: if too sweet add juice of lemon, if too stodgy add more of the tinned fruit juices. For special occasions add a wineglass of sherry. Serve with custard, whipped or pouring cream or just plain.

Will keep for some days in fridge and can be topped up when in a hurry with more apples and leftovers in the fruit bowl. SERVES 8.

Barbara Wickalls, Berkhamsted, Hertfordshire

FRUIT SURPRISE

300 ml/½ pint whipping cream
150 ml/¼ pint natural yogurt
honey to sweeten (about 2
    teaspoons)

raspberries and/or strawberries
    (225–450 g/8 oz–1 lb, depending
    on availability and flavour
    required)

WHIP cream, add all other ingredients. Put in fridge until required. SERVES 4.

Mary Barber, Bowsden, Northumberland

FIVE MINUTE RASPBERRY CREAM

2 egg whites
300 ml/½ pint whipping cream
2 tablespoons dry sherry

450 g/1 lb fresh raspberries
castor sugar

WHISK egg whites, set aside. Whip cream, add sherry, fold in egg whites. Sprinkle raspberries with sugar to taste.

Layer raspberries and cream in a glass dish or individual goblets, top with a few raspberries. SERVES 4.

Mrs Gwenda Bendall, Marksbury, Bath

INDEX

Adstone summer chicken 157
Almond:
  Almond nutty apples 171
  Almond pastry 185
  Almond puff 191
  Almond raspberry tart 188
Angela's autumn apple pie 184
Apple:
  Almond nutty apples 171
  Angela's autumn apple pie 184
  Apple and blackberry soufflé
    pudding with sherry sauce 192
  Apple and brandy cream flan 228
  Apple cake 250
  Apple chutney 260
  Apple crisp 180
  Apple hedgehog 172
  Apple and marzipan tart 185
  Apple meringue 202
  Apple and mint stuffing 64
  Apple posset 209
  Apple and tomato chutney 262
  Aunt Alice's summer apple pie
    176
  Autumn apple cake 251
  Baked pork chops with apple
    and onion sauce 79
  Blackberry and apple delight 181
  Blackberry and apple strudel 186
  Blushing apples 200
  Bramble dessert 202
  Bramley pork pie 128
  Coburg pie 185
  Crisp-topped apple pudding 180
  Egg, mincemeat and apple flan
    184
  Hot apple slice 187
  Lemon apple slice 183
  Millin apple charlotte 181
  Norfolk apple and blackberry
    pudding 192
  Pommy rabbit 115

Pork and apple dish 85
Pork and apple savoury 78
Prunes and apples hare 117
Sausagemeat, apple and onion
  pie 130
Somerset lamb 62
Sour cream pie 186
Spicy apple cake 251
Swiss toffee apple 199
Tuna and apple salad 159
Apricot:
  Apricot braised lamb 63
  Apricot cream cashew 254
  Apricot-stuffed shoulder 66
  Lamb with apricots and
    coriander 69
  Lamb chops and apricots 58
  Princess charlotte 219
  Sweet poached eggs 222
Aunt Alice's summer apple pie 176
Autumn apple cake 251
Autumn chicken casserole 101
Autumn chicken stew 98
Autumn fruit chutney 262
Autumn pancakes 197
Autumn pheasant casserole 110
Autumn pork casserole 81
Autumn sausage 267
Autumn slow bake 48
Autumnal pot roast 66
Avocado:
  Salmon and avocado mousse 22
  Shrimps and avocado pears 263

Bacon:
  Bacon beany 92
  Bacon casserole 94
  Bacon chops with creamed
    mushrooms 92
  Bacon Italian 266
  Bacon and pea hot pot 140
  Bacon and potato puff 138

Chibble pasty 128
Crispy cheese and bacon dish 139
Farmhouse bean and bacon soup
   13
Haynes Landrace au gratin 94
Winter bacon warmer 90
Banana meringue pie 190
Barbecue meat loaf 52
Bean:
  Bacon beany 92
  Bean gunge 140
  Butter bean and fish pie 32
  Farmhouse bean and bacon soup
    13
  Green bean chutney 261
  Guernsey bean jar 141
  Sausage and bean supper 86
Beef. See also Corned beef
  Autumn slow bake 48
  Barbecue meat loaf 52
  B.B.C. casserole 39
  Beef casserole surprise 43
  Beef cosmopolitan 45
  Beef and pork loaf 146
  Beer stew 40
  Brisket hot pot 44
  Cheese and beefburger pie 142
  Curried spaghetti mince 49
  Curried vols-au-vent 148
  Family casserole 40
  Family warm-up casserole 43
  Farmhouse beef casserole 41
  Fruity Scotch beef 42
  Grandma's farmhouse pie 125
  Irish hot pot 42
  Mince roll 267
  Mince and yogurt pie 126
  Mum's surprise 127
  Nethercott noshup 48
  Peanut chop 51
  Puff-topped beef and wine pie
    126
  Steak and kidney with savoury
    crust 44
  Steaming hot pot of chilli con
    carne 47

  Summer curry 46
  Summer steak parcel 38
Beer stew 40
Biscuits *see* Cakes etc.
Black cherry cheesecake 235
Blackberry:
  Apple and blackberry soufflé
    pudding with sherry sauce 192
  Blackberry and apple delight 181
  Blackberry and apple strudel 186
  Blackberry clouds 210
  Blackberry cream 210
  Blackberry roll 186
  Bramble delight 221
  Bramble dessert 202
  Bramble and hazelnut sponge
    179
  Bramble mousse 211
  Norfolk apple and blackberry
    pudding 192
  Purple pudding 198
  Yorkshire bramble pudding 179
Blackcurrant:
  Blackcurrant delight on biscuit
    base 229
  Blackcurrant flummery 211
  Blackcurrant royale 201
  Blackcurrant velvet 212
Blushing apples 200
Bombe princesse 242
Bramble *see* Blackberry
Bramley pork pie 128
Brandy cream, pear tart with 188
Brisket hot pot 44
Buckling and potato salad 160
Butter bean and fish pie 32

Cabbage:
  Callcannon 161
  Red cabbage and pork 75
Cakes, teabreads and biscuits:
  Apple cake 250
  Apricot cream cashew 254
  Autumn apple cake 251
  Boiled fruit cake 249
  Carrot cake 248

Cakes, etc – cont.
Cherry ginger cake 249
Easter gâteau 253
Grandmother's shortbread 254
Hazelnut ring 252
Mother's lambing cake 250
Oat biscuits 255
Ovaltine loaf 247
Royal horns 256
Shortbread date slices 255
Spicy apple cake 251
Spring lemon cake 252
Tea cakes 248
Callcannon 161
Canes Farm rabbit casserole 118
Carrot:
Carrot cake 248
Carrot and watercress mousse
  with tarragon cream 15
Luxury carrots 162
Cashew and gooseberry stuffing 65
Cassoulet 74
Cauliflower:
Cauli crisp 152
Cauliflower soufflé flan 121
Cauliflower starter 16
Fluffy cauliflower bake 163
Celery:
Chicken with bacon and celery
  105
Chicken, celery and walnut salad
  156
Pork chops in celery sauce 77
Charlotte delight 219
Cheese:
Baked cheese and salmon mould
  265
Cheddar mackerel pâté 19
Cheese and beefburger pie 142
Cheese and chops 268
Cheese shrimp 263
Cheesy farmhouse flan 120
Cheesy vegetable bake 167
Cotswold cheese crescents 17
Cottage cheese fruit salad 153
Crispy cheese and bacon dish 139

Economical cheese, marrow and
  tomato bake 164
Ham and cheese flan 119
Melted cheese and onions 271
Onion cheese 136
Spinach cheese soufflé 26
Winter warmer 137
Cheesecakes:
Black cherry cheesecake 235
Chicken and mushroom
  cheesecake 106
Cucumber cheesecake 25
Fluffy pineapple cheesecake 236
Mandarin and chocolate
  cheesecake 237
Summer cheesecake 234
Tangy lemon cheesecake 234
Waistline honey and nut
  cheesecake 237
Cherry:
Black cherry cheesecake 235
Cherry ginger cake 249
Chestnut:
Pheasant aux marrons 108
Chibble pasty 128
Chicken:
Adstone summer chicken 157
Autumn chicken casserole 101
Autumn chicken stew 98
Chicken with bacon and celery
  105
Chicken, celery and walnut salad
  156
Chicken divine 269
Chicken fricassée 103
Chicken galantine 106
Chicken and grape salad 158
Chicken and hunky dory sauce
  100
Chicken mousse 25
Chicken and mushroom
  cheesecake 106
Chicken pot roast 96
Chicken and sausagemeat pie 132
Chicken surprise parcels 102
Chicken surprise salad 157

Creamed chicken and leeks 103
Devilled chicken with savoury
    topping 99
Dressed summer chicken 158
Farmer's chicken pie 131
Favourite chicken casserole 104
Fowl rice pudding 97
Fricassée of chicken 270
Lazy chicken 100
Lemon chicken 97
Mexican chicken 102
Picnic chicken 148
Saighton chicken 98
Spinach chicken 105
Spring rabbit and chicken loaf
    116
Summer chicken 270
Tipsy chicken 269
Topsy turvy chicken pie 131
Chilli con carne 47
Chocolate:
    Charlotte delight 219
    Chocolate ginger delight 232
    Hazelnut meringue cake with
        brandy chocolate filling 240
    Individual chocolate strawberry
        gâteaux 226
    Mandarin and chocolate
        cheesecake 237
    Shades of delight 218
Christmas pudding, mock 193
Chutney 260–2
Cider:
    Pheasant in cider 108
    Prawn and cider mousse 23
    Sausages in cider 87
    Strawberries in cider 201
    Stuffed pork tenderloin with
        cider and tomato sauce 83
Citrus summer sweet 220
Citrus wham 238
Cloutie dumpling 195
Coburg pie 185
Cockle pie 124
Corned beef hot pot 266
Corned beef pie 127

Corned beef surprise 143
Cottage cheese fruit salad 153
Country cassoulet 74
Country kebabs 70
Country timbale with a tomato
    sauce 50
Courgette:
    Courgette and mushroom dish
        164
    Courgette, onion and tomato
        bake 136
    Courgette pie 26
    Salmon-stuffed courgettes 18
Cream of vegetable soup 10
Creamed chicken and leeks 103
Creamed leek and potato soup 10
Creamy potatoes 162
Crindleykes Seville surprise 221
Crispy cheese and bacon dish 139
Crumbled pork casserole 75
Crunchy potato salad 152
Crunchy raspberry cream 205
Crusty baked tomatoes 16
Cucumber cheesecake 25
Cucumber mousse 23
Curd cheese cakes 190
Curried dishes:
    Curried rabbit 118
    Curried spaghetti mince 49
    Curried vols-au-vent 148
    Egg prawn curry 264
    Monday curry 142
    Sausages in curry sauce 90
    Summer curry 46

Dabs with Sage Derby and a
    strawberry salad 266
Dad's broth 11
Dairy cream pudding 241
Delicious pudding 194
Devilled chicken with savoury
    topping 99
Dormers 141
Drambuie dream baskets 232
Dumpling pudding 95
Dumplings, herb 78

Dutch flummery 214

Easter gâteau 253
Eggs:
  Egg, mincemeat and apple flan
    184
  Egg pâté 20
  Egg prawn curry 264
  Egg and sultana pudding 198
  Egg and tomato boats 20
  Egg and tomato patty 146
  Sweet poached eggs 222
Elderberry pie 187
Elderflower sorbet 244

Family casserole 40
Family salad 153
Family warm-up casserole 43
Farmer's chicken pie 131
Farmhouse bean and bacon soup 13
Farmhouse beef casserole 41
Farmhouse broth 12
Farmhouse sausage casserole 88
Favourite chicken casserole 104
Field fare or game with mushrooms
    112
Finnan chowder 13
Fish. See also Dab, Haddock etc.
  Butter bean and fish pie 32
  Fish suprême 33
  Quick and easy fish dish 264
  Smoked fish bake 32
  Surprise baked fish soufflé 31
Flans and tarts, savoury:
  Cauliflower soufflé flan 121
  Cheesy farmhouse flan 120
  Egg and tomato patty 146
  Ham and cheese flan 119
  Salmon and spinach flake 125
  Savoury spinach flan 122
  Savoury tomato quiche 121
  Seafood quiches 124
Flans and tarts, sweet. See also
  Pies, sweet
  Almond raspberry tart 188
  Apple and brandy cream flan 228

Apple and marzipan tart 185
Blackcurrant delight on biscuit
    base 229
Chocolate ginger delight 232
Egg, mincemeat and apple flan
    184
Fresh berry torte 230
Gooseberry flan 150
Kiwi and peach flan 231
Pear and plum harvest flan 225
Pear tart with brandy cream 188
Summer fruit flan 226
Summertime flan 239
Fluffed rhubarb cream 208
Fluffy cauliflower bake 163
Fluffy pineapple cheesecake 236
Fluffy stuff 212
Fowl rice pudding 97
French style spring salad 158
Fricassée of chicken 103
Fricassée of chicken or turkey 270
Fricassée of trout 28
Frisky lamb chops 56
Fritters:
  Herb fritters 169
Fruit. See also Apple, Apricot etc.
  Autumn fruit chutney 262
  Boiled fruit cake 249
  Cottage cheese fruit salad 153
  Easy summer sweet 207
  Fluffy stuff 212
  Fruit sponge 224
  Fruit surprise 273
  Fruited lamb steaks with risotto
    60
  Fruity lamb chops 59
  Fruity Scotch beef 42
  Glazed fruit gammon 93
  Hedgerow cheese 259
  Lee salad 151
  Midsummer glories 243
  Quick and easy pink pudding 206
  Simple fruity ice cream 244
  Speedy, easy and luxurious 272
  Steamed fruit roly-poly 193
  Summer cheesecake 234

Summer fruit flan 226
Variety fruit soup 14
Winter crumble 182
Winter fruit salad 272

Game:
  Field fare or game with
    mushrooms 112
  Game pie 133
Gammon:
  Glazed fruit gammon 93
  Knuckle pasties 130
  Scottish platter 159
Gardener's salad 156
Ginger:
  Cherry ginger cake 249
  Chocolate ginger delight 232
  Ginger pork 84
  Pears with ginger sauce 170
  Sticky gingerbread 149
Gooseberry:
  Cashew and gooseberry stuffing
    for lamb 65
  Gooseberry amber 174
  Gooseberry flan 150
  Gooseberry honeycomb 212
  Gooseberry meringue pie 189
  Gooseberry sorbet 244
Grandma's farmhouse pie 125
Grandmother's shortbread 254
Grannie's rhubarb cake 178
Granny's English lamb 64
Grape:
  Chicken and grape salad 158
Grapefruit cream 216
Green bean chutney 261
Green pea with mint savoury ice
    cream 17
Grouse delicacy 112
Guernsey bean jar 141

Haddock:
  Finnan chowder 13
  Scottish platter 159
Ham:
  Ham and cheese flan 119

Potato and ham soufflé 139
Hampshire goose 89
Hare:
  Casserole of hare 116
  Hare pie 134
  Prunes and apples hare 117
Haynes Landrace au gratin 94
Hazelnut:
  Bramble and hazelnut sponge 179
  Encased lamb with hazelnuts and
    redcurrant sauce 72
  Hazelnut meringue cake with
    brandy chocolate filling 240
  Hazelnut ring 252
Heatwave lemon 213
Hedgerow cheese 259
Herb dumplings 78
Herb fritters 169
Herring:
  Baked stuffing herrings 27
Hollandaise sauce 36
Honey and nut cheesecake 237
Honeyed Welsh lamb 61

Iced puddings:
  Bombe princesse 242
  Dairy cream pudding 241
  Elderflower sorbet 244
  Gooseberry sorbet 244
  Green pea with mint savoury ice
    cream 17
  Lemon ice cake dessert 242
  Midsummer glories 243
  Quick and easy ice cream 241
  Raspberry cream delight 245
  Simple fruity ice cream 244
  Strawberry ice cream 246
  Strawberry sorbet 246
I.I. special 85
Irish hot pot 42

Jamaican crunch pie 231
Jellied rhubarb delight 208

Kebabs:
  Country kebabs 70

Kidney:
  Sausage and kidney 87
  Steak and kidney with savoury
    crust 44
Kiwi and peach flan 231
Knuckle pasties 130

Lamb:
  Apricot braised lamb 63
  Apricot-stuffed shoulder 66
  Autumnal pot roast 66
  Casseroled chops and mushrooms
    54
  Cheese and chops 268
  Country kebabs 70
  Dormers 141
  Encased lamb with hazelnuts and
    redcurrant sauce 72
  Frisky lamb chops 56
  Fruited lamb steaks with risotto
    60
  Fruity lamb chops 59
  Granny's English lamb 64
  Honeyed Welsh lamb 61
  Lamb with apricots and
    coriander 69
  Lamb chops and apricots 58
  Lamb chops in cream sauce 57
  Lamb chops and pepper-style
    omelette 57
  Lamb in devil sauce 268
  Lamb and leek casserole 53
  Lamb and maître d'hôtel butter
    58
  Lamb surprise 71
  Leftover lamb 53
  Leg of English lamb with apple
    and mint stuffing 64
  Mince and yogurt pie 126
  New season lamb hot pot 70
  Peanut chop 51
  Ploughman's pie 149
  Red-glazed lamb 61
  Roast loin of lamb with cashew
    and gooseberry stuffing 63
  Saturday spring lamb stir fry 68

Seasonal lamb 67
Shepherd's casserole 56
Shepherd's harvest 52
Somerset lamb 62
Spring lamb parcel 55
Stuffed lamb rolls 73
Stuffed marinated leg of lamb 62
Summertime lamb 68
Wenceslas wassail 54
Lazy chicken 100
Lee salad 151
Leek:
  Creamed chicken and leeks 103
  Creamed leek and potato soup 10
  Lamb and leek casserole 53
  Stuffed leeks 135
Leftover lamb 53
Lemon:
  Dutch flummery 214
  Glazed lemon slices 231
  Heatwave lemon 213
  Jamaican crunch pie 231
  Lemon apple slice 183
  Lemon batter pudding and lemon
    sauce 196
  Lemon chicken 97
  Lemon curd meringue 238
  Lemon fool 215
  Lemon haze 213
  Lemon ice cream dessert 242
  Lemon pudding (cold) 214
  Lemon pudding (hot) 195
  Lemon sponge mousse 224
  Lemon and tuna baskets 18
  Lemon yogurt soufflé 215
  Oranges and lemons pudding 182
  Rhubarb and lemon cooler 150
  Spring lemon cake 252
  Tangy lemon cheesecake 234
Lettuce soup 8
Liver:
  Stuffed liver roast 93
Logger's warming casserole 89

Macaroni:
  Macaroni fireside supper 143

Tuna macaroni 265
Mackerel:
 Cheddar mackerel pâté 19
 Savoury mackerel 28
Maître d'hôtel butter 58
Mandarin and chocolate cheesecake
 237
Marrow:
 Economical cheese, marrow and
 tomato bake 164
 Stuffed marrow rings 137
Meat. See also Beef, Lamb etc.
 Meat sauce concoction 49
 Meat and vegetable soup 7
 Meatballs 50
 Monday curry 142
Melting milky hot-pot 138
Meringue citrus crumble 196
Mexican chicken 102
Michaelmas pears 258
Midsummer glories 243
Mile high pie 227
Millin apple charlotte 181
Mince roll 267
Mince and yogurt pie 126
Mincemeat 257; rich 258
Mint and currant pasty 191
Mock Christmas pudding 193
Mock crab 146
Monday curry 142
Mother-in-law's mushroom
 soup 8
Mother's lambing cake 250
Mousse:
 Carrot and watercress mousse
 with tarragon cream 15
 Chicken mousse 25
 Cucumber mousse 23
 Lemon sponge mousse 224
 Prawn and cider mousse 23
 Salmon and avocado mousse 22
 Tuna mousse 24
Mum's surprise 127
Mushroom:
 Bacon chops with creamed
 mushrooms 92

Casseroled chops and mushrooms
 54
Chicken and mushroom
 cheesecake 106
Courgette and mushroom dish
 164
Field fare or game with
 mushrooms 112
Mother-in-law's mushroom soup
 8
Mushroom and watercress soup 9
Mushrooms in garlic 17
Simple supper 136
My grannie's curd cheese cakes
 190

Nellie's harvest chutney 260
Nethercott noshup 48
Nettle:
 Nettle soufflé 165
 Wayfarers' soup 9
Norfolk apple and blackberry
 pudding 192
Nut roast 271

Oat biscuits 255
Omelette:
 Lamb chops and pepper-style
 omelette 57
Onion:
 Melted cheese and onions 271
 Onion cheese 136
 Tomato and onion savoury 141
Orange:
 Crindleykes Seville surprise 221
 Orange mousse 216
 Orange pudding 175
 Oranges and lemons pudding
 182
 Raspberry and orange creamy
 dessert 204
 Rhubarb and orange meringue
 175
 Tomato and orange soup 8
Oslo sauce 95
Ovaltine loaf 247

Pancakes. See also Fritters
　Autumn pancakes 197
　Spanish pancakes 144
Parsley sauce 29
Parsnip:
　Swede and parsnip soup with
　　cinnamon 11
Pasties:
　Chibble pasty 128
　Knuckle pasties 130
　Mint and currant pasty 191
　Mum's surprise 127
Pâtés:
　Cheddar mackerel pâté 19
　Egg pâté 20
　Smoked trout pâté 19
Pea:
　Bacon and pea hot pot 140
　Green pea with mint savoury ice
　　cream 17
Peach:
　Kiwi and peach flan 231
　Peach pudding 203
Peanut butter pie 233
Peanut chop 51
Pear:
　Michaelmas pears 258
　Pear conserve 258
　Pear and plum harvest flan 225
　Pear tart with brandy cream 188
　Pears with ginger sauce 170
　Spicy cream baked pears 200
Pheasant:
　Autumn pheasant casserole 110
　Peasant's pheasant 109
　Pheasant casserole 110
　Pheasant in cider 108
　Pheasant aux marrons 108
　Pheasant à la Marshalls 109
　Potted pheasant 111
Pickled plums 259
Picnic chicken 148
Picnic surprise 147
Pies, savoury:
　Bacon and potato puff 138
　Bramley pork pie 128

Butter bean and fish pie 32
Cheese and beefburger pie 192
Chicken and sausagemeat pie 132
Cockle pie 124
Corned beef pie 127
Courgette pie 26
Farmer's chicken pie 131
Game pie 133
Hare pie 134
Mince and yogurt pie 126
Ploughman's pie 149
Puff-topped beef and wine pie
　126
Sausagemeat, apple and onion
　pie 130
Somerset pork pie 129
Speedy sausage pie 268
Topsy turvy chicken pie 131
Vegetable harvest pie 123
Wholemeal vegetable pie 122
Pies, sweet:
　Angela's autumn apple pie 184
　Aunt Alice's summer apple pie
　　176
　Banana meringue pie 190
　Chilled rhubarb pie 228
　Coburg pie 185
　Elderberry pie 187
　Gooseberry meringue pie 189
　Jamaican crunch pie 231
　Mile high pie 227
　Peanut butter pie 233
　Raspberry cream pie 245
　Soda cracker pie 233
　Sour cream pie 186
Pigeon, braised, with whisky and
　raisins 113
Pineapple:
　Fluffy pineapple cheesecake 236
　Pineapple fluff 207
　Pineapple meringue pudding 173
　Pineapple pudding (cold) 207
　Pineapple pudding (hot) 171
　Plum and pineapple flambé 173
　Spiced pineapple 172
Ploughman's pie 149

Plum:
Pear and plum harvest flan 225
Pickled plums 259
Plum castaways 174
Plum and pineapple flambé 173
Plum sunshine 176
Pommy rabbit 115
Poor man's ratatouille 166
Pork:
Autumn pork casserole 81
Baked pork chops with apple
and onion sauce 79
Beef and pork loaf 146
Bramley pork pie 128
Cheese and chops 268
Country cassoulet 74
Crumbled pork casserole 75
Ginger pork 84
P.S. pork 84
Pork and apple dish 85
Pork and apple savoury 78
Pork casserole 73
Pork chops in celery sauce 77
Pork chops with herbs and lemon
78
Pork cobbler 80
Pork hot pot 80
Pork in a rich cream sauce 82
Pork Stroganoff 81
Pork in tomatoes 74
Ragoût of pork with herb
dumplings 78
Red cabbage and pork 75
Somerset pork pie 129
South Brook pork 82
Stuffed pork tenderloin with
cider and tomato sauce 83
Tarted-up chops 77
Tipsy pork chops 79
Wealdon spare-rib of pork 76
Potato:
Bacon and potato puff 138
Buckling and potato salad 160
Callcannon 161
Creamy potatoes 162
Crunchy potato salad 152

Melting milky hot pot 138
Potato and ham soufflé 139
Potted pheasant 111
Prawn:
Egg prawn curry 264
French style spring salad 158
Prawn and cider mousse 23
Salmon and prawn slice 37
Primroses, crystallised 224
Princess charlotte 219
Prunes and apples hare 117
Puddings, cold. See also
Cheesecakes, Iced puddings,
Flans and tarts (sweet) *and*
Pies (sweet)
Apple meringue 202
Apple posset 209
Blackberry clouds 210
Blackberry cream 210
Blackcurrant flummery 211
Blackcurrant royale 201
Blackcurrant velvet 212
Blushing apples 200
Bramble delight 221
Bramble dessert 202
Bramble mousse 211
Charlotte delight 219
Citrus summer sweet 220
Citrus wham 238
Crindleykes Seville surprise 221
Crunchy raspberry cream 205
Drambuie dream baskets 232
Dutch flummery 214
Easy summer sweet 207
Five minute raspberry cream 273
Fluffed rhubarb cream 208
Fluffy stuff 212
Fruit sponge 224
Fruit surprise 273
Gooseberry honeycomb 212
Grapefruit cream 216
Hazelnut meringue cake with
brandy chocolate filling 240
Heatwave lemon 213
Individual chocolate strawberry
gâteaux 226

Puddings, cold – cont.
Jellied rhubarb delight 208
Lemon curd meringue 238
Lemon fool 215
Lemon haze 213
Lemon pudding 214
Lemon sponge mousse 224
Lemon yogurt soufflé 215
Orange mousse 216
Peach pudding 203
Pineapple fluff 207
Pineapple pudding 207
Princess charlotte 219
Quick and easy pink pudding 206
Raspberries in port jelly 206
Raspberry chiffon 220
Raspberry marshmallow cream 204
Raspberry and orange creamy dessert 204
Rhubarb spring pudding 203
Rich raspberry trifle 222
Rolled raspberry delight 223
Scottish delight 216
Shades of delight 218
Sheil's strawberry special 218
Snow pudding 217
Southern cream splendour 217
Speedy, easy and luxurious 272
Spicy cream baked pears 200
Spring blancmange 208
Strawberries in cider 201
Strawberry and redcurrant Pavlova 240
Strawberry yogurt jelly 206
Sweet poached eggs 222
Swiss toffee apple 199
Tangy rhubarb mousse 209
Winter fruit salad 272
Puddings, hot. See also Flans and tarts (sweet) *and* Pies (sweet)
Almond nutty apples 171
Almond puff 191
Apple and blackberry soufflé pudding with sherry sauce 192
Apple crisp 180

Apple hedgehog 172
Autumn pancakes 197
Blackberry and apple delight 181
Blackberry roll 186
Bramble and hazelnut sponge 179
Cloutie dumpling 195
Crisp-topped apple pudding 180
Delicious pudding 194
Egg and sultana pudding 198
Gooseberry amber 174
Grannie's rhubarb cake 178
Hot apple slice 187
Lemon apple slice 183
Lemon batter pudding and lemon sauce 196
Lemon pudding 195
Meringue citrus crumble 196
Millin apple charlotte 181
Mint and currant pasty 191
Mock Christmas pudding 193
My grannie's curd cheese cakes 190
Norfolk apple and blackberry pudding 192
Orange pudding 175
Oranges and lemons pudding 182
Pears with ginger sauce 170
Pineapple meringue pudding 173
Pineapple pudding 171
Plum castaways 174
Plum and pineapple flambé 173
Plum sunshine 176
Purple pudding 198
Raspberry cream pudding 177
Raspberry ripple sponge 177
Rhubarb crisp 182
Rhubarb delight 178
Rhubarb and orange meringue 175
Spiced pineapple 172
Steamed fruit roly-poly 193
Sussex pond pudding 194
Walnut pudding 197
Winter crumble 182
Yorkshire bramble pudding 179

Puff pastry leaves 29
Puff-topped beef and wine pie 126
Purple pudding 198

Quiches *see* Flans and tarts

Rabbit:
  Canes Farm rabbit casserole 118
  Casserole of rabbit 116
  Curried rabbit 118
  Pommy rabbit 115
  Rabbit feast 115
  Rabbit Marengo 114
  Rabbit in red wine sauce 114
  Spring rabbit and chicken loaf
    116
Raspberry:
  Almond raspberry tart 188
  Crunchy raspberry cream 205
  Five minute raspberry cream 273
  Fresh berry torte 230
  Fruit surprise 273
  Raspberries in port jelly 206
  Raspberry chiffon 220
  Raspberry cream delight 245
  Raspberry cream pie 245
  Raspberry cream pudding 177
  Raspberry marshmallow cream
    204
  Raspberry and orange creamy
    dessert 204
  Raspberry ripple sponge 177
  Rich raspberry trifle 222
  Rolled raspberry delight 223
Ratatouille, poor man's 166
Red cabbage and pork 75
Redcurrant sauce 72
Red-glazed lamb 61
Rhubarb:
  Chilled rhubarb pie 228
  Fluffed rhubarb cream 208
  Grannie's rhubarb cake 178
  Jellied rhubarb delight 208
  Rhubarb crisp 182
  Rhubarb delight 178
  Rhubarb and lemon cooler 150

Rhubarb and orange meringue
    175
  Rhubarb spring pudding 203
  Spring blancmange 208
  Tangy rhubarb mousse 209
Rice:
  Fowl rice pudding 97
  Rice and nut salad 152
  Risotto 50, 60
Royal horns 256

Saighton chicken 98
Salad dressing 160
Salads:
  Adstone summer chicken 157
  Buckling and potato salad 160
  Cauli crisp 152
  Chicken, celery and walnut salad
    156
  Chicken and grape salad 158
  Chicken surprise salad 157
  Cottage cheese fruit salad 153
  Crunchy potato salad 152
  Dressed summer chicken 158
  Family salad 153
  French style spring salad 158
  Gardener's salad 156
  Lee salad 151
  Quick tossed salad 155
  Rice and nut salad 152
  Sausage twist salad 154
  Scottish platter 159
  Spring salad for farm hands 155
  Spring salad ring 24
  Supreme summer salad 154
  Tuna and apple salad 159
Salmon:
  Baked cheese and salmon mould
    265
  Baked salmon and tomato sauce
    35
  Salmon and avocado mousse 22
  Salmon cushion with hollandaise
    sauce 36
  Salmon mould 21
  Salmon and prawn slice 37

Salmon – cont.
  Salmon pudding 34
  Salmon and spinach flake 125
  Salmon-stuffed courgettes 18
  Salumber 20
  Special salmon puff 34
Saturday spring lamb stir fry 68
Sausage, sausagemeat:
  Autumn sausage 267
  Bean gunge 140
  Chicken and sausagemeat pie 132
  Chicken and sausagemeat
    casserole 88
  Hampshire goose 89
  I.I. special 85
  Layered sausage bake 91
  Logger's warming casserole 89
  Mum's surprise 127
  Picnic surprise 147
  Sausage and bean supper 86
  Sausage hot pot 91
  Sausage and kidney 87
  Sausage loaf 145
  Sausage twist salad 154
  Sausagemeat, apple and onion
    pie 130
  Sausages in cider 87
  Sausages in curry sauce 90
  Savoury cottage pie 86
  Speedy sausage pie 268
  Stuffed marrow rings 137
  Sussex sausage casserole 88
Savoury pudding 76
Scalloped tomatoes 163
Scampi à la livornese 34
Scottish delight 216
Scottish platter 159
Seafood quiches 124
Seasonal lamb 67
Shades of delight 218
Sheil's strawberry special 218
Shepherd's casserole 56
Shepherd's harvest 52
Sherry sauce 192
Shooting party chutney 261
Shortbread 254

Shortbread date slices 255
Shrimp:
  Cheese shrimp 263
  Shrimps and avocado pears 263
Simple supper 136
Smoked fish bake 32
Smoked haddock *see* Haddock
Smoked trout pâté 19
Snow pudding 217
Soda cracker pie 233
Sole suprême 30
Somerset lamb 62
Somerset pork pie 129
Sorbets 244, 246
Soufflés:
  Cauliflower soufflé flan 121
  Lemon yogurt soufflé 215
  Nettle soufflé 165
  Potato and ham soufflé 139
  Spinach cheese soufflé 26
  Surprise baked fish soufflé 31
Soup:
  Cream of vegetable soup 10
  Creamed leek and potato soup 10
  Dad's broth 11
  Farmhouse bean and bacon soup
    13
  Farmhouse broth 12
  Finnan chowder 13
  Lettuce soup 8
  Meat and vegetable soup 7
  Mother-in-law's mushroom soup
    8
  Mushroom and watercress soup 9
  Swede and parsnip soup with
    cinnamon 11
  Tomato and orange soup 8
  Variety fruit soup 14
  Wayfarers' soup 9
  Winter vegetables soup 12
Sour cream pie 186
South Brook pork 82
Southern cream splendour 217
Spaghetti:
  Bacon Italian 266
  Curried spaghetti mince 49

Spanish pancakes 144
Spiced pineapple 172
Spicy apple cake 251
Spicy cream baked pears 200
Spinach:
  Salmon and spinach flake 125
  Savoury spinach flan 122
  Spinach cheese soufflé 26
  Spinach chicken 104
Spring blancmange 208
Spring lamb parcel 55
Spring lemon cake 252
Spring rabbit and chicken loaf 116
Spring salad for farm hands 155
Spring salad ring 24
Starters. See also Soup
  Carrot and watercress mousse
    with tarragon cream 15
  Cauliflower starter 16
  Cheddar mackerel pâté 19
  Chicken mousse 25
  Courgette pie 26
  Crusty baked tomatoes 16
  Cucumber cheesecake 25
  Cucumber mousse 23
  Egg pâté 20
  Egg and tomato boats 20
  Green pea with mint savoury ice
    cream 17
  Lemon and tuna baskets 18
  Mushrooms in garlic 17
  Prawn and cider mousse 23
  Salmon and avocado mousse 22
  Salmon mould 21
  Salmon-stuffed courgettes 18
  Salumber 20
  Smoked trout pâté 19
  Spinach cheese soufflé 26
  Spring salad ring 24
  Tuna mousse 24
  Tuna surprise 18
Steak and kidney with savoury
  crust 44
Strawberry:
  Dabs with Sage Derby and a
    strawberry salad 266

Fresh berry torte 230
Fruit surprise 273
Individual chocolate strawberry
  gâteaux 226
Mile high pie 227
Royal horns 256
Sheil's strawberry special 218
Strawberries in cider 201
Strawberry ice cream 246
Strawberry and redcurrant
  Pavlova 240
Strawberry sorbet 246
Strawberry yogurt jelly 206
Summertime flan 239
Stuffed lamb rolls 73
Stuffed leeks 135
Stuffed liver roast 93
Stuffed marinated leg of lamb 62
Stuffed marrow rings 137
Stuffed pork tenderloin with cider
  and tomato sauce 83
Summer cheesecake 234
Summer chicken 270
Summer curry 46
Summer fruit flan 226
Summer steak parcel 38
Summertime flan 239
Summertime lamb 68
Supreme summer salad 154
Sussex pond pudding 194
Sussex savoury casserole 88
Swede and parsnip soup with
  cinnamon 11
Swiss toffee apple 199

Tarted up chops 77
Tarts see Flans and tarts
Tea cakes 248
Teabreads see Cakes etc.
Tipsy chicken 269
Tipsy pork chops 79
Tomato:
  Apple and tomato chutney 262
  Baked salmon and tomato sauce
    35

Tomato – cont.
  Crusty baked tomatoes 16
  Egg and tomato boats 20
  Egg and tomato patty 146
  Pork in tomatoes 74
  Savoury tomato quiche 121
  Scalloped tomatoes 163
  Shooting party chutney 261
  Simple tomato sauce 51
  Tomato and onion savoury 141
  Tomato and orange soup 8
Topsy turvy chicken pie 131
Tossed salad, quick 155
Trifle 222
Trout:
  Summer trout 30
  Trout fricassée 28
  Trout souchet 28
Tuna:
  Lemon and tuna baskets 18
  Tuna and apple salad 159
  Tuna macaroni 265
  Tuna mousse 24
  Tuna surprise 18
Turkey:
  Fricassée of turkey 270
  Savoury turkey balls 107

Vegetable. See also Bean, Cabbage
    etc.
  Cheesy vegetable bake 167
  Cream of vegetable soup 10
  Hot vegetable layer 168
  Meat and vegetable soup 7

  Mixed vegetable chutney 260
  Summer vegetable terrine 168
  Vegetable harvest pie 123
  Vegetable medley 167
  Vegetable stew 166
  Wholemeal vegetable pie 122
  Winter vegetable soup 12
Venison casserole 113
Vols-au-vent, curried 148

Walnut:
  Chicken, celery and walnut salad
    156
  Walnut pudding 197
Watercress:
  Carrot and watercress mousse
    with tarragon cream 15
  Mushroom and watercress soup 9
Wayfarers' soup 9
Wealden spare-rib of pork 76
Wenceslas wassail 54
Wholemeal vegetable pie 122
Winter bacon warmer 90
Winter crumble 182
Winter fruit salad 272
Winter salad 262
Winter vegetable soup 12
Winter warmer 137

Yogurt:
  Lemon yogurt soufflé 215
  Mince and yogurt pie 126
  Strawberry yogurt jelly 206
Yorkshire bramble pudding 179